D0364166

Lost and Found

JULES MONTAGUE

lost

and

found

Memory, Identity, and Who We Become
When We're No Longer Ourselves

SCEPTRE

First published in Great Britain in 2018 by Sceptre
An Imprint of Hodder & Stoughton
An Hachette UK company

1

Copyright © Julie Phukan 2018

The right of Julie Phukan to be identified as the Author of the Work has been
asserted by her in accordance with the Copyright, Designs and Patents Act 1988.

The stories throughout this book are grounded in reality. The names and
identifying features of patients have been substantially changed to protect
privacy, ensure confidentiality and guarantee complete anonymity. Some scenarios
are a composite of events from different experiences and different times.

A CIP catalogue record for this title is available from the British Library

Hardback ISBN 978 1 473 64694 0
Trade Paperback ISBN 978 1 473 64695 7
eBook ISBN 978 1 473 64693 3

Typeset in Sabon MT by Hewer Text UK Ltd, Edinburgh
Printed and bound in Great Britain by Clays Ltd, St Ives plc

Hodder & Stoughton policy is to use papers that are natural, renewable
and recyclable products and made from wood grown in sustainable
forests. The logging and manufacturing processes are expected to
conform to the environmental regulations of the country of origin.

Hodder & Stoughton Ltd
Carmelite House
50 Victoria Embankment
London EC4Y 0DZ

www.sceptrebooks.co.uk

Contents

Introduction

It had started with headaches, just niggling ones that settled with paracetamol at first, but then they didn't. And soon she was slurring her words and seeing double.

Years before, she had driven Anna and me home from tennis lessons and teenage discos – now, Anna was asking me about brain tumour stages and experimental treatments for her mother.

And then one day, a different sort of conversation.

Her mother, Anna explained, had begun tearfully telling the family that she loved them, repeatedly. She had never done this – in fact, she had been remote during Anna's childhood, indifferent and seemingly unaffectionate for the most part. Anna asked me what it meant. Was this her mother's true personality coming to the surface – an authentic pronouncement? Or was it simply an effect of the inoperable tumour on the frontal lobes of her brain – a hollow declaration of love that represented only a declaration of disease?

I was able to answer the questions about tumour stages and experimental treatments. But these questions about her mother's true self? That wasn't so easy.

There is a solemn tradition in medicine called grand rounds. A junior doctor stands at the front of an auditorium. She or he faces an audience of consultants – some predictably wearing bow ties – trainees and medical students. The junior doctor presents the medical history of a patient invariably plagued by an esoteric disorder. The gowned patient is then walked or wheeled in, sometimes attached to a drip or a catheter or oxygen. They field questions from the room, are examined, and then depart.

Another junior doctor is now grilled: what is the diagnosis, how will you investigate, how will you treat? The replies are often nervous, tentative. Reputations are made and fractured. Then the discussion is opened to the floor. Experts hold court.

Behind the Socratic ritual there lies utility. Once you see a mysterious case and the unveiling of its Delphic diagnosis, you'll never forget it. 'Ah, I've seen this type of thing before. At grand rounds once upon a time.'

Meanwhile, patients benefit from the diagnostic acumen and treatment expertise of a roomful of doctors, some of whom saw this sort of thing once upon a time. They matter, their cure matters.

Grand rounds happen every week in some shape or form in just about every hospital in the world – the tuberculosis clinics I visited as a medical student in Guyana, the sprawling wards where I teach each summer in a port town of Mozambique, the hospital where I work in leafy Hampstead, north London.

At grand rounds, we speak of lung fibrosis and cardiac output, seizures and rashes, fevers and abdominal aneurysms, kidney failure and liver toxicity. We point to dilated pupils and uneven thyroid goitres. We palpate enlarged spleens and angry lymph nodes. We percuss the abdomen and tap the reflexes.

In the two decades since starting at medical school, I have never heard the word 'identity' spoken. Grand rounds, the very heartbeat of medical learning, are not a place for philosophical musings or profound emotional questions. Diagnostic labels gathered there speak more to the patient and less to the person. We talk about loss of blood and loss of lung function but we do not contemplate the loss of person and loss of self.

In Anna's mother, had the brain tumour made her more or less herself? Was she still the same person as before? The answers to these questions, I realised, would not be revealed at grand rounds.

Instead, I have gone back to the stories I hear each day as a neurologist. The patients who walk into my clinic room are tube drivers and teachers, lawyers and cabbies. White witches with potions and prophecies, and restless criminals cuffed to silent prison guards. There are women in burkhas, men in boubou and nuns in habits. There are elderly women who can only express pain in their own language ('beesh, beesh'). There are atheists and religious fundamentalists. And there are women and men newly landed here; they show me the ragged scars of their torture.

But outside of their sartorial, ethnic, religious and forensic diversity, what they all share is their willingness to tell stories. They tell of memories lost or limbs weakened. Of choking and shaking, of aching and staggering. And behind those symptoms are stories of spouses who have supported them or deserted them, benefits provided or denied, death feared or welcomed.

Those stories ultimately lead me to diagnoses and from there on to treatment.

But in the midst of those tales, there are also deeper insights into who we become. Not just if we develop a brain tumour or dementia or lose consciousness, but even if we embellish a story or forget something for just a moment, or dream or sleepwalk or take drugs.

This book is about the exceptional patients and families I have met along the way but it is also about the rest of us. About our continuity of experience and who we become when that continuity falters in some way.

The truth is that I answered Anna without hesitation. I told her that this was really her mother speaking. Not the cancer. That her mother's declaration of love was real, that she was more herself now than ever.

But since then, I have wondered how I could be sure of this. If her mother had become less affectionate, more hostile, would I also have claimed that this was her mother's true self?

Perhaps I had only claimed her mother's pronouncement of love was authentic because Anna desperately wanted to hear it, because I desperately wanted to believe it.

I still do.

Part I

Memory

A childhood memory is misplaced, an autobiography embellished. False memories are created and true ones erased. Reminiscences are cropped and filtered and shared.

Faces are forgotten and lifetimes lost. A word dances on the tip of the tongue, a name momentarily fades. Car keys are lost and phones mislaid and why did I go upstairs?

In remembering and forgetting, we become ourselves or perhaps distant strangers.

Here are stories of nomadic amnesiacs, confabulating liars and fabricating fraudsters. Of reporters who misreport, politicians who misstate and witnesses who devastatingly misremember.

Of you and me.

On this voyage, our selves might be discovered or destroyed.

Let's begin.

I

Missing

You stand in the kitchen. A recipe book in front of you. On its cover a woman licks a spoon made from chocolate. Did you leave that there? What goes where and how and why? Here's a spear. With a handle. A silver spear and a handle. And a wooden rectangle. A board. A chopping board. Ah, it was a knife! And all these clocks on the oven with numbers and signs. Dials, dials. What time does the clock open? Start the fridge. Phone inside. Did you turn the gas on? Was it someone else? Someone else sneaked into the kitchen and turned the oven on when you were looking in the fridge and tried to kill you but you caught them just in time.

David Attenborough on TV. He's getting a bit older, you think. And here are the animals. Pigs, maybe? Rhinos, the TV voice tells you. Almost the same thing. Similar shape, similar shadow. Lights flicker.

You remember the old times and linger there. Memories embrace and envelop. Mint ice cream with chocolate chips. The heat of the day melts it, the cone overflows, you lick your fingers one at a time. Your face pressed up so hard against the fence that the tip of your nose pokes through. Giraffes in the sky. Nobody to say, 'I told you that already.' They weren't there and these are your stories. Your stories to remember and forget as you please.

Names. First, your neighbour around the corner. You see

her every Wednesday when she lugs her trolley to the shops, her spine bent and skin grey and cough full of phlegm and orthopaedic shoes with surgical stockings. Tales of insomnia and emphysema. You remember the first letter of her name, sometimes. And when you hear her name, it rings a bell. A good sign, surely.

Soon, a different name evaporates. It's your best friend, she tells you. Green uniforms, Bunsen burners with orange rubber tubing, wooden desks with books inside. Periodic tables of mercury and zinc. The name is gone. Soon the face becomes unfamiliar, too.

And later still. That's your daughter, they insist. It can't be, you think. She is a new one. That's your son, your brother and your sister. The picture frames in the hall are filled with strangers. Liars. They're trying to take your money and your things and you must stop them.

It's cold outside. Sweater letters front. Jumper. Jumbled. Jumble sale. Car. Air out, cigar smoke. Give me a vowel, Carol. Your fingers are all a colour. Red? Blue? White nose. Snow. Ice. Ice cream. Policeman is here. Bobby. Must be Bobby. Blanket Bobby. Home, he says. Strangers at the front door. Bobby knows them. Shaking hands. Nodding. His mother had been the same way, Bobby says. What same way?

The brain betrays.

What is happening as you forget, as you lose memories and things and people? As people lose you?

Lost by the Lighthouse

One day, Patrick found his wife's handbag in the fridge. They had spent the previous half-hour looking for it and there it was. On the second shelf, next to the cream cheese.

As Alzheimer's disease eroded Anita's brain, nerve connections malfunctioned, abnormal proteins gathered and neurotransmitters failed. She asked Patrick the same questions repeatedly. Words vaporised and sentences misplaced structure. She muddled up faces and names.

She had noticed the problems first, she said. Before the rest of the family. Occasionally losing things, missing the usual exit off the motorway, searching for words that returned sluggishly to her mind, long after a conversation had ended.

She was just tired, she thought. These were senior moments. She reassured herself, others reassured her.

But soon there was little room for reassurance. 'I just told you that!' they told her, exasperated. You didn't, she argued. 'I just told you that!' An accusation and a refrain.

The Bog of the Frogs walk. They did it four times a year. A three-hour walk that loops up the promenade of the fishing village of Howth, about nine miles north-east of Dublin's city centre. Up the path over Balscadden Bay by W.B. Yeats' childhood home, along the cliffs watching peregrines and kittiwakes and razorbills, towards the old Baily Lighthouse of 1814 looking out to Dublin Bay, through the Bog of Frogs, a circle of the Ben of Howth and back along the tramline to the harbour for seafood chowder, watching the sea lions as the day faded away.

Patrick wasn't able to make it that afternoon – he'd sprained his ankle – and so she went with the rest of the group from book club. Somehow she had fallen behind, lost sight of them for just a moment. Then she was alone, looking at the little purple and green and blue arrows on wooden posts that marked the route and they were pointing to the right one minute and to the left the next. She decided to try one way, which way she couldn't remember now, but it was hopelessly wrong. On a small muddy path, the voices of fellow walkers grew distant as panic soared, then another path to nowhere, and another. A man from the golf course had found her, shivering and bawling and unable to figure out how to dial Patrick's number.

Anita sat in front of me now at clinic, Patrick by her side. I think they already knew. She looked lost all over again.

She had got dressed up for this day. Fuchsia handbag matching her fuchsia earrings. Patrick had brought along a black Moleskine notebook and fountain pen.

She could remember childhood summer trips to Butlin's Holiday Camp at Mosney: the Holiday Princess Competition. HB cream ices, chalets and treasure hunts. Skirmishes over Lego with her little brother, the time she got given lines for talking in class ('I am a chatterbox, I am a chatterbox').

But ask her what she did that morning or the week before and the room swelled with silence.

'Apple', 'table', 'penny', I asked Anita to say three times, to etch the words into her brain. A minute later, I asked her to repeat them. She couldn't. She knew the month and the year but not the day or date. I asked her to draw a clock; she bunched up all the numbers to one side. Doctors are taught to look for asymmetry, outliers, differences. That's where pathology lies. I asked her to copy a drawing of a cube. The lines she drew criss-crossed each other in a diagram of disarray.

The temporal lobe takes the hit initially in Alzheimer's disease, years before symptoms even emerge, its sea-horse-shaped hippocampus and entorhinal cortex shrinking away early. Episodic memory suffers – the ability to travel back in time, the capacity to encode, store and retrieve your personal experiences: how you celebrated your birthday last year, what you had for breakfast this morning, where you went on holiday last summer.*

There are other forms of dementia, disorders that affect cognition – things like learning, memory, language, social cognition and executive function – but Alzheimer's is by far the most common form of all and is the one that typically manifests with this sort of memory impairment as an early symptom.

The disease spreads outwards after that, encompassing the rest of the temporal and parietal lobes and moving towards the front of the brain. You ask the same questions over and over, you misplace things, get lost while walking to the shops. Your family hides the car keys after the morning you swerved into an oncoming car. Your speech is hesitant, halting, you cannot name objects: maybe a saucepan first, then a fridge, then a pen. Gloves become socks, tigers become cats. You cannot figure out 'how' – how to button up a shirt, how to change channels. As neurons at the front of the brain are lost, you cannot plan your day or do two things at once. You are anxious and irritable, perhaps depressed and paranoid.

* This reliving of personal experience also depends on the temporal lobe's connections with the frontal lobe and the limbic system, among other parts of the brain that play a supporting role in the operation of memory.

Anita's story was in some ways similar to that of others who develop Alzheimer's every year, some 47 million worldwide, one new case every 3.2 seconds. Ultimately, age is the greatest risk factor for developing Alzheimer's and usually the first symptoms begin after the age of sixty-five, around the same age as she developed hers. The incidence of Alzheimer's doubles every five years after this. I see plenty of younger patients at my cognitive clinic, too. Whether or not you develop Alzheimer's seems to depend on a host of genetic and environmental factors, but inheriting risk genes does not guarantee that you will develop the condition.

Around 25% of cases are clearly familial, with two or more family members affected. Similarly, age, obesity, head trauma and high blood pressure are only risk factors for Alzheimer's; they are not causative in isolation. The thing about Alzheimer's – all diseases – is that generalisations are only useful to a point. Though the results of her memory tests told a well-worn tale, this particular journey was hers alone. The process of forgetting and remembering is familiar, but Anita's own memories and personality would shape the trajectory of her dementia.

'Did I ever tell you, Doctor?' And she almost always had. That couple who were having an affair at book club and the clam chowder and the HB cream ices. I could tell that she had told Patrick too, each day. But there was a warmth to her stories, a place of comfort and sameness and a connection with her past.

'That thing, you know that thing, that thing. Lions the wet. Carcan leap deep parz. Children sea.' Pronouns disappeared, syntax ebbed away.

Despite the gradual transformation of speech and of

thought and of being, wasn't there something of Anita still present throughout? Wasn't Anita still, in a sense, Anita?

The Mountain of Memories

Anita's memories, it seems to me, are her story, her continuous narrative, her record of herself. Those earlier experiences link present Anita to past Anita; they seem to make her the same person. And this sameness is at the core of identity – the confluence of things that make you *you*, over time.

And so, really, what I want to understand is this: if we lose our memories, do we lose ourselves?

Let's try an experiment. Gather all your memories into a cardboard box – of building sandcastles and breaking wine glasses, of first loves and lost loves, of road trips and car crashes, of sunsets and storms. Emotion trickles through each memory – sorrow for a friendship allowed to fade carelessly, the elation of a relationship rekindled. Once the box is full, stand at the foot of the mountain. While you're doing that, I'm standing at the top of the mountain and I'm emptying my brain of each and every memory it has ever held.

Next, a volunteer takes the box you've filled (it's heavier than she expected!) and ascends towards me. She tips your box of memories into my brain.

Where are *you* now? The essence of who you are? At the foot of the mountain bereft of those memories? Or at the top, in a different physical body?

I think most of us would intuitively feel that we are wherever our memories lie – of those first loves and lost loves, and sunsets and storms; memories of the things and people and times that we sense made us who we are today.

You are now at the top of the mountain.*

Yet when I wonder if Anita is the same person as before, I suspect that memory is not the only answer. I can't remember everything I did as a six-year-old – nobody could say that I am not the same person as her, though, despite this. For that matter, she of course does not 'remember' the grown-up me; it does not follow that sameness is radically lost. There must be more to us all than a box of memories, no matter how easy or difficult that box is to carry.

A Succession of Selves

I'd like you to transport yourself to Dublin if you're not already there. You decide to walk the Bog of Frogs today because you've just read about it in some book that happens to merge tourist information with philosophy. You realise that it would be useful to buy a map of the area. Mid-morning you buy that map and plan your

---

* John Locke, seventeenth-century philosopher, certainly felt this way. In his thought experiment, he transplanted a prince's soul and its consciousness (consciousness taken to mean memory) into the body of a cobbler. The cobbler's memories simultaneously entered the body of the prince. The person in the cobbler's body is now the prince, according to Locke. 'As far as this consciousness [memory] can be extended backwards to any past action or thought, so far reaches the identity of that person; it is the same self now it was then; and it is by the same self with this present one that now reflects on it, that that action was done.' Without memory, said Locke, there is no person.

walking route. Then you take the train out to the village of Howth. There are already connections building up, moment to moment; intentions, goals and desires. You wanted to walk to the Bog of Frogs when you woke up this morning. It still feels like a good idea. We could map your route out of Dublin as a succession of selves, each looking at the one behind and the one ahead in this train carriage, a wave of definite recognition between them each time. You walk the Bog of Frogs, taking in the view of Dublin Bay, watching the peregrines and kittiwakes and stopping off at the pub by the harbour afterwards. As you sway yourself back home, you remember standing on the cliffs and breathing in the sea air earlier that day. The you of this evening maintains strong connectedness to the you of this afternoon on the cliffs; the you on the cliffs connects to the you of this morning as you were planning your trip. Links on a chain were formed throughout. You can easily extend these chains from day to day, week to week and so on. Identity is steeped in connectedness.

But we need a second step to maintain sameness over time: continuity. In the pub you remember walking the Bog of Frogs, but you probably don't remember yourself, aged four, building that sandcastle. You in the pub don't hold the same intentions or beliefs as you on the beach. But how much does that matter? As long as a series of intermediate links carries memories, intentions and beliefs to each subsequent link, identity does persist. The first link of the chain might not appear to share strong connectedness with the very last, at first glance, but there are enough solid overlapping connections from stage to stage for us to argue that you remain the same person.* There are enduring psychological traits even though these may ebb and flow throughout your life. There's a fair chance that the sociable you in your late teenage years is now the gregarious you at a cocktail party. And it's quite likely that the conscientious punctual you at your last job is the self-disciplined and dependable you at your current one. Even though your cells have been replaced many times over, you are still you.†

Yet many would contest this, arguing that the loss of these connections in dementia withdraws personhood entirely. The American philosopher, bioethicist and now Professor Emeritus at Harvard Dan Brock has argued:

> I believe that the severely demented, while of course remaining members of the human species, approach more closely the condition of animals than normal adult humans in their psychological capacities. In some respects the severely demented are even worse off than animals such as dogs and horses who have a capacity for integrated and goal-directed behaviour that the severely demented substantially lack.

---

* Being the same person in philosophical terms is all about numerical identity; being one and the same – there cannot be two versions of Anita, for example. In the numerical manner of speaking, two things are never identical. Robert Galbraith and J.K. Rowling are identical, not simply similar. They are one and the same. Ronnie and Reggie Kray might have been identical twins but were not one and the same. Drake sings to Rihanna: 'If you had a twin, I would still choose you.' Rihanna and her imaginary twin are similar but not the same.

† This idea of overlapping stretches of 'psychological connectedness' was built on the concepts developed by British philosopher Derek Parfit in his 1984 book, *Reasons and Persons*.

The dementia that destroys memory in the severely demented destroys their psychological capacities to forge links across time that establish a sense of personal identity across time and hence they lack personhood.

Anita might be unrecognisable in certain ways as her dementia progresses but most of us, Anita's family included, would soundly reject Brock's argument.

The words of Barbara Pointon provide the perfect counterpoint to Brock's view. Even connectedness and continuity only go so far. Her husband, Malcolm Pointon, was a pianist and lecturer from Thriplow, a village in Cambridgeshire. Diagnosed with Alzheimer's, aged fifty-one, his last eleven years were filmed in a groundbreaking documentary, *Malcolm and Barbara: Love's Farewell*, by film-maker Paul Watson. In 2007, Barbara wrote about her husband's last months:

> Malcolm is surrounded by love. We reach out to communicate with him at a profound level − often through eye contact and gentle whispering and touch − and from him flows a deep childlike trust, luminosity and reciprocating love − as though it were his very self, the self he was born with, that we are privileged to glimpse . . . Does it matter what we call it − spirit, soul, inner self, essence, identity − so long as we have experienced it?

Denying Descartes: Reimagining Loss

As her dementia evolved, Anita appeared more vague, more fragile, more vulnerable with each clinic visit. Eyes wider, hands trembling, gait shuffling. But she still bore a physical resemblance to the person who had walked into this room three years before. She was recognisable, notwithstanding the loss of psychological connections I've mentioned before, and the box of memories being emptied one by one.

Our *physical* form, despite its constant turnover of cells, ageing or alteration of consciousness, is stable enough to make us familiar to ourselves and to others. You are the past or future being that has your body, goes the argument. By this idea, Anita is still Anita.

Yet I know that her physical appearance is not enough to ground Anita as the same person as her dementia evolves. Anita is more than her cells and molecules, her legs weakened and shoulders slumped. She is also her relationships with others, her engagement and inter-action, her looking outwards. Philosophers such as Martin Heidegger thought that human beings are always relating to other people and things in the world – an existential interaction rather than a topographical or spatial one. Dasein, 'being there', is Heidegger's term for the human being, but in Heidegger's mind this is a nod towards exist-ence, of being in the world and engaged with it, of not being isolated from it.

Yet, 'Cogito ergo sum,' wrote Descartes instead. 'I think, therefore I am.' The body is simply a possession – in Alzheimer's it becomes obsolete or even a hindrance. Bodies are envisioned as a battleground to clean and control, monitor and survey, secure and constrain, restrict and restrain. There are alarm bells and safety fences. (Consensual) sexual expression and intimacy are path-ologised. A body is to be clothed in easily wipeable fabrics, quick-to-manage drawstrings and Velcro shoes in the preparation of a 'lounge-standard' resident.

But switch the filter and another view emerges: it's not just that we have bodies; we *are* bodies, we are embodied. Bodies that interact with the world, engage with it, are embedded within it. Dementia does not annihilate these capacities. As French philosopher Maurice Merleau-Ponty (1908–61) wrote, 'The world is not what I think but what I live through.'

Take Raymond's story. Five years before, he had driven himself to A&E with an internet diagnosis of a flesh-eating bug. It transpired to be athlete's foot; it could, he figured, have gone either way. But now, as he mixed up friends' names and got lost repeatedly on his way to work, his worst fears had been realised. He did not need the internet to diagnose himself this time; he had dementia. Just like Lieutenant Columbo, he knew who the bad guy was even before the whole story had unfurled.

Early on, I glimpsed his fear of physical contact – his shoulders tensed, his fists clenched even as a nurse checked his blood pressure. Later, he could not verbalise the horrific abuse of his childhood but told the story without words. He shuddered uncontrollably when a male carer attempted to shave his beard. He shouted whenever the parish priest passed by his home. In the past, his wife told me, he had switched channel at the first sight of a religious programme (and there were plenty of those in Ireland at the time). In this new parish priest, Raymond saw the priest of his childhood. He shouted in order to switch the channel.

Raymond was the increasingly blurred photographs he took.

He was the tears he cried when his brother put a hand on his shoulder.

He was the sternotomy scar of his heart surgery.

He was the way he bounced his granddaughter on his knee.

He was his weathered skin from years on a construction site.

He was his tender embrace of his wife.

His was a newfound language, calling out for translation. His gestures, habits and actions were embodied. His existence was resolutely embedded in his physical experiences, perceptions and interactions.

Could this concept of embodiment also allow Anita to still be Anita? Yes: if we exist in the context of the surrounding world, are truly ingrained within it, dementia should not steal this away.

Despite this, our medical model of dementia continues to revolve around inability and invisibility; it insists that Anita is defined by her fading away rather than her stepping forth. In Alzheimer's, it is a formidable task to see anything but obliteration – of expression, agency, autonomy and independence.

When I ask patients with mild or moderate Alzheimer's if they think they are the same person they were before, although they frequently answer in the affirmative, there often follows a list of what they physically cannot do any more, their families joining in: I can't speak as well as I used to, can't walk as well as I used to. I can't put the bins out any more, I can't play nine holes of golf.

Impairment in the ability to perform day-to-day tasks is even a core diagnostic criterion for dementia – as doctors, we cannot tell you that you have dementia until we know what you can't do. And so we ask questions about what's missing rather than what remains.

Trying to move away from a negative definition of dementia is not the same as disputing the impairment it brings; it is re-evaluating how we have chosen to imagine it. There is more to dementia than loss and failure.

When a loved one with Alzheimer's has wandered out of the house or appears angry or apathetic or paranoid, these concepts around recognising embodiment are difficult, perhaps impossible, to process. Philosophy is not the policeman who will find the missing person with dementia.

Laurie Graham, speaking to the BBC for their feature *Dementia Diaries*, spoke about caring for her husband: 'The person I'm dealing with, the person I'm yelling at, the person who's making me weep with frustration, is like a stranger. He looks like my husband, but Howard's gone.'

Would these ideas around embodiment, around reimagining loss in dementia, have helped Laurie Graham in her greatest moments of despair? No doubt on her better days – fewer of those as time went on – she had already lived these very ideas and desperately translated the subtle signs that proved her husband was still in there somehow. She and her husband had done all they could to search for sameness, to express it, to enable it, to cling on to it as tightly as they could.

The truth is that there is no special formula here – no simple protocol to see beyond inability, no simple pathway towards valuing presence. But certainly in the medical setting, our view of dementia is often short-sighted – a reductionist biomedical model that desperately needs to be reimagined: assumptions challenged, communication reinterpreted and agency repositioned. Otherwise Anita's identity can only hurtle towards annihilation.

Shift the pinhole focus on dysfunction to a broader visual field of enablement, engagement and expression. Everyday conversations, art classes or dance therapy become not just pastimes but conduits of expression and connection.

Take away the dark corridors of residential homes and imagine them into social spaces: design streets in these homes with meeting points, benches, streetlights and village squares. How can anyone belong if they are brutally removed from the world?

Embodiment pulls identity solely from the realm of cognition. We are all, undeniably, present. In some ways at least.

The Stories We Tell

John Bayley, writing about his wife Iris Murdoch's evolving dementia, describes how their communication persisted without words, 'like underwater sonar, each bouncing pulsations off the other, and listening for an echo'. Despite advancing dementia, 'Iris remains her old self in many ways.'

Communication persists beyond language; through a smile or a grimace, a shrug of the shoulders, a nod of assent, a clenched fist or a handshake, crossed arms or a roll of the eyes. Without a word spoken, much can be conveyed – joy, distaste, gratitude, admiration, encouragement, warmth and empathy.

Anita couldn't really speak as time went on. Or at least she couldn't speak the way she used to. Grammar was lost, tenses were mixed up, the sequence of events differed in the retelling.

And yet, I still had a sense of who she was.

'I made the cut, the As and Bs. Proved them wrong!'

Among her tales of holidays and hill walks, here was a story of an ambitious woman who became the first in her family to go to university. She still could impart that university story, until her dementia was very advanced, albeit with fewer words and more gestures – making the motion of opening and closing a book, peering down a microscope, struggling across cobblestones in high heels, excitedly throwing an imaginary mortar-board hat into the air, her enthusiasm infectious throughout. Whenever she hesitated, encouragement from me or from her husband would reignite the rest of the story, reignite her animation. And she would transport us away from that room with its hand-washing posters, 'hazard: asbestos above' sign and straw-yellow walls.

A coherent autobiography, a chronicle of self, links your past to your present and perhaps your future. Morals, behaviour and beliefs exist between the lines. We are the tales we tell.

Dementia interrupts this storytelling, true, but what if even these seemingly chaotic and repetitive stories cement rather than decimate identity in Alzheimer's, even as stories are repeated, words disappear, sequence and temporal binding are fractured or confabulation holds forth? What if they allow those with dementia to make sense of themselves and others? The chaos and repetition might be our problem, not theirs.

Anita's communication embodied her values: she owned and knew her own mind when others doubted her. Even in severe dementia, self-expression persists and simple gestures have agency. A first-person 'I' perspective rather than only a third-person one. Implicit rather than explicit.*

These stories reflected Anita's past and present identity even through tales as tangled as the proteins that clumped within her brain.

Mirrors

> Did you ever observe that the face of the person looking into the eye of another is reflected as in a mirror; and in the visual organ which is over against him, and which is called the pupil, there is a sort of image of the person looking?
>
> Alcibiades I, Socrates

Identity incorporates how we are seen as well as how we see ourselves. 'Self' refers primarily to the experience of the individual (a sense of one's own being), but 'identity' encompasses the views and observations of others. Your identity is not just about you – it's collaborative.

There was a way they'd always had, Anita and Patrick. She'd lock the front door on the way out and Patrick would open the car's passenger door for her. Recently, Patrick told me, when the ambulance men used to arrive to transport her to hospital appointments (she could no longer manage by car), they would let him pull open the back doors of the

---

* Canadian philosopher Charles Taylor subscribes to this idea in his 1995 book, *Philosophical Arguments*: 'Our understanding is itself embodied. That is, our bodily know-how, and the way we act and move, can encode components of our understanding of self and world ... My sense of myself, of the footing I am on with others, is in large part also embodied.'

ambulance in ceremonial fashion. 'Your carriage awaits, m'lady.' She still smiled at it.

Ar scáth a chéile a mhaireann na daoine, goes the Irish saying. Under the shelter of each other, people survive.

Of course identity is not binary in practice; it is not simply there or not there. Her family might occasionally get a glimpse of the Anita they knew from far away, like looking at a face through binoculars as you twist the lenses in and out of focus. They might feel she is less herself now, that she was a bit more Anita a few months ago, even though she already had dementia at that point. Even through the fog of amnesia, there are degrees of psychological continuity or connectedness.

In conditions that change personality, let's say a tumour of the frontal lobe, family and friends are more likely to say, 'She's not herself.' With traumatic brain injury such transformation can be chaotic; identity switches instantaneously. But there is something different about Alzheimer's, at least in its less advanced stages. Memory changes develop insidiously. Strangers emerge in Alzheimer's, if at all, in later stages when personality changes have often superseded memory ones. Nancy Reagan said of her husband, 'Ronnie's long journey has finally taken him to a distant place where I can no longer reach him.'

When a loved one loses memories in this way, perhaps some memories never conveyed to us in the first place, there naturally comes with this a sense of loss and perhaps mourning. Our own identity might be anchored in the memories they have of us, too.

But if identity incorporates the views and observations of others, this suggests that a change in 'what we are known for' might threaten identity, more so than incremental memory loss.

What are the traits, beliefs, ambitions, routines that people associate you with? Generosity of spirit, eternal optimism, relentless cynicism, dogged determination, skilled diplomacy? This approach to identity chimes more with the psychological than the philosophical; it speaks to not just what we value most in ourselves, but also what others value in us. These facets might change over time, yet they do not inevitably mark us as different persons with each change in code. We act differently in different situations: at work versus at home; at home versus on holiday. We might be treated differently on each occasion as a result. Samuel Barondes, Professor of Psychiatry and Neurobiology at the University of California, San Francisco, says despite this we remain 'the same person – replete with the inconsistencies and contingent behaviours and the unconscious motives and the self-deceptions that each of us has in considerable measure'.

In his description of his wife Iris Murdoch's dementia, John Bayley writes that as she is 'sailing into the darkness', she is unaware of her formidable achievements: 'The power of concentration has gone, along with the ability to form coherent sentences, and to remember where she is or has been. She does not know that she has written twenty-seven remarkable novels, as well as her books on philosophy; received honorary doctorates from major universities; become a Dame of the British Empire.' This was 'what she was known for', the lens through which she was viewed. As her literary abilities diminished, the image blurred, rendering her unrecognisable at times to her family, beyond even her memory loss.

Murdoch's last novel was *Jackson's Dilemma*, published in 1995. In a study conducted five years after her death,

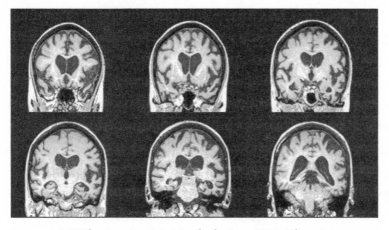

MRI brain scan, Iris Murdoch, June 1997. There is
global volume loss with profound atrophy of the
hippocampi. Iris Murdoch died two years later.

neuroscientific analysis confirmed that her language had
begun to change a year before Alzheimer's was diagnosed.
Her vocabulary was now more restricted, her language less
abstract and more concrete and she introduced fewer new
words in this book than in her earlier ones. This was
reflected by its unwittingly prescient reviews (well before
the critics and indeed Murdoch herself realised that she
was developing dementia). A.S. Byatt concluded that the
structure of the novel was akin to an 'Indian Rope Trick' in
which the characters 'have no selves and therefore there is
no story and no novel'. Penelope Fitzgerald said that the
economy of the writing made it appear 'as though Murdoch
had let her fiction wear through almost to transparency',
while Hugo Barnacle described it as reading 'like the work
of a 13-year-old schoolgirl who doesn't get out enough'.
Brad Leithauser, reviewing for the *New York Times*, was
bewildered: 'Could even Murdoch's staunchest admirers

explain why the phrase "then suddenly" should appear three times in a single paragraph?' He concluded, 'The story is a psychologically rich tale of romances thwarted and revived. The writing is a mess.'

Iris Murdoch was viewed differently because she did differently. She was not, in the eyes of others, 'herself'. The 'what she was known for' had shifted.

Does this mean we are complicit in damaging the identity of those with dementia? Along the same lines, do we have the capacity to maintain it?

Psychologists Steven Sabat and Rom Harré argue that others endanger self in Alzheimer's rather than the disease. Selves are joint productions, they explain; we can choose to edit or enhance those interactions, to make or break others.

J.B. was an academic, teacher, administrator and author. Diagnosed with Alzheimer's four years previously, he was an integral participant of Sabat and Harré's wider study. He met the researchers on a weekly basis. But J.B. opted out of scheduled activities at the daycare centre (games and discussions and the like); instead he took walks, read or spent time with staff.

The initial assumption might be that J.B. is a misanthropic recluse, loath to socialise, an outsider and an aimless wanderer. But J.B.'s narrative discounts that assumption.

Yes, well, my wife and I are very strong academic people and, uh, so we start talking to each other, we talk at a very high level right away. Uh, and uh, I mean, uh, most of these people here, most of them here are good. But when I get closer, uh, I, uh, get, information that's much, uh, that Trivial Pursuit – I wish I could find out how to make it break.

And so evaporates the character of an asocial, confused wandering recluse. Instead J.B. is an academic socialising with those he sees as being on a similar level, a man wishing to avoid, in his mind, mindless pursuits, a man who likes to walk with purpose instead of wander in confusion. He no longer fulfils his academic role in the conventional sense; this does not render the role irrelevant.

> I have the feeling, some feeling that I don't necessarily have status, um, because it's not really something that I'm piddling with. And you know I feel a way is that, I feel that this is a real good, big project and I'm sure you do too. This project is a sort of scientific thing.

The danger of grasping only this approach, the idea that the nature of the self is contingent on social interaction or the 'what she was known for', would be at its extreme to place blame at the feet of those who care for someone and love someone with Alzheimer's, to suggest (and this is incendiary) they are complicit in or even responsible for dehumanising and marginalising those with dementia by creating a 'malignant social psychology' as Professor Tom Kitwood termed it: a social environment that actively infantilises, intimidates, stigmatises and objectifies those with dementia.

Kitwood, a psychologist, hoped, through this approach, to end the dehumanisation of those with dementia. His theories drove strategies now used internationally to provide patient-centred care and to empower families.

But the approach also does not allow much for the inevitable alteration in identity (or personhood) that dementia imposes, irrespective of social environment. And it is a devastating interpretation for families, friends and carers. Dementia can be cruel enough; for the most part I believe we strive to shelter one another.

Anita

In the corner of the room stands a younger Anita. She is watching an older version of herself turn to her husband. Younger Anita, the one from before dementia, watches her older self struggle with words, with expression. But there is recognition; the younger Anita cares what happens to her older self, does not disown her, sees the likeness, the connectedness.

Anita returned to clinic. She could not repeat lists of words or draw clocks or copy pentagons now. Over time, I stopped asking her to do these things.

Was she the same person as before? Was she even a person towards the end? I believe that her continuity of being lay far beyond the accuracy of her memories or the fluency of her speech or the dexterity of her movements. Beyond the abnormal proteins gathering in her brain or the nerve cells disappearing with each passing day. Not to deny her dementia and its inexorable progression until her death, not to deny its ramifications for her and her family, but instead to refuse its capacity to withdraw personhood. To see her, still. Anita resolutely was present in the world.

I remember her each time I go back to Ireland and walk up by Balscadden Bay, along the cliffs, back by the tramline. Where she was lost, but found again.

2

The Honest Liars

Charlie was cachectic. His muscles wasted, body trembling, bulging purple veins under translucent skin. His palms shone red, his fingernails yellow-tinged. Serrated scratch marks on his forearms oozed.

Yesterday had been different, he told me. Yesterday, he had fired his butler, Harry. Twelve years of loyal service and Harry had stolen a combine harvester and driven it up the main street. Maybe it was the recession; it seemed to be breaking all of us, didn't it Doctor? Those Irish politicians.

Not half an hour before I had arrived, Charlie had stepped out of the hospital to visit a local children's charity. He had presented prizes at their egg and spoon race (even the child who finished last got a prize) and had a go on a pink trampoline. No, the trampoline was purple. It was definitely purple.

I pressed my stethoscope to Charlie's chest as I felt his pulse – it was irregular and faint. On his upper torso were tiny pink spider-like formations: spider angiomata, they are called. Each body of the spider representing an enlarged blood vessel, several others radiating outwards as spider legs. These tiny pink spiders told me that Charlie's liver was damaged. I asked Charlie to look to the right and then to the left. His eyes jerked chaotically, back and forth involuntarily. Nystagmus, this is called: his brain was damaged, too.

The bottle of alcohol gel stuck to the wall was empty.

He'd have to leave in a few minutes for a board meeting, he said. But it was very nice to meet you, Doctor.

Charlie was unkempt and dishevelled. He was also endlessly polite and amiable and had drunk one or two bottles of vodka every day for the past twenty years. He was in and out of homeless shelters and police stations around Dublin and our emergency department. Everybody knew Charlie.

Charlie didn't have a butler. Not now, not before. There were no board meetings for him to go to. Yesterday his only trip had been to the ultrasound department on the first floor for a scan of his liver; no trampolines and no egg and spoon races.

But these were not lies. Not really. Charlie did not seek to deceive.

He was confabulating.

The term 'confabulation' describes false memories that arise, not deliberately, but instead in the context of a neurological disorder – strokes, brain infections, traumatic brain injury or a condition of amnesia called Korsakoff's. This last one was Charlie's.

Charlie had initially developed Wernicke's encephalopathy, a syndrome of thiamine deficiency (one of the B vitamins). Most frequently seen in alcoholics, it is also associated with other conditions of malnutrition: anorexia nervosa, refeeding after starvation, gastrointestinal diseases. Charlie had its hallmark signs: confusion, unsteadiness and abnormal eye movements.

Without thiamine replacement, 20% of patients die. Left untreated, up to 85% of survivors develop Korsakoff's – a condition of severe amnesia with confabulation.

The patient with implausible tales cannot remember that he cannot remember.*

Confabulators fabricate. Occasionally there are relatively minor embellishments and elaborations. But sometimes there are bizarre, evocative stories without any obvious motive.

The medical literature is filled with such case studies: patients convinced of being a pirate on a spaceship, a pilot in Saddam Hussein's air force, a rescuer of drowning children. One man said he had been attacked by enemy aircraft when boarding a submarine. Another insisted he had just discussed a building job with then Prime Minister Harold Wilson.

Russian neuropsychiatrist Sergei Korsakoff described one such patient in 1889:

> In telling of something about the past, the patient would suddenly confuse events and would introduce the events related to one period into the story about another period . . . Telling of a trip she had made to Finland before her illness and describing her voyage in fair detail, the patient mixed into the story her recollections of the Crimea, and so it turned out that in Finland people always eat lamb and the inhabitants are Tatars.

* Barbizet, J. (1963), 'Defect of memorizing of hippocampal-mammillary origin: A review', *Journal of Neurology, Neurosurgery and Psychiatry*, 26, pp.127–35.

Korsakoff's, frontal lobe trauma, aneurysms of the anterior communicating artery – confabulation is primarily seen in disorders that affect the front of the brain. Take the case of a sixty-eight-year-old woman with hydrocephalus who was a hardened confabulator: an honest liar. When she awoke from a shunt operation to correct the hydrocephalus, the lies had disappeared. The operation, the authors ventured, had led to recovery of the hippocampal connections to other parts further forward in the brain. Confabulation removed, surgical success.

Could understanding the mechanisms of confabulation in these patients with brain damage help us to understand other, more quotidian, false memories a little better? Perhaps then we might make sense of the inaccuracies that surface as we summon a remote memory or the inconsistences that infiltrate the tales we tell. You and I, our stories might be different from Charlie's, but our remembering might not be.

Dogs and Doubts

Confabulators will insist upon leaving for a non-existent business meeting or job interview – they fail to abandon plans that are no longer applicable. And this suggests that patients like Charlie cannot situate memories correctly in time – chronological confusion sees past memories floating into the present even though they are not pertinent to the reality of now. Charlie was unable to suppress or deactivate old memory traces even though they were now irrelevant.

The Swiss authors of the chronological theory later circled back to Pavlov and his description of extinction to explain this.

In Pavlov's classic conditioning experiment, first, the dog associates a stimulus, perhaps a metronome or a buzzer, with the arrival of food. The dog salivates whenever the stimulus is activated – Pavlov called this 'psychic salivation'. Now the stimulus is activated but no food emerges. The dog figures out what's going on and stops salivating at the tick of the metronome or the buzz of the buzzer. The anticipated outcome (of food) does not occur and therefore the dog learns not to anticipate it. This archaic learning process is called 'extinction', and it has even been described in sea slugs and fruit flies. However, confabulators fail to adapt their behaviour in this way. There is no meeting with a business colleague, no job interview, but confabulators will anticipate these things all the same.

As the Pavlovian experiments suggest, this process is closely tied in with the brain's reward system. This makes sense: the orbitofrontal cortex is linked to reward, and the orbitofrontal cortex is frequently damaged in Korsakoff's.

Nonetheless, distortion of time or of filtering cannot explain all instances of confabulation. Take the case of a sixty-four-year-old man with an aneurysm. At a party the night before, he had met a woman with a bee's head. His neurologists realised that although the memory of going to a party could be a true memory displaced in time, the memory of a woman with a bee's head could not.

This suggests that something beyond chronological confusion must account for some cases. And that's gut feeling. Charlie did not just have trouble salvaging or

strategically searching for memories but his ability to monitor them was impaired. Usually, we have a fast-acting auto-
matic feeling of rightness (with a slower checking process to
follow as needed) that allows us to instinctively reject memories that could not possibly be true. 'There's something not
quite right about this,' we say. This feeling of rightness is
linked to the front of the brain – areas such as the orbitofrontal cortex and the adjacent ventromedial cortex – and
could be disrupted in confabulators. We have an unconscious checking system, which 'tags' thoughts that require
extra conscious checking.* This tag is accompanied by the
normal doubt we all experience. In confabulation, the
checking system falls apart, doubt disappears and patients
are entirely convinced their memories are true. Because their
doubt tag is missing, there is no reason for confabulators to
consciously check their thoughts. Charlie was insistent that
he judged an egg and spoon race and then jumped on that
trampoline and had no reason to believe otherwise.

But Charlie is not the only one who imparts impossible
memories with quite such conviction.

Heroic by Association

25 March 1996, Bosnia. Hillary Clinton: 'I remember landing under sniper fire. There was supposed to be some kind
of a greeting ceremony at the airport, but instead we just
ran with our heads down to get into the vehicles to get to

* Turner, M. and Coltheart, M., 2010, 'Confabulation and delusion: A
common monitoring framework', *Cognitive Neuropsychiatry*, 15(1–3),
pp.346–76.

our base,' she said. Video footage soon emerged of her calmly disembarking from a US Air Force plane with her daughter, Chelsea, greeting troops and talking to an eight-year-old girl who presented her with a poem.

Clinton called the faulty recollection a 'minor blip'. 'I say a lot of things – millions of words a day – so if I misspoke, that was just a misstatement,' she said. 'This has been a very long campaign. Occasionally, I am a human being like everybody else.'

Misstatements cross political lines.

President Bush recalled more than once seeing the first plane hit the north tower of the World Trade Center before he entered a classroom in Florida on 11 September 2001. And yet there was no live footage available at the time.

Meanwhile, Donald Trump insisted that after 9/11 he watched news footage of 'thousands of thousands of people' celebrating in northern New Jersey, 'where you have large Arab populations'. He had not.

When memories are lost or manipulated, what lies beneath? Where does embellishment end and fabrication begin?

The saga of Brian Williams raises these very questions.

NBC Nightly News with Brian Williams was the highest-rated newscast in the US. His official NBC profile celebrated his twelve Emmy Awards, eleven Edward R. Murrow Awards, the duPont–Columbia University Award, the Walter Cronkite Award for Excellence in Journalism and the broadcasting industry's Peabody Award, awarded for exemplary storytelling. In 2006, *Time* magazine named him one of the 100 most influential people in the world.

His signature: his intrepid ability to bear witness.

Williams, a former New Jersey firefighter, spoke on the *David Letterman Show* in 2013; the story he told would transform his career. Letterman's guests that week at the Ed Sullivan Theater on Broadway included Donald Trump and Bill Cosby. (Their lives would change too, but for different reasons.)

Williams describes an assignment to cover the Iraq invasion. He speaks to Letterman with supreme confidence: without hesitation, deviation or repetition. Black suit, white dress shirt with top button fastened, collar taut, a tie with diagonal black and white stripes. Behind Letterman, the famous Brooklyn and George Washington bridges, or rather miniature replicas that were part of the show's stage set.

Flying aboard a Chinook helicopter, Williams had come under fire from a rocket-propelled grenade (RPG).

'Two of our four helicopters were hit by ground fire, including the one I was in. RPG and AK-47 . . . we got hit, we set down, everyone was OK, our captain took a Purple Heart injury to his ear in the cockpit.'

The story was rich with detail: 'we landed very quickly and hard and we put down and we were stuck – four birds in the middle of the desert'. US Bradley fighting vehicles and Abrams tanks arrived, he said, happening upon the stricken helicopter crew and protecting them for three days during an epic sandstorm. Later: 'Our travelling NBC News team was rescued, surrounded and kept alive by an armoured mechanised platoon from the US Army 3rd Infantry.' And finally in one transcript: 'A jagged hole in the skin of a helicopter, a symbol for the unexpected challenges faced by US soldiers.'

In early 2015, NBC was covering a tribute New York Rangers hockey game at Madison Square Garden for Command Sergeant Major Tim Terpak. Williams had invited Terpak to thank him for the protection he and his NBC team had received in Iraq.

It was a step too far. Crew members who had been on the under-fire Chinook were watching the broadcast and finally spoke out.

Williams had never been on that Chinook. He had arrived an hour afterwards. Lance Reynolds, a flight engineer: 'It was something personal for us that was kind of life-changing for me. I know how lucky I was to survive it. It felt like a personal experience that someone else wanted to participate in and didn't deserve to participate in.' Mike O'Keefe, a door gunner on the damaged Chinook, also called out Williams: 'I can't believe he is still telling this false narrative.'

It was only after the debate emerged on social media that Williams confessed. He claimed he held:

no desire to fictionalise the experience and no need to dramatise events as they actually happened . . . I spent much of the weekend thinking I'd gone crazy. I feel terrible about making this mistake . . . I don't know what screwed up in my mind that caused me to conflate one aircraft with another . . . I want to apologise. Nobody's trying to steal anyone's valor. Quite the contrary: I was and remain a civilian journalist covering the stories of those who volunteered for duty. This was simply an attempt to thank Tim, our military and Veterans everywhere – those who have served while I did not.

A mistake and a mix-up. Recant and regret.

But if it had happened once, had it happened more than that? Questions were now raised about his reporting of Israel's military action against Hezbollah in Lebanon and that of Hurricane Katrina in 2005. Williams had claimed that he had seen bodies float by after the hurricane hit, his hotel overrun by gangs. He had caught dysentery from the floodwaters, he reported. These claims were disputed by some health officials, local residents, outreach workers and non-profit groups.

NBC News President Deborah Turness spoke after an NBC internal investigation: 'It then became clear that on other occasions Brian had done the same while telling that story in other venues,' she wrote. 'This was wrong and completely inappropriate for someone in Brian's position. In addition, we have concerns about comments that occurred outside NBC News while Brian was talking about his experiences in the field.'

Williams was suspended without pay for six months in February 2015. It was September that year before he returned, demoted to MSNBC, a smaller cable-news channel.

Did Williams unintentionally amplify the central detail of a Chinook under fire, inadvertently incorporate footage of helicopter crashes into his own narrative?

We judge the intent behind falsehoods through a unique lens: what did he get out of it? Williams earned over ten million dollars each year, the trust of his audience and more than ten million nightly newscast viewers.

David Letterman said to Williams, 'I have to treat you with renewed respect, that is an incredible story . . . you are a true journalist and a war hero.'

All of those awards at least partially recognised his assumed credibility, his valour and honesty. His memories, his retelling of them, stood for who he was. Williams was on the Board of Directors of the Congressional Medal of Honor Foundation. 'The mark of a true hero,' the organisation states, 'is to have the moral courage to do what needs to be done because it is the right thing to do.'

I was on call the night Charlie was transferred to our intensive care unit, heading towards the end of a thirty-six-hour shift. Ventilators hummed, cardiac monitors bleeped. He was wheeled in, his temperature rising, his blood pressure plummeting as sepsis surged through his body. His skin was pale and clammy. I drew a tourniquet from the pocket of my green scrubs, placed a line into his arm, dripped antibiotics into his veins, dispatched intravenous fluids through his circulation. I waited for him to tell stories again.

A Wolf in the Forest. Perhaps.

The stories of Brian Williams, Hillary Clinton, George Bush – could they be our stories, too?

The common thread is the highly emotional circumstances surrounding these memories. Bush was being told about 9/11. Clinton was visiting a region that had seen war (even if she wasn't in any way under attack). Williams had been embedded with US troops. Could an emotional surge compromise the accuracy of recollection?

Flashbulb memories were described by psychologists Roger Brown and James Kulik in 1977 as 'memories for the circumstances in which one first learned of a very surprising and consequential (or emotionally arousing) event'. Vivid, startling, like photographs taken with a flash-bulb. They were, as William James – philosopher and psychologist – described in 1890, 'so exciting emotionally as almost to leave a scar upon the cerebral tissues'.

Brown and Kulik thought that memories infused with emotion, such as the assassination of John F. Kennedy, would create not just vivid recollections, but accurate ones, too. These memories, formed through a unique remembering mechanism, would resist forgetting. Consider your own flashbulb memories – do they seem more concrete, more ingrained than others?

The theory was persuasive but these original studies examined memories reported many years after the index event without comparison to the participants' memories of the early aftermath, or indeed of neutral events.

A later study by a different group examined flashbulb memories following the 11 September terrorist attacks. Their study recruited 3,000 adults from seven US cities.

After a year, participants' memories were consistent with their original accounts only 63% of the time. That figure was 57% at three years. Even their memory of emotions changed over time. Strong emotional reactions such as sadness, anger, fear, confusion, frustration and shock were remembered poorly, even more so than non-emotional features such as where and from whom one learned of the attack.

Emotion seems to enhance the recollective experience: the subjective vividness of the memory, the sense of reliving the event and confidence in the accuracy of the memory. But accuracy itself does not follow.

Recollection works better in soft paragraphs than hard bullet points.

These soft paragraphs bear surprising levels of conviction. Clinton, Williams, Bush and others remained seemingly certain of their memories until video footage or collateral accounts proved otherwise. In studies of 9/11 and of the space shuttle *Challenger* explosion, conviction in flashbulb memories rose even as accuracy fell. Emotion changes how and what we remember and how sure we are.

'I could have sworn it happened like that.'

Personal experience is also key. Where were you during the last World Cup or Olympic Games? The memory circuits drawn into action as you watched Lionel Messi, Simone Biles or Usain Bolt seem to vary according to whether you had ringside seats or a remote control. The same goes for distressing memories of a traumatic event – being enveloped by an experience modifies how you remember it.

A 2006 study found that people closer to the 9/11 attacks in downtown Manhattan seemed to have a different response compared to those a few miles away in midtown.

More of the downtown group had seen the smoke, heard the noise, watched the planes crash. 'I saw with my own eyes: the towers burning in red flames, noises and cries of people.' 41% of them had come under direct personal threat, trying to avoid falling debris, for instance.

None of the midtown group encountered direct threat, although 60% had direct sensory experiences related to the attacks – seeing buildings collapse, for instance. Most experienced the events second-hand. 'I was in the office and heard about the attack. I looked on the internet'; 'I remember watching TV news coverage at Café Tacci and presumably hearing sounds of explosions on TV.'

Researchers scanned each group with functional MRI to assess brain activity as they recalled the events of 9/11, and found that there was enhanced activation of the hippocampus in all participants. This makes sense since the hippocampus mediates memory formation, retention and retrieval.

But scanning of the downtown participants showed selective activation of the amygdala as they recalled 9/11. The amygdala, a structure in the temporal lobe, is important for processing emotional information. It seems to encourage retention of emotional memories, linked to the release of cortisol, influencing their consolidation and storage.

And so as the amygdala and hippocampus connected, emotion and memory interacted.

Flashbulb-focus on this crucial thing, the amygdala advises us, when information with high emotional content surges towards us. Memories moulded by the amygdala, emotional memories, seem more vivid. With these sorts of memories, we have a sense of reliving the event. We often bear absolute confidence in their truth.

Ringside and remote control memories diverge. Close personal experience seems to engage different neural circuitry that draws upon the amygdala. That's not to say that these memories are more accurate. The amygdala thrives on gist, not detail.*

---

* Since the amygdala is involved in enhanced memory for gist rather than details of complex stimuli, the theme of a memory is captured but encoding of contextual details can be compromised. Compare this with the hippocampus – its particular strength lies in focusing on contextual recollection of a neutral scenario.

Something else happened to the downtown participants as they remembered 9/11. There was decreased activation in the parahippocampal cortex, a region linked more closely to processing and recognition of details of a scene. Perhaps this also explains why being up close and personal to a highly emotional event leads to us losing the specifics.

There's a lot to be said for gist as assisted by the amygdala, particularly if it confers evolutionary advantage.

Picture this. You are confronted by a terrifying wolf-like creature in an isolated part of the forest. As it happens, you were in a similar part of the forest a couple of months ago and experienced another terrifying encounter with a similar animal. It doesn't really matter if today's animal is quite the same as the one a couple of months ago; the general impression is what counts. Your past experience, or at least what you recall of it, will inform your behaviour this time round. So in an emotional situation (isolated part of forest, terrifying animal), vivid memories for selected critical details seem more important in guiding your actions.

Conversely, contextual detail is more useful in neutral situations when it comes to decision-making. Who cares if your memory for the forest/animal is entirely accurate? If you're confident in the accuracy of emotionally charged memory (despite its utter inaccuracy), no harm done because that's potentially an adaptive mechanism – you act quickly based on the essentials, on inference, and you escape the wolf-like creature in an isolated forest. Spending time thinking about overall memory quality would just slow you down.

Drawing upon the wolf story, Elizabeth Phelps and Tali Sharot from New York University and University College

London propose that the rich, subjective experience of recollection that occurs with emotion allows for faster decision-making. If a stimulus previously led to a strong emotional response such as fear, encountering a similar (albeit not necessarily identical) stimulus now tells you that this situation requires prompt action.

We grow ever more confident in our memories as they develop blurred edges. We are blissfully impervious to their haziness. If we escape the dangerous animal in the forest, that lack of focus is a price worth paying. Run, just run.

Construction Site: Work in Progress

Take yourself back to your first kiss. Maybe it was on a date – a moonlit night, stars sparkling and waves gently crashing. Maybe it was by a cloakroom with the DJ playing 'Come On Eileen', the smell of cigarette smoke and cheap gin.

Either way, when you remember that moment, you are not really remembering *that* moment. Instead, you're remembering the last time you remembered it – retrieving what you recalled before and infusing that memory with the experiences and perceptions you've gathered since then. With remembering, there is rebuilding. And that is the thing about memory: it's a home constantly under reconstruction, not a video playing on a loop.

When Brian Williams remembered, he remembered the last time he remembered. Us too.

It was the work of Karim Nader, Glenn Schafe and Joseph Le Doux in 2000 that challenged conventional understanding of what happens when memories are reignited. But to understand how memories were made, they first had to block them. Nader was a graduate student in his early thirties who had an idea that he could erase fear memories in rats. His results would shake the foundations of memory research.

He and his fellow researchers trained rats to fear a neutral tone by associating it with an electric shock. Hear the tone, remember the shock. When just the neutral tone was played later, without the shock, the rats experienced the same fear response – they froze.

The formation of new memories requires the manufacture of proteins. The conventional dogma suggested that the proteins had done all their work the day before when the fear memory was constructed and consolidated for good. So if you were to call up the fear memory the next day (by playing that tone again), you wouldn't need the same proteins to all kick into action.

There is a neat way to test this. Anisomycin is a drug that interrupts the active manufacture of those proteins. If the old dogma is true, you wouldn't expect the anisomycin to have any effect when you reactivate yesterday's fear memory today (since you're not creating a new memory, no active protein formation is happening). The memory from yesterday has been already consolidated – put into long-term storage and resistant to change – said conventional thinking; the proteins had kicked in yesterday. All we're now doing here is taking a bound book out of the library. You'd expect anisomycin to be redundant.

But here's what happened to the mice instead. The tone was replayed the following day to reactivate the memory and anisomycin was injected into the lateral amygdala, an area important for fear. The rats who received the drug soon after hearing the tone forgot their fear. This meant a new collection of proteins had unexpectedly been summoned into action, giving anisomycin something to do – block active proteins. That's how the fear response from the day before was forgotten. Reactivation of the memory drove it to a vulnerable fluid state where it could be rewritten, reconstructed.

This represented a seismic shift in the understanding of memory. Recollection was not hard-wired after all; instead of memories becoming fixed once initially stored, they were inherently flexible.*

And there seems to be value to this despite any compromise in precision. As we update a memory, its relevance is enhanced – we incorporate what we have learned and felt since the last time it was taken out of the library. There is potentially another benefit, too, with each update: preparation for the future. Like a software update that learns from the past, crowdsources feedback, and looks beyond today.

The work from Nader and his colleagues suggests that at least under some circumstances, each time we remember something we remembered before, a novel rebuilding process occurs. That first kiss of yours – retrieve the memory, reactivate the trace, see those proteins gather and cells shift, watch the circuit spark, add a coating of what you know now that you didn't know then and store the memory for another day.

---

* Donald Lewis, a Rutgers psychologist, and his team had performed similar animal experiments in the late 1960s (using electroconvulsive shocks instead of anisomycin), but the findings were so contrary to conventional theories of memory that his experiments and similar ones were largely dismissed over the next decade.

If these theories of reconsolidation and rewiring certain memories are correct, the potential for therapy is intriguing. Let's say you carry a traumatic memory. A psychiatrist speaks to you to reactivate it. As it is brought to the surface, the memory is malleable. It's a small window of opportunity, only a matter of six hours or so, but you are injected with a drug or receive intensive psychological therapy just as the memory starts to reconsolidate. And so you have a chance to rewrite the memory, add a filter of your choosing and store it away without the fear that enveloped it before. This is solely about removing the fear association of a memory rather than erasing the memory itself (don't believe the sensational headlines about your memories being annihilated entirely . . . yet).

Despite an initial flurry of studies that convincingly replicated Nader's results in animals, not all have supported this model of reconsolidation in humans over the last five years or so. A small electrical shock to the foot of a mouse does not equate to the experience of human combat or assault, nor does it allow for the extent and depth of trauma or how remote that trauma was.

But if our understanding of reconsolidation is expanded in humans in the next few years, could Brian Williams be vindicated? The emotions he experienced during his time in Iraq might well have enhanced the vibrancy of his memories, the sense of reliving those events (remember the downtown 9/11 experiments and the amygdala being called into action) and his confidence in the accuracy of his memories. And as he reactivated his memory of the Chinook attack while talking to David Letterman and many others, you could decide he rewrote it with each remembering, and stored it away afterwards, transformed. Ready for the next telling. Ready for the next remembering.

But it's one thing to rewrite the emotional response of a traumatic event and another to rewrite the memory in its entirety. To transform that memory so radically that Brian Williams remembered being on a Chinook helicopter under fire, shielding himself from rocket-propelled grenades and watching as a brave and bloodied pilot sitting next to him landed that Chinook in a desert sandstorm. Could all of us so catastrophically misremember? How far are we really from Brian Williams?

The Childhood You Never Had

In the 1990s, psychologists Elizabeth Loftus and Jacqueline Pickrell convinced a quarter of participants they had been lost in a shopping mall as a child even though they had not been. 'I was crying and I remember that day . . . I thought I'd never see my family again,' one said. The 'Lost in the Mall' study confirmed to Loftus and others that therapists could inadvertently implant false memories of childhood sexual abuse in their clients. Later studies by her group and others convinced participants that in childhood they had, variously, almost drowned, witnessed demonic possession, taken a hot-air balloon trip, knocked over a wedding cake or been attacked by vicious animals.

More recently, Julia Shaw and Stephen Porter, from the universities of Bedfordshire and British Columbia respectively, drew upon suggestive memory techniques to convince undergraduate students that they had a criminal history.

After three interviews, 70% of study participants had false memories of committing a crime in early adolescence (theft, assault or assault with a weapon) that led to police contact, and even volunteered a detailed false account. Here is a transcript:

> Subject: I remember the two cops. There were two. I know that for sure . . . I have a feeling, like, one was white, and one maybe Hispanic . . . I remember getting in trouble. And I had to, like, tell them what I did. And why I did it, and where it happened . . .
>
> Interviewer: You remember yelling?
>
> Subject: I feel like she called me a slut. And I got ticked off and threw a rock at her. And the reason why I threw a rock at her was because I couldn't get close to her . . .
>
> Interviewer: So you threw a rock instead?
>
> Subject: That was bad. That was bad. Bad scene . . . Oh wow, that's crazy.

The study was ended prematurely.

Even those with a highly superior autobiographical memory (HSAM; also known as hyperthymesia) are susceptible to memory distortion. HSAM individuals can remember the day of the week a date fell on and details of what happened that day and every other day of their lives from around the middle of childhood. When those details are verified, HSAM individuals are correct 97% of the time. Yet on tests that do not focus on autobiographic memory, they only score in the average range.

Lawrence Patihis and his colleagues tested HSAM participants in a 2013 study. One was asked what happened on 19 October 1987: 'It was a Monday,' she immediately responded, correctly. 'That was the day of the big stock market crash and the cellist Jacqueline du Pré died that day.' The group was then asked about (non-existent) footage of the United 93 crash in Pennsylvania. Written information was provided first: 'video footage of the plane crashing taken by one of the witnesses on the ground has been well publicised'. This was followed by the suggestive question, 'Have you seen the video?'

20% of HSAM individuals and 29% of controls indicated they had seen the footage.

Where does this leave Brian Williams and Charlie and the rest of us with false memories? There are commonalities between us all – we transpose and embellish, memories intrude and disrupt, an incomplete narrative is presented as complete. And so I believe Charlie's confabulation might hint towards what we are all capable of. But not all researchers would agree.

In the literature around confabulation, you'll often see mention of just two types: spontaneous and provoked, with unique underlying pathology in each case.

Spontaneous confabulators are characterised, these researchers suggest, by stories produced with no external trigger or encouragement: the sort of thing Charlie did. Patients act upon these stories, which are often more vivid and elaborate than provoked confabulations. In contrast to those with more quotidian false memories, spontaneous confabulators usually have clear structural brain damage with disorientation and a profound derangement of thought; one patient with a ruptured aneurysm was convinced that she had to go home to feed her baby (the patient was fifty-eight at the time, her daughter over thirty). This is quite distinct from a moment of memory embellishment, a fleeting discrepancy, your decision to subtly spice up your featureless holiday story.

Conversely, provoked confabulations arise in response to an external trigger – direct questioning or psychological testing, for example. Provoked confabulation is not consistently linked to a specific region of brain damage and might be more representative of our everyday imprecise memories – filled with conflation and tinged with confusion. Brian Williams fits into this provoked category.

But I think that this represents a false dichotomy and instead that a spectrum of confabulation exists. Some patients with ruptured brain aneurysms, for example, initially have so-called spontaneous confabulation and later provoked confabulation (and later still, none) as their condition improves. We can all confabulate – especially, I believe, when emotion overrides our doubt tags. Confabulation exposes the fragility of memory; at the very least it forces us to doubt our memories as veridical recordings. Charlie is just further down the line than Brian Williams. We might not be too far behind.

Bearing False Witness

The fallibility of memory comes under sharp focus on the witness stand.

21 December 1988. Pan Am flight 103 explodes over Lockerbie. All 259 passengers die. Eleven people on the ground are also killed. Abdelbaset al-Megrahi is later

convicted of mass murder and sentenced to life with a minimum jail term of twenty-seven years.

In 2013, Elizabeth Loftus examined case evidence as part of the post-conviction review. Loftus is Distinguished Professor of Psychology and Social Behaviour and Professor of Law at the University of California, Irvine. She has been an expert witness or consultant in hundreds of well-known cases, including the trial of officers accused in the Rodney King beating, the trial of Oliver North, the Ted Bundy murder case and litigation involving Michael Jackson, Martha Stewart, Scooter Libby and the Duke University lacrosse players.

The testimony of a Maltese shopkeeper, Mr Tony Gauci, was central to Megrahi's conviction and pivotal to Loftus's analysis.

During the search investigation around Lockerbie, fifty-six fragments of a hardshell Samsonite suitcase were discovered. Clothing thought to have originally been packed into the suitcase included a blue Babygro, men's shirts, Yorkie-brand men's trousers and a herringbone jacket. Within the fibres of the Babygro was a 'Made in Malta' label; this would later be traced back to Tony Gauci's store in Silema, a coastal town there.

The suitcase in turn was thought to contain explosives concealed in a Toshiba radio cassette player. Investigators soon linked a fragment of a timer circuit board found during their Lockerbie search with a Swiss electronics firm who had sold twenty such timers to Libya, aiming to secure a contract with their military. Owner Edwin Bollier had met Megrahi in Libya during this sale and later rented an office to him in Zurich.

One of the investigators' tasks was to place Megrahi at Tony Gauci's shop, Mary's House, in Silema in late 1988.

Interviewed in September 1989, some nine months later, Gauci described the shopper as 'six feet or more in height, big chest, large head, clean-shaven, wearing a dark-coloured two-piece suit and speaking Libyan'. He recalled the shopper buying a blue Babygro, Yorkie-brand men's trousers and a herringbone jacket.

Gauci was called upon two weeks later to create a photofit and worked with a police artist to produce a sketch that he felt was more accurate.

The first of many photo viewings took place the following day. Of the nineteen photos, he felt one bore a resemblance to the shopper but was too young.

During another viewing on 6 December 1989, he failed to make an identification of one Abu Talb but later thought that he resembled the shopper when his brother showed him a *Sunday Times* story. He did not make any identification during a subsequent viewing of thirty-nine photos that included Abu Talb. By 15 February 1991, Gauci had made a 'highly tentative' identification of Megrahi from a selection of twelve photos. The man in photo number 8, he said, would have to look ten years older to look like the shopper and would have to have shorter hair.

Four days before a 1999 line-up, Gauci saw a photograph of Megrahi in a magazine story that linked him to the bombing. During the line-up, he picked out Megrahi.

Football matches and Christmas decorations: where innocence and guilt are determined. Around nine months after the clothing purchase, Gauci said he had met the shopper 'one day in the winter of 1988' in his store. In his initial testimony, he had stated that Christmas decorations were not up. He remembered being in the shop on his own as his brother was watching the football.

The football matches helped narrow the dates to 23 November or 7 December. Megrahi was apparently in Malta around the first week in December. But the absence of Christmas lights would date the purchase instead to 23 November, when Megrahi was not documented to be in Malta.

In his 2000 trial testimony, Gauci said 'there were Christmas lights on already, I'm sure.' His altered testimony now crucially favoured the December date (also favoured by the prosecution) and was one factor that incriminated Megrahi.

Think back to Christmases gone past. Can you remember whether the Christmas lights were up in your home or on the high street on a given day last year, let alone ten years ago? Imagine being interviewed about this formally twenty-three times over twelve years and being visited by detectives fifty times – as Gauci was. Would your confidence grow or diminish over the years?

Some eleven years after that very first police interview, Gauci was asked if he saw the shopper in the courtroom. He pointed to Megrahi and said, 'He is the man on this side. He resembles him a lot.'

Elizabeth Loftus points to a number of factors that could have influenced this eyewitness testimony.

For one, over two years had passed between the clothing purchase and Gauci's first 'identification' (quotation marks: hers) of Megrahi.

Familiar can be as good as guilty. Gauci would have seen many photos of Megrahi, including the one his brother showed him, dead-or-alive posters and even pictures on matchboxes in Libya and its neighbouring countries at the time. Megrahi had been on the FBI's Ten Most Wanted Fugitives list since 1995.

Imagine that you volunteer, as an innocent person, to be included in a series of mugshots. As you would hope, the witness does not identify you. Next you participate in a second line-up being inspected by the same witness, who has seen your mugshot. You are now rather worryingly identified by the witness as a perpetrator. If your photograph is seen before a line-up, the chances of being falsely identified as a criminal rises to 20%, even more so if there are fewer mugshots or when the real suspect is absent. Almost 80% of US judges in a 2004 survey acknowledged this mugshot-induced bias phenomenon to be true.

Your days as a mugshot volunteer are over.

To date, 342 people in the United States have been exonerated by DNA testing via the Innocence Project, including twenty who served time on death row. 75% of these wrongful convictions involved erroneous identifications from victims or witnesses. More errors occur when a member of one race attempts to identify an unknown person of another race (compared to a stranger of the same race). An innocent suspect is more likely to be identified as a culprit if (s)he is wearing clothes similar to those of the suspect viewed by the eyewitness.

There are attempts to avoid the shortcomings of current practices – using double blinded line-ups, standardised witness instructions, videotaped identification processes and expert testimony during court proceedings on eyewitness reliability.

But as long as memory remains fallible, the legal process is, too. If physical trace can be contaminated at the crime scene, so can memory beyond it.

Back to Lockerbie.

Mohammed Abu Talb was an agent (General Commando) for the PFLP-GC, the People's Front for the Liberation of Palestine, a radical Palestinian splinter group. Investigators soon learned that he had visited Malta twice in October and November 1988. Clothing bought in Malta was found in his flat. Although Abu Talb was a suspect initially, the timeline of events didn't seem to fit with Gauci's testimony. Investigators also thought his Egyptian accent would have been recognised by the shopkeeper. Instead, Abu Talb later acted as a prosecution witness in Megrahi's trial. He and other members of the PFLP-GC were subsequently linked to Lockerbie by investigators who were, it is important to acknowledge, commissioned by Megrahi in preparation for a second appeal.

In 1989, Abu Talb was given a life sentence in Sweden for carrying out bombings in Copenhagen and Amsterdam. Since being released, he continues to deny any link to the Lockerbie bombing and says he was babysitting on the day Pan Am flight 103 fell from the sky.

Megrahi was convicted on 31 January 2001 and sentenced to life imprisonment. His first appeal was unsuccessful. In 2007, the independent Scottish Criminal Cases Review Commission (SCCRC) concluded that his conviction could have been a miscarriage of justice and granted him leave to appeal for a second time. Megrahi dropped his second appeal to avoid any delay in his 2009 release on compassionate grounds. He died in Tripoli of prostate cancer, aged sixty, on 20 May 2012.

The conviction remains contentious, not solely because of Gauci's account but because of a litany of concerns around forensic evidence, political interests and discredited witnesses. In October 2009, legal reports revealed that Tony Gauci and his brother Paul had received rewards of up to three million dollars under the US Department of Justice's 'reward-for-justice' programme.

I look back and think that it was the memory of a Maltese shopkeeper on trial as much as it was Megrahi. Justice can stand or fail on the success or failure of how we remember.

During a search of Abu Talb's home, terrorist investigators found a calendar on the kitchen table. On it, the date of 21 December 1988, the day of the Lockerbie bombing, was circled.

He had circled it to remind himself of something. To remember.

Who Do You Think You Are?

Memories reflect personal stories, narratives we weave through our inner perspective. These are not perfect transcripts; instead, stories are adapted around our values and hopes. In most cases our memories are not closely scrutinised – listening to someone's story is not usually a fact-checking exercise. In our minds, unless we are actively trying to deceive, these memories are true to what we experienced, albeit with a filter of our choosing. The story is cropped a little here and there. That filtered photo is posted and becomes the new original. Click 'like'. Subjectivity does not equate to deception.

And so who are we when those stories are filtered – are our identities threatened? There's a narrative view of identity which suggests that, to an extent, we are our stories. As psychologist Dan McAdams says: 'People create unity and purpose in their lives, and they make sense of the psychosocial niches they inhabit in adulthood through stories, even if they must rely on more than one story to do so.'

We have a conception of ourselves that is enduring and that can be expressed.

Self-told tales are filled with ambitions to be realised, tasks to be completed, beliefs to be shared and the past and future to be owned. Connections are woven between past and present, between self and others.

I am reluctant to embrace the narrative account in its entirety. Not all of my patients can tell stories in this way; the narrative view might exclude them. Anita's embodiment, for example, went beyond the accuracy or veracity of a given story. Although storytelling might help us coherently and wholly construct and understand ourselves, it seems strange to say that we must tell a story to do so. The narrative might simply be the vehicle for driving where we were going to get to anyhow. And quite simply, not everyone chooses to frequently remember and tell stories about themselves.

At most, narrative is important for many, crucial for some, but it isn't the imperative by which we define identity. On this, Galen Strawson, British analytic philosopher and literary critic, is emphatic: 'There are deeply non-Narrative [sic] people and there are good ways to live that are deeply non-Narrative [sic]. I think the [narrativity theses] hinder human self-understanding, close down important avenues of thought, impoverish our grasp of ethical possibilities, needlessly and wrongly distress those who do not fit their model, and are potentially destructive in psychotherapeutic contexts.'

Where stories are told, when memories are recalled, sustaining identity might simply depend upon some form of continuity to the narrative – in moral perspective or character, for instance. So, a person who turns up at your door without any life story to tell, with an entirely empty box of memories (as seen in fugue states, Benjaman's story outlined later in this book), might be discontinuous with his or her former self.

False memories undeniably have all sorts of forensic, moral and social consequences. The exposure of Brian Williams' imperfect memories (embellished, deceitful or otherwise) led to his fall from grace. Flawed witnesses lead to miscarriages of justices. Our narratives might, on occasion, be marked by chronological confusion and conflation just the way Charlie's were; by embellishment and elaboration. But those inaccuracies and inconsistencies generally do not change the essence of who we are, the sameness of our characters from year to year. We remain ourselves.

Charlie was out of Intensive Care within a fortnight. His sepsis had settled but his liver function was fading fast. He still spoke of Harry the butler and egg and spoon races and purple trampolines. I realised that the memory tests I had performed when we first met told me much about the depth of his amnesia but little about the character of his remembering.

He absconded from the ward three days later, an intravenous cannula still in his arm and the bottle of alcohol gel empty once again. He made his bed before he left.

I never saw Charlie after that but I hope that he later found happiness or comfort or validation in the memories that were true to him. In a way, he taught me that that's what we all try to do.

3
Mugshots

During the summer holidays, my parents took us on trips back to their homeland – the state of Assam in north-eastern India.

And so formed childhood memories of death-defying rickshaw rides, men chewing paan and lounging about in brown toe-loop sandals. Women gliding by in vibrant sari-like mekhela chador. Our cheeks forever pinched and heads forever patted by a series of loving aunties and uncles. Fans swirling and swishing hot, acidic air. Vats of pungent daal, masor tenga, aloo paratha and laru. Army guards holding up my Irish passport to the light, golden harp etched onto its front cover; chins stroked and notes counted. Cool, refreshing, sheets of rain thud, thud, thud, wash the streets clean.

And yet so many of my early memories of Assam seem to have evaporated. How could I have forgotten weeks of conversations with my late grandparents, a safari to find a one-horned rhinoceros with my uncle (we found one, my parents tell me), even small earthquakes and a large landslide? There were my parents trying their very best to create lifelong memories and I couldn't even hold on to them.

We all have experienced islands of memory loss, moments irretrievable from our past. There are parts of certain experiences, memories and perceptions that are inaccessible to us at times. As if looking through a storm drain on a pavement, streetlights overhead flickering and then fading.

What lie ahead are the stories of our everyday forgetting, followed by tales of wandering amnesiacs and fraudsters. Memories unearthed and buried. But unlike the stories earlier, of Anita with Alzheimer's dementia or Charlie with Korsakoff's syndrome, everybody you will read about next has no brain damage to explain their memory loss. By that I mean none of the abnormal proteins of Alzheimer's under the microscope, none of the brain atrophy you might see on Charlie's MRI scan. In fact, you might find yourself featured in quite a few of these stories. And in each case, you might join me in wondering if amnesia should ever be treasured.

The Disappearance of Disney

Think back to your three- or four-year-old self. A few early recollections might shimmer. Are they enough to fill a page, a small notebook, a tome? Most of us are unable to retrieve memories of our early lives. Memories are sparse if not absent from the years before we started to speak. We rarely recall events before the age of three and can only summon up fragmented memories from between the ages of three and seven.*

---

* Although the average age of first memories is perceived to be three and a half years, recent research suggests childhood memories could instead date back to the age of two; as we get older, we date our earliest memory to more than a year after it actually happened. This post-dating of memories is known as a telescoping error – an object appears closer when viewed through a telescope.

'Forgetting,' said Martin Heidegger, is 'more primordial than remembering.' Childhood amnesia, decided Freud, 'veils our earliest youth from us and makes us strangers to it' – a defence mechanism against childhood trauma.

It turns out, however, that young children do indeed create memories but lose some just as quickly. Take the 1991 research paper entitled 'Memories of Mickey Mouse: Young children recount their trip to Disneyworld'. Children around the ages of three to four years old were asked to recall details either six months or eighteen months after their holiday.

Not many scientific papers have a paragraph like this one:

48 subjects interacted with a variety of characters such as Mickey Mouse and Goofy, and 81% of all children went on the Jungle Boat ride and It's a Small World. In addition, 79% of the children went on the Dumbo ride, 73% went on a train ride, and over 50% of all subjects went on the merry-go-round and the Tea Cup ride.

Children remembered plenty of accurate information, a mean of forty propositions, regardless of what age they were or the interval since the trip. Younger children recounted just as much as older children though needed more questions and prompts to provide the same level of Disney detail.

Not for long, though. A US study recorded conversations between mothers and their children, starting when the children were three. By the age of seven, they remembered 64% of the events they had talked about four years before. Eight-year-olds remembered only 36% of these past events.

Now summon up a childhood memory that seems quite solid to you. Perhaps an early birthday. You might swear you remember the preparations in the days beforehand or the games you played that day. But even the things we think we remember from childhood could simply be a reconstruction of stories told to us, ideas and facts layered on to experiences and photographs from that time. Not necessarily that rich evocative sense of something truly, viscerally recalled. When you pack your suitcase of childhood memories and the person at customs asks if you've packed your luggage yourself, the truth is that many people have helped you.

Understanding childhood amnesia requires stepping briefly into a world of mice and running wheels. New neurons rapidly grow within infants' brains, a process called neurogenesis. It's a process that slows down with later childhood and adult life.

A group of Toronto researchers began their experiments by subjecting adult mice to electric shocks in a box. After they had been shocked, some of the mice were allowed to remain deservedly sedentary while the others were provided with a running wheel. Brisk exertion on a running wheel triggers neurogenesis in the brain's hippocampus. After six weeks, each group of mice was placed back into the box. The sedentary mice demonstrated fear (they froze); the running-wheel mice showed no such response. In other words, running-wheel mice (who had more neurogenesis) were more likely than sedentary mice to forget experiences.

This remains an open research field but these findings could lend themselves to an explanation of childhood amnesia: brisk neurogenesis around the age of two or three leads to remodelling in the hippocampus, the seat of learning and memory. These new neurons compete with existing ones to form novel connections. Earlier memories are now inaccessible – the equivalent of forgetting the shocks in the mice experiment – or they vanish entirely.

Childhood amnesia allows us to fine-tune our memories and to create rich, multimodal recollections.

Forgetting allows for remembering.

Where Did I Leave My Phone/Car/Keys?

Memory glitches persist as language develops but some glitches might be worthwhile.

Na-vonotootse'a is a Cheyenne word that describes the singular moment of a word being there but not quite there.

Harvard psychologists Roger Brown and David McNeill described the experience in 1966: 'The signs of it were unmistakable; he would appear to be in mild torment, something like the brink of a sneeze, and if he found the word his relief was considerable.'

In this tip-of-the-tongue (TOT) phenomenon, the elusive word is tantalisingly close. We typically have partial recall: we know the type of word we are looking for (that tyre-thing you put on the side of a boat) or one that sounds fairly close (lender, fader) but the real word (fender) is temporarily inaccessible.

The TOT metaphor is far-reaching enough with a place in just about every lexicon, identified in about 90% of native speakers of fifty-one languages. There is 'on the tip/point of the tongue' in Afrikaans (*op die punt van my tong*), 'at the head of the tongue' in Estonian (*keele otsa peal*), 'on the top of the tongue' in Irish (*ar bharr theanga agam*), 'sparkling at the end of the tongue' in Korean (*hyeu kkedu-temam-dol-da*), and 'I have lost it on my tongue' in Cheyenne (*na-vonotootse'a*).

Five languages use 'in the mouth' to describe the experience: (Cantonese Chinese, Mandarin Chinese, Hindi, Hausa and Ibo). Several West African languages captured this temporary inaccessibility through the metaphor 'hole in the head'. In sign language, the 'tip of the fingers' phenomenon parallels TOT.

No equivalent TOT idiom has been identified in Icelandic, Indonesian or two sub-Saharan African languages, Kalenjin and Kiswahili.

There are two views as to why TOT occurs. The first suggests that the unretrieved word directly causes the TOT experience. The TOT state directly detects the word's presence in your memory. This detection of presence is strong enough to trigger TOTs but not the word, at least temporarily. The sneeze not sneezed.

However, more captivating is the inferential view, described by researchers at Dartmouth College in 1993: clues and cues, rather than the unretrieved word, drive the experience of feeling that the word is just within reach. We infer it's there. Let's take the moon landing – if you're asked the name of the first person on the moon, the answer (Neil Armstrong) might not be available to you but you might instead be familiar with the Apollo programme. So, that feeling of familiarity relates to the cue (Apollo programme) rather than the target answer (Neil Armstrong). This cue familiarity triggers the TOT. And hopefully the sneeze.

Although TOT becomes more frequent with age, the phenomenon might be adaptive, increasing our efforts to retrieve words and memories; we sense they are there, we search harder: 'Don't tell me, don't tell me, I know it, don't google it!'

Many of the patients I see at my cognitive clinic don't have cognitive impairment. Instead, they arrive with concerns around their everyday forgetting. Might this be a harbinger of something more serious, they wonder? They provide a meticulous account of their symptoms; usually they are more perturbed than their families (who often have not noticed anything amiss at all), their neuropsychological results are stellar, their brains look wonderfully plump and healthy on MRI scans and they go back to their normal lives after our assessment, reassured.

'I forgot why I went upstairs' is a classic form of everyday forgetting that people worry about. Actually, it's a constructive form of mental block. Revealed over the past decade as a compartmentalisation effect, entering and exiting doorways creates event boundaries in the mind. We leave perceivably less useful information from the last room behind us and instead focus on the next space, a location-updating effect. Thoughts and memories are separated and organised; we travel across borders taking only what we need (or so we think). The irritating part is that compartmentalisation frequently results in impaired retrieval of thoughts that were formulated only a few feet away, through a doorway in another room.

Here's another example of everyday forgetting. Every now and then, I lose my car. I wander around a multi-storey car park, disheartened as I press the key fob repeatedly, listening for that reassuring ping and click. I sometimes even have to go up a level or down a level until I hear it, fairly sure that my ineptitude is the afternoon entertainment for the

CCTV security staff. Forgetting where I parked my car occasionally does not affect my daily functioning. It's not the same as forgetting what my car looks like or repeatedly going to the wrong car park across the city; these things might be more ominous.

Writing about the seven sins of memory, Daniel Schacter, Professor of Psychology at Harvard, labels absent-mindedness as one of these sins, which occurs either when encoding memories or retrieving them.

The encoding errors represent inattention: you were on autopilot when you parked your car (the same applies to when you can't recall where you left your phone). You were more focused on what you needed to get from the shops or what route you were going to take home. Add a poor night's sleep, stress, chronic pain, a hangover or sedatives to the mix and your attention is further compromised – how can you call upon your memory when the memory was not really encoded in the first place?

Absent-mindedness also develops during memory retrieval. I must remember to go to the dry-cleaners later, I must remember to close the window before I go to bed, I must remember to take my medications. These are examples of prospective memory: 'I must remember to' instead of 'remember that time when'.

Being absent-minded about the dry-cleaners is one thing. Being absent-minded flying an airplane is another. Pilots and their fellow crew members call upon prospective memory constantly; they need to remember to remember.

In one study of memory failure in pilots, seventy-four of seventy-five self-reported errors were prospective ones – inadvertent omissions of a normal procedural step. In the

United States between 1987 and 2001, the National Transportation Safety Board (NTSB) identified crew error as a causal factor in twenty-seven major airline accidents. Prospective errors played a pivotal role in five of these.

Northwest Airlines flight 255 crashed in August 1987 just after take-off from Detroit. The NTSB attributed the accident to 'the flight crew's failure to use the taxi checklist to ensure that the flaps and slats were extended'. This was compounded by an electrical power fault at take-off that failed to trigger a warning system.

All six crew members were killed, as were 148 passengers. Just one survived – a four-year-old girl pulled from the burning wreckage in which her parents and brother had died. Now in her thirties, Cecelia Cichan went on to recover from multiple fractures and third-degree burns. Although she cannot remember the crash, she has a tattoo of a plane on her left wrist: 'So many things, scars were put on my body against my will, and I decided to put this on my body for myself.'*

There are, reassuringly, a whole host of safety mechanisms introduced by the aviation industry to protect against these failures. Prompts to remember to remember.

But ultimately, 'I must remember to' really means 'I must not forget to'.

Humans are intrinsically forgetting creatures: *animal obliviscens*, as described by Harald Weinrich, German literary scholar and linguist. But these moments of everyday forgetting are usually not moments that alter our identities

* *Sole Survivor*, film, directed by Ky Dickens. USA: Yellow Wing Productions, 2013.

and when infrequent, they don't interrupt our narrative formation. We don't need to encode and retrieve all information with the same level of detail and effort. There's no point remembering today where you parked your car yesterday if you didn't park it there today. Remembering everything and everywhere has the power to paralyse.

So far, it seems that there is some value in everyday forgetting, despite the exasperation inherent within it. But how about when forgetting is more pervasive, when we forget a lifetime instead of a moment?

Found, but Still Missing

Benjaman is found at 5 a.m. on 31 August 2004. He is lying by a dumpster behind a Burger King outlet in Richmond Hill, Georgia. Unresponsive and semi-naked. Later, he regains consciousness in hospital. He is distressed, at times hysterical. He does not know who he is or who he was. He retains no memories of any time before this moment. He assumes the name Benjaman Kyle. Initials B.K. – Burger King. His mugshot appears on news bulletins even though he has committed no crime. His loss goes viral. He is listed as missing even though you can see him standing right there, in front of the cameras, bewildered.

Before he ended up behind those bins, Benjaman Kyle was somebody else. He had stories to tell, stories of his own. Today, the narrative of his past is missing. He is in a state of fugue, a form of dissociative amnesia.

For sufferers of dissociative amnesia, autobiographical information lies out of reach; personal memories, often of a stressful or traumatic nature, are erased, A crash or an assault, abuse or combat. Minor stressors and major ones.

Autobiographical memories fill the relived story of your own life as you time-travel backwards. This sort of memory is more than recalling personal experiences: it's not just 'I remember a car crash I was in'. It's also more than the simple memory for facts known as semantic memory: the date of the crash, the speed you were driving at or the location. Instead, it's a rich multimodal construct: the sensory experience, your interpretation of it, what the story portrays about you to others. Your understanding of your very own narrative includes the infused emotions around the personal facts. When people read your autobiography, you hope that they'll understand who you were, who you have become, perhaps who you might be in the future.

And this is the very thing that is fractured by dissociative amnesia: autobiographical memory. Usually, it's just islands of memory loss in the aftermath of trauma but occasionally the memory loss is more profound: swathes of memories for a given period of time; perhaps three months of combat, that year of a tumultuous relationship. Frequently, the amnesia has quite a sudden starting point. Memories often, but not always, return.

At its most extreme, you lose your name and your past and turn up dishevelled and perplexed at a police station or a hospital with no idea of who you are or who you were. This is a state called dissociative fugue and this is Benjaman's story. The impulsive, and sometimes compulsive, wanderer (*fugue* is Latin for 'flight'), can end up several thousand miles from the place they set off from. Distressed fugeurs are led to prison cells or emergency departments – found and yet still lost.

All of us can have memory blanks, of course. Fragmented recollections of an uneventful holiday. Splintered memories from a minor car crash. But those in a state of fugue do not simply misplace moments of distress. Instead, an entire memory canvas lies blank. Personal identity is decimated – who am I? At best, there are dashes of grey. Over time, Benjaman would recall part of his social security number, sparse information about siblings and hazy memories of eating grilled cheese sandwiches at the Indiana State Fair. But little more.

For some, fugue lasts days or weeks. For others, years pass without a hint of the past reaching their consciousness. Recovery, if it comes, can be gradual or instant. The recovered find that access is granted again to memories before the fugue. Memories from the period of fugue are, however, denied. The time of bewildered, empty wandering is forgotten. Perhaps all the better.

In dissociative amnesia there is no damage on a brain scan that could account for this profound memory loss. No contusion to point to or bleed to stem or tumour to resect.*

And so people with dissociative amnesia, if they do seek medical attention, are treated by psychiatrists and

---

* There is a distinction, albeit with some overlap, between dissociative amnesia and post-traumatic stress disorder (PTSD). PTSD specifically follows exposure to actual or threatened death, serious injury or sexual violence. The picture of PTSD is more broad: re-experiencing of the event with distressing flashbacks; hyperarousal (such as angry outbursts and hypervigilance); avoidance of anything to do with the original trauma (such as people and places); persistent negative alterations in mood; and more pervasive and profound memory loss. To meet diagnostic criteria, both conditions must result in clinically significant distress or impairment in social, occupational or other important areas of functioning.

psychologists rather than neurologists. Various terms have been used over the years to capture these disorders of memory that persist without contributory brain damage: 'psychogenic', 'hysterical', 'functional'. Despite an estimated 6–7% lifetime prevalence, many never reach medical attention: the memories filter back or they live to accept their vanishing.

Either way, Benjaman Kyle as we know him now did not exist before August 2004.

A Plague of Nervousness

In the nineteenth century, 'fugue' was a broad term that described any number of bewildered wanderers. There were vagrants traversing nations. There were war deserters escaping duty. There were epileptics staggering down alleyways in the aftermath of a seizure. There were hallucinating alcoholics drifting through villages. And itinerants driven demented by the syphilis that seeded their brains. Fugue back then was not inevitably associated with amnesia for one's past or lost personal identity. Most knew who they were, many knew where they were.

Fugue was medicalised in Bordeaux around 1887. Philippe Tissié's thesis *Les Aliénés Voyageurs* contained a collection of cases centred around one of his own, Albert Dadas. Albert's travels began when he was twelve. His peregrinations took him to Paris, Marseilles, Algeria, Aix, Liège, Nuremberg, Linz, Vienna, Prague, Berlin, Posen, Moscow, Constantinople and Algeria. Occasionally Albert would simply hear of a foreign land and off he would go, irrespective of the distance he had to cover or the fate he might face. This was not, Tissié emphasised, just the tale of a wanderer. Albert lost his identity, frequently. And when he came to, befuddled and without money or identification papers, he ended up destitute or in prison or in hospital. He endured several years of forced labour. When he could not identify himself, others tried. A policeman in Moscow approached him: 'I know who you are!', only to confuse him with a known nihilist. Dadas was imprisoned for three months for appearing to be someone else.

> In his normal state, at home, in the factory, or as a cook in the army, he was a good worker, timid, respectful, shy with women. He never drank and when he was on a fugue had a particular hostility to alcohol. At home he would have a regular and uneventful life. Then would come about three days of severe headaches, anxiety, sweats, insomnia, mastur-bation five or six times a night, and then – he would set out.

His fugues were said to have been eventually calmed by falling in love. And hypnosis. Tissié's suggestions to him: (1) You won't masturbate any more; (2) You won't leave Bordeaux any more; and (3) You will come to see me next Sunday at 10 a.m.

Fugue at the time was seen as a form of hysterical amnesia; memories vaporised in a state of stress and excitement. Hysteria had long been the preserve of women, (*hystera*, the Greek word for 'womb'; *hysterikos* – 'of the womb'); a plague of nervousness, sleeplessness, fainting, irritability, erotic fantasy, sensations of heaviness in the abdomen, lower pelvic oedema and, tellingly, 'a tendency to cause trouble for others'. Even Hippocrates and Plato had referred to the restless and migratory uterus. It was diagnosed in up to 50% of women in the Victorian era and there was a host of treatment options: smelling salts, sexual activity or conversely sexual abstinence, genital massage by physicians and vibrators to induce 'hysterical paroxysms'.

The First and Second World wars saw hysteria described in men, variably termed 'war neurosis' and 'shell shock'. Some received psychotherapy; others were subjected to chamber isolation and electric shock treatment.*

Later, the diagnostic label 'fugue' fell out of favour. Medical conditions such as schizophrenia and epilepsy accounted for many cases, and newer theories discredited the concept of hysteria and its pejorative connotations. Psychologist Pierre Janet (1859–1947) coined the terms 'dissociation' and 'subconscious': the mind could double or split, identities could multiply or fragment in the absence of a single brain lesion.

By 1980, hysteria was omitted from diagnostic classifications. Hysterical fugue became dissociative fugue.†

And so fugue was redefined for our times. But some of these people never went away, these people who lost themselves and their place in the world.

---

* The competing cause of fugue, according to neurologist Jean-Martin Charcot (1825–1893) of Pitié-Salpêtrière, was epilepsy. These patients were treated with potassium bromide rather than hypnosis. Nowadays, we can deduce whether a confused, wandering patient is in the midst of a seizure by performing an electroencephalogram (EEG) – a simple non-invasive test that takes around twenty minutes.

† The American Psychiatric Association describes dissociation as 'the disruption of and/or discontinuity in the normal integration of consciousness, memory, identity, emotion, perception, body representation, motor control and behavior.'

Fugue is now thought to carry a 0.2% prevalence in the general population. But how many cases do we really know about? How many other Benjamans are out there waking up behind a dumpster in some alley?

Fugue: Friend or Foe?

Whoever he was, Benjaman's personal showreel has malfunctioned. The clips of his past are grainy, distorted, absent. Benjaman's brain scan might be normal but this only undermines his impairment, his loss.

Earlier, I mentioned that there are occasional upsides to memory loss. Forgetting childhood memories in order to remember later ones, or the adaptive advantage of the 'tip-of-the-tongue' phenomenon, or our ability to filter relatively trivial information in order to hold on to what matters most.

But what about dissociative amnesia and its desperately blank memory canvas – could Benjaman really benefit from an amnesia so sudden and stark?

Paul Schilder and Milton Abeles, junior psychiatrist and clinical director respectively of New York's Bellevue Hospital, wrote in 1935 that hysterical amnesia, as it was then labelled, was a mechanism of evasion, a form of psychological defence.

N.C., a thirty-eight-year-old woman, approached a policeman in the street. She was depressed and agitated: 'I don't know anything about myself.' She was admitted to Bellevue Hospital at 2 a.m. and her life story re-emerged some eight hours later. Her first marriage, she told Schilder and Abeles, had ended when mumps had rendered her husband sterile. She had remarried some ten years ago but she and her second husband had not had sex for five years. Eight months before her hospital admission, she travelled to Florida and fell in love with another man: 'She would like to have stayed in Florida. She also would have liked a divorce but did not want to disrupt her social life. She enjoyed sexual relations and missed them.' But with reluctance, she returned to New York. On the evening of her admission, she recalls feeling hungry, cold, shaken up. She spontaneously recovered at Bellevue but the hours of fugue remained blank.

'The psychogenesis in the case is clear,' the doctors decided. 'From the warm climate of Florida where she found love, she came to a colder climate. She felt "hungry and cold" before the attack. She wanted to be warm and with the man she loved in Florida.'

Amnesia was thus a representation of deeper sentiments, a suicide of sorts: 'In many cases one finds a deep disappointment in the love object. One is dead for the love object. One removes oneself (suicide), but one removes the others at the same time.'

A new identity is created. The previous one is killed off.

This all sounds rather archaic – could an unconscious defence mechanism really situate Benjaman by a dumpster, behind a Burger King outlet in Richmond Hill, Georgia?

Contemporary theories instead merge the psychological and the neuroscientific. Psychological trauma, say supporters of one of these theories, provokes a neurotoxic surge of stress hormones from the adrenal glands that in turn blocks memory retrieval from the hippocampus and amygdala. An intriguing concept but no more than that.

Another possibility is that fugeurs are simply swayed by cultural and media expectations. They are suggestible and susceptible to fantasy and to false memories. They step on stage, eager to play the bemused protagonist. 'Do you know this man with no name?' we are asked as the spotlight lands upon them. We are captivated by the theatre of it all.

Putting aside these putative theories around fugue, isn't it just sometimes convenient to forget? Are the fugeurs nothing more than elaborate fraudsters? Amnesia manufactured to mask a sinister past, to abdicate from legal and financial responsibilities?

Amnesia, writes Professor Michael Kopelman in *The Handbook of Memory Disorders*, is claimed by 25–45% of offenders in cases of homicide, approximately 8% of perpetrators of other violent crimes and a small percentage of non-violent offenders.

Others create a novel identity for nefarious reasons. In 2002, John Darwin, a prison officer from Durham, faked his own death in a North Sea kayak accident in calm waters. His wife of thirty years, Anne, played grieving widow and collected over £500,000 in life insurance payouts while he hid in a bedsit next door with a secret passage through a wardrobe to their home. He obtained a false passport, assuming the identity of John Jones – stolen from a child of the same name who had died a few weeks after birth. Darwin travelled to Cyprus, Gibraltar and the United States to view properties and catamarans. He and his wife then fled to Panama but, five years later, he returned to the UK, walked into a police station and claimed amnesia. This was his statement:

The last clear thing I remember before any of this is a holiday in Norway in the year 2000. I have hazy recollections of being in a kayak, but I cannot remember the accident or anything leading up to it at all. It is, therefore, true to say that I do have some form of amnesia. It was some years later (I am still not sure when) that I turned up at the family home, though I don't know how I got there, and my wife was understandably shocked given that she thought I was dead . . . To stress again, I have limited memory of what occurred between 2000 and the year I regained my memory, which is still unclear.

I have read back the above and can confirm that it is true.

It was not. The ruse was quickly unearthed. A 2006 photograph of the happy couple at an estate agent's in Panama surfaced online. Anne had known all along. They had spent one million dollars on land in Escobal and bought properties elsewhere. Darwin was christened 'Canoe Man' by the media; this seemed infinitely catchier than 'Kayak Man'. Sentenced to over six years each for fraud and money-laundering, John and Anne Darwin were released after three. The couple divorced in 2011.

Financial gain is not the only motive for feigning amnesia. I was once asked to consult on a patient in a forensic psychiatric unit. As is often the way with these places, it lay several minutes away from the main hospital building, unmarked. You probably won't see these units signposted by the hospital entrance. Or else they'll be called the Bluebell Unit or Daffodil Ward or something equally benign. Details are divulged on a need-to-know basis. Security guards buzzed me through. I was ordered to hand over my stethoscope and reflex hammer, suddenly visualised as instruments of strangling and of stabbing. Up two flights of stairs, through three sets of impenetrable doors and there I was in Aryan's room. Prison guards stood close to him but not close enough, I thought.

'Who am I, Doctor? What's my name? I don't know who I am but you look like my sister.'

He had shot his sister six times in the head. And two months into his prison sentence he had claimed sudden amnesia. My cognitive assessment revealed this memory loss was contrived; he suspiciously claimed he had forgotten every single moment from his crime onwards – in true amnesia, there are usually islands, momentary glimpses even, of memory preservation. Unlike Benjaman Kyle, Aryan still knew who he was; he had not lost his personal identity. And unlike most with genuine amnesia, he was bizarrely unconcerned about his memory loss – at one point he told me he was enjoying the experience. I needed more concrete evidence, though, to be certain he was faking his symptoms; the court would, too. I showed him a series of pictures – one by one, three seconds on each, images of a hammer, a chair, a car, and so on. Then I showed him pairs of pictures instead – I started with the hammer that had been in the first series accompanied by a chair that had not. Which of these two pictures did I show you the first time? The chair, he answered. One incorrect answer – hardly unusual. So I showed him the next pair of pictures – he chose incorrectly again. Fifty pairs of pictures we went through and almost every time he chose the wrong option. This was odd; I would have expected him to randomly get half of the questions correct – instead, he performed far below chance, a classic sign of malingering.[*]

He was returned to prison soon after. His court case was a high-profile one and so I saw pictures of his sister regularly in news reports. I did look a bit like her. Aryan had remembered her well.

But Benjaman wasn't faking it, he told Reddit users in 2012:

There are more than 7 billion people on this earth. Most have never heard of me and of the ones that have heard of me there are bound to be some who are not going to believe me. I don't let it worry me. The people that are most familiar with me and my friends believe, so that is enough. Like everything else in this world you are going to have to decide for yourselves where the truth lies.

Was the character of Benjaman Kyle a cover for a criminal past? Over the course of a decade, he was subjected to an FBI investigation, DNA analysis and facial recognition technology. He was listened to by linguists and hypnotised by hypnotists and still, nothing. An appearance on the *Dr Phil* show did not bring forth friends or family, nor did features elsewhere – the BBC, CNN, the *Guardian*, NPR, Fox, CBS and ABC. And they did not bring forth victims

---

[*] 'Malingering' is defined by the American Psychiatric Association as 'the intentional production of false or grossly exaggerated physical or psychological symptoms, motivated by external incentives such as avoiding military duty, obtaining financial compensation, or evading criminal prosecution'. It takes more than one cognitive test on one day to establish if someone is malingering and so I took Aryan through an extended assessment – there were dozens of inconsistencies. In the end, there was no doubt. His was wilful deception.

either. A man trying to hide an unlawful past probably does not willingly provide a mugshot to the international press.

If it was big money that Benjaman was after, the ploy failed spectacularly. Without a legal identity, he was unable to obtain a social security number, driver's licence or bank account and he was not eligible for benefits or food stamps. In any case he refused many donations and initially spent time at a homeless shelter. He worked for a time in low-paid jobs – mowing lawns and then washing dishes in a restaurant – all off the books since he did not officially exist.

Katherine Slater was a nurse at the shelter where Kyle moved to after his hospital discharge. Making it her mission to solve the mystery of his past, she reached out to message boards, scoured missing persons' lists and eventually sought out the media. She later took Kyle into her own home but soon wondered why he seemed less interested in finding his true identity than did others.

In a 2016 interview with the *New Republic*, long after Kyle had moved out following a series of arguments about his hoarding and unfinished building projects around the house, she questioned his motives:

'I'm dead sure there was trauma,' she said. 'But I think he likes being stuck in the place he's stuck in. All these people, all over the country, trying to solve this case? That's a hell of a drug.'

Disconnected

The found Benjaman is an adopted identity. Reborn.

Remote memories seemingly lie inaccessible to Benjaman; a new persona has emerged. And so begins the process of laying down new memories, cementing them and consolidating them. A new narrative will form. A continuous chronicle of self.

In the absence of evidence of fraudulent motives, perhaps trauma really has rendered certain memories inaccessible to him. We allow for memory loss in post-traumatic stress disorder in soldiers after conflict or in victims of assault, even when there is no brain injury. Benjaman, I think, deserves the same allowance.

You might decide that there are elements of his amnesia that have been elaborated – as Benjaman says, 'Like everything else in this world you are going to have to decide for yourselves where the truth lies.'

But his story is a profound lesson in how autobiographic memory shapes identity, whether those personal memories are involuntarily irretrievable or wilfully suppressed. When you cannot fill the pages of your autobiography, or choose not to, how do you know who you are? How can you tell us who you are when the pages lie blank?*

Is there anything Benjaman shares with the person who went missing? The man who set off that day in August 2004, probably within view of the Ogeechee River, knowing who he was as much as any of us do?

If the autobiographical memories we hold become the stories we tell, Benjaman in his failure to retrieve his past exists without narrative.

---

* In the last year, three otherwise healthy and high-functioning people have been described by researchers in Canada and Sweden as never having been able to mentally relive personal experiences – there is no movie they can watch from a first-person perspective even when the facts are known to them. They live only in the present; their past is experienced in the absence of recollection.

Although Benjaman's personality, morals and preferences might share common ground with the ones from years gone by, we have no way of knowing, no friends of his to ask. There isn't anyone to recognise Benjaman, to sit with him and to tell him about himself. The city where he was found, Richmond Hill, has a population of just over 9,000 inhabitants, none of whom could fill in the gaps. Nor could anyone elsewhere, despite his highly publicised case. Identity is collaborative; it embraces the views and observations of others. Years of shared experiences that in Benjaman's case seemed beyond reach.

One fugeur was found on a park bench and remained in a fugue state for several weeks. He was identified by friends after a press conference and only then learned about his personal past.

'When he entered a pub in his area, the waitress reportedly asked him "The same as always?" and then brought him rosé wine. This discovery of his previous preference reportedly took [him] by surprise. Similarly, he was surprised to learn that he used to smoke a special brand of cigarettes and to like dogs.'

Another patient was an avid car driver before his amnesia but afterwards decided that cars were too fast for human beings and refused to sit in them.

Benjaman had one form of memory that remained intact. Although the fugeur might not recall how he or she learned to do things, the ability to do those things, procedural memory, is preserved. Muscle memory maintains the ability to drive a car or tie shoelaces.

In 2013, doctors reported the case of A.Z., a man found in the central railway station of a harbour city in Germany.

He did not know who he was or why he was there, but his slang and his discovery by the harbour hinted towards a nautical past. His medical team asked him to produce some sailing knots:

'Only mentioning to him the name of the respective knot led him to manufacture this type of knot by using the un-plugged electrical cable of a lamp.'

The book *The Bourne Identity* captured this idea. Assassin Jason Bourne (played in the film by Matt Damon) loses his life history. Fishermen discover him floating in the Mediterranean, his body riddled with bullets. There is a bank code embedded in his right hip. But his procedural memory persists through his dissociative fugue. In a pivotal scene in the film Bourne realises:

'I know the best place to look for a gun is the cab of the gray truck outside, and, at this altitude, I can run flat-out for a half mile before my hands start shaking. Now why would I know that? How can I know that and not know who I am?'

But this muscle memory is devoid of the emotion that filters through autobiographic reminiscence. These skills alone do not truly allow Benjaman to feel or be just the way he used to be.

To make things worse, he is unable to tell stories from his past. As Canadian philosopher Charles Taylor wrote, one of the basic conditions of making sense of ourselves is that we grasp our lives in a narrative. To have a sense of who we are, Taylor explains, we have to have a notion of how we have become, and of where we are going.

It is true that our autobiographic memories, even for those of us who are not fugeurs, are hardly omniscient. They are filled with elaboration and embellishment, suppression and repression, false and falsified memories. The stories we create sometimes portray the picture we wish to paint or the painting we want to hide. We edit and copy and paste and cut. We hope that others will hit 'like'.

Accuracy is not mandatory in defining continuity and sameness. But there is a difference between telling inaccurate stories about your past and not having any to tell at all.

This absence of an autobiography matters deeply for Benjaman's identity, I believe. It robs him of the possibility of sameness – the confluence of things that make him *him*, over time. There isn't even the faintest outline of continuity of memory in Benjaman as far as anyone can tell, not a hint of those chains of psychological connectedness.

Writing about Anita earlier in this book, I suggested that her gestures and manner of speech and communication in the midst of Alzheimer's were embodied, that we understood a bit of who she was even if the syntax was disrupted, even if her stories were unconventionally told, even through her neologisms and paraphasias. But hardly anything of Benjaman's past seems to be available to him, nothing to allow for embodiment of his old self. Just vague memories of eating grilled cheese sandwiches at the Indiana State Fair and a later recollection that George W. Bush had been President and that the US had invaded Iraq the year before. Only dashes of grey across the canvas.

One crucial component of autobiographical memory is autonoetic consciousness: the ability to reflect upon ourselves and to distinguish ourselves from others around us. Autonoetic consciousness enables us to mentally represent and become aware of protracted existence across subjective time. And with this emerges a sense of 'sameness' over days and months and years; an ability to relive our prior experiences through mental time travel to the past. I am the person today I was last year. I have a sense of self in time.

The new Benjaman ostensibly lacks these skills. He cannot travel back in time to relive subjective experiences. Establishing a continuum of sameness is not an option.

I'm running out of 'sameness' options for Benjaman. He shouldn't really need us to validate his identity but as it happens, we can't recognise Benjaman; clearly nobody can, because nobody has come forward to claim him. He looks at his reflection with shock. Speaking to National Public Radio in 2014, he said, 'I looked at myself in the mirror, and I just could not believe that that was me that I was looking at. I was so old. I felt like I should be in my forties, and here I'm looking at an old man in the mirror.'

A connection to his physical past is only borne out by the trauma that marks him:

'Two parallel surgical scars on left elbow (from reparative surgery for broken elbow that may involve pins/plates implantation). Surgical scar on front of neck appears to be from cervical discectomy. Small round scar on left side of face near chin appears to be a puncture-type wound but believes it may be related to former tooth abscess. No tattoos. No body piercings.'

I do not want to grasp for sameness only through his scars.

Ultimately, I think that Benjaman shares little with the person he was before. No autobiographical memories to access, no overlapping psychological connections, an uncertainty of past character, no hope of anyone emerging from his past to resolve this chaos. Benjaman Kyle can only look to the future.

Benjaman: Found

Here is Benjaman Kyle's Facebook post from 16 September 2015.

> MY IDENTITY HAS BEEN FOUND! It is now the start of the eleventh year since this began and I never thought this day would come. A little over two months ago I was informed by CeCe Moore that that (sic) they had established my Identity using DNA.

He would soon have a Social Security card; he could finally reclaim his former self. His long-lost relatives live in Indiana; his childhood memories of eating grilled cheese sandwiches at the Indiana State Fair now seem accurate.

His real name: William Burgess Powell.

Bit by bit, the story has come together. William's father, Furman Powell, was a flight engineer in the Second World War and died in a boating accident in 1969. His mother, Marjorie, a photographer, died of cancer in 1996. His brother, Furman Junior, remembers that William was abused by his father; the abuse was 'regular and brutal', he says. William held a string of odd jobs in Lafayette for several years before suddenly disappearing in 1976 with a drinking buddy, leaving all of his possessions behind. His station wagon was found abandoned by the Oakdale Dam. He was soon found by police in Boulder, Colorado, working as a restaurant cook, only to disappear again. His mother was distraught. She died believing that William had been lost for ever. And perhaps he almost was.

William Powell was last seen in Colorado in 1977. Benjaman Kyle was found in Richmond Hill in 2004. What happened in those intervening years? Although Benjaman Kyle had no past to speak of, William Powell barely left a footprint either – no address on file for nearly three decades, no phone number, employment record, benefits claims, traffic tickets, lawsuits, loans, marriage certificates or divorce proceedings.*

William has moved back to Indiana now, a few minutes away from his childhood home – his brother, Furman, still lives there. But William hasn't felt able to enter the house yet. Not all childhood memories vanish easily.

The grave of William's father, Furman Ansel Powell, lies in a Lafayette cemetery. Section J, Lot 280. It is difficult to ignore that middle name. Ansel Bourne was the first ever documented case of dissociative fugue – a carpenter turned preacher who disappeared from his Rhode Island home in

* In 2016, journalist Matt Wolfe wrote for the *New Republic* magazine 'The Last Unknown Man', a long-form story that delved into William Powell's earlier years and Benjaman Kyle's later ones. He has conducted a painstaking search of twenty-seven years of public records for evidence of William Powell, to no avail.

January 1887. He was last seen withdrawing $551 from a Providence bank. His family reported him missing, his case made the papers, the police searched for him in vain – foul play was suspected.

A drifter, Albert John Brown, arrived in Norristown in Pennsylvania two weeks later to set up a small shop, where he lived and worked, selling 'stationery, confectionery, fruit and small articles'. He acquainted himself with some of the locals and attended church regularly. After two months as Albert, he woke to find himself suddenly Ansel Bourne the preacher once again, bewildered as to how on earth he had ended up a shopkeeper in Pennsylvania. He might have lost himself for two months but Ansel Bourne gained an identity as the world's most famous fugeur. Less than a century later, he would become the inspiration for the character of Jason Bourne.

The Burger King in Richmond Hill, the one where Benjaman Kyle was found, no longer exists. Other connections have evaporated, too. Kyle walked out of Katherine Slater's house in 2011 after a series of arguments, setting fire to some of his old mail as he did so. He and Slater have not spoken since. He took out a cease and desist order against Colleen Fitzpatrick, a self-styled 'genealogical detective' who met Kyle in 2009. Fitzpatrick had worked on his behalf on a voluntary basis, sifting through government records, maps and DNA databases, even managing to get as far as the Powell family name. But just when she had almost cracked the code, Kyle accused her of denying him access to his DNA data (a claim she denies) and cut off contact.

The last Facebook posts of 'Benjaman Kyle' included a video of children reading to shy shelter dogs, news stories of sexual abuse by clergy, the crash of a robot car and National Cat Day pictures.

And then, nothing.

Benjaman Kyle has disappeared.

Part II

Personality

Plot the essence of you over time – do you see yourself disrupted and dissociated from one day to the next, or instead a character perpetually continuous and connected? The same person throughout on this graph of yours or rather a series of different selves?

This is an exploration of how personality shapes us, who we become when it switches in some way.

Brain injuries that propel some from savagery towards humanity, others from compassionate towards cavalier. Seizures that release creativity, and dementia that allows for artistry. Psychotic painters on dopamine and obsessive authors on amphetamines.

We'll meet criminals seeking freedom because 'it wasn't the real me, Your Honour'. I'll introduce you to therapists who will try to hypnotise you, coaxing you to be someone else, to be many people at once. And we'll watch ordinary people who become, even for a few moments, extraordinary heroes.

These are tales of who we are and who we are capable of being.

4
The Stranger

He had been, said one of his female friends, a little wist-fully perhaps, 'the most attractive bachelor in the village'. Martin, in his early fifties, lived on the west coast of Ireland. He was a member of the local Tidy Towns committee with specific responsibility for walls, fences, hedges and grass verges. He sang in the village church choir, pitch-perfect, with a solid baritone. He ironed his trousers with a line down the front of each leg and wore braces and cufflinks.

I later discovered that Martin had played hurling in his younger days, brandishing a sliotar at county level, broad-shouldered, a steady and consistent presence on the field. Not, perhaps, with the pace of some of the others, but with a reliability and loyalty that ensured his selection at almost every game. I cobbled together his story piece by piece from those who knew him – his niece Tara, the wistful female friend, his local GP.

He stood in the corner of my clinic room that morning. Kneading his hands, watching flakes of skin tumble towards the floor. He cracked his knuckles, rocked back and forth on his heels, whistled the national anthem. He spat at nobody in particular. No, I wouldn't like to sit down, Doctor. Distracted by a sheaf of papers piled on my desk, he took one page, folded it as small as it would go. Two minutes passed: folding and unfolding. Then he started masturbating. He stopped just as suddenly, pulled his trousers up and spent the next ten minutes searching for coins on the floor. There weren't any, but he kept searching.

Those who knew him told me that the changes had been subtle at first. Martin gradually withdrew from his social circle. He often skipped council meetings and was ill-tempered when he did turn up, blunt and uncharacteristically combative. He no longer chatted to neighbours over the fence, no longer asked after their children. He stared through them, beyond them.

Within a year he was swaying, gesticulating and swearing as he staggered down the street. Malodorous and unkempt, his greying hair straggled and greasy. Urine stained his crotch. He wore shoes without socks and the same crumpled pair of trousers for weeks on end. People saw Martin, averted their gaze and crossed the street. He bought armfuls of chocolate (the large discounted bars – the ones you're supposed to share) at the local shop each day. He went to the funeral of a cousin and laughed and laughed during the Mass. Nobody knew what to do, where to look.

When Martin's GP was finally granted access for a home visit, she'd discovered hundreds of teabags laid out in neat piles across the living room. Newspapers were stacked up methodically, blocking doorways, full of stories that Martin would never read. Credit card bills lay unpaid, letters from the bank unopened.

When we talked, Martin denied there was a problem, disputed the evidence that he was a changed man. When he wasn't distracted (and there were windows of stillness), he could tell me his name, birthday, where he lived, who the Prime Minister was.

'Lemon, key, ball, apple, penny,' I said. Flawlessly, he repeated the words back to me; his gaze was intense, and he whispered the last two into my ear. He could remember them all after a five-minute delay, too. This was not, I realised, advanced Alzheimer's; his memory and orientation were intact – it could not be.

I tried a different approach.

'Martin, as many words as you can in a minute beginning with the letter "S"?' I asked.

'Sailor. Sailor. Salt.'

'Anything else?'

'Sailor, pepper.'

Two correct answers in a minute; I'd have expected fifteen or so. This test of letter fluency provides insight into frontal lobe function but can also be compromised by damage elsewhere in the brain – I would need some other tests to localise the problem. I moved on to proverb interpretation.

'Too many cooks spoil the broth,' I said. 'What does that mean?'

'Lots of cooks in the kitchen,' he replied. 'Lots.'

Cognitive estimates call upon strategy and reasoning – another way to interrogate the frontal lobes and their connections:

'How many hippos in Belgium?' I asked.

'A million,' he answered. He had his hand on my shoulder now.

I had my diagnosis by this point. A scan confirmed that the frontal lobes and parts of the temporal lobes of his brain were atrophied. The areas that mediated his judgement, insight, empathy, abstract thinking and behaviour were all irreparably damaged. Martin had frontotemporal dementia, an insidious-onset but relentlessly progressive condition that disassembles personality. Less common than Alzheimer's disease, it is more likely to affect younger people, typically in their fifties but sometimes as early as their twenties.

There is a significant inherited component – far, far more so than Alzheimer's; genetic mutations are identified in up to 25% of cases. An additional 40% of patients have a family history of dementia or a psychiatric disorder. So there was every chance that Martin was predestined from birth to become demented. And to die within five years. There is no cure.

I had made the diagnosis. But what did I really have? I didn't have answers for his family, who wanted to know where the old Martin, the one they knew and loved, had gone. Was he still accessible in some way? How did the person he was now relate to the person he had been? Had this new Martin somehow always been inherent in the old one?

I had plenty of questions for Martin. But I had few answers in return.

The hallmark of frontotemporal dementia (FTD) is behavioural change initially rather than memory loss (which follows later).* Disinhibition is typical: kissing strangers, urinating in public, a tendency towards crude or sexually explicit remarks and a failure to pick up on

* There are three main clinical FTD syndromes. Behavioural variant FTD (bvFTD) is the most common and the one referred to in this chapter. There are also language variants termed progressive non-fluent aphasia and semantic dementia.

social cues – patients who go on talking, not sensing if others look bored or uncomfortable. Martin's neglect of his personal hygiene was characteristic of FTD. Some patients show out-of-character behaviour in public: flatulence, masturbation, belching or spitting without concern. There is a diminished sense of personal space – standing a bit too close for a bit too long. A lesser number carry out inappropriate sexual acts or commit crimes. Appetites are never satisfied – patients with FTD hoard, obsess, develop food fads, crave carbohydrates, try to eat inedible objects.* There are repetitive movements too: rubbing hands, clapping, scratching, repeating the same words over and over.

Others become apathetic rather than disinhibited – inertia predominates, motivation and drive fade. Constant prompting is needed: to get out of bed, bathe, get dressed, to leave the house, to opt back into life. A battle for families against the person, against the disease. Chances are, the person with FTD will see a psychiatrist or a police station long before they see a neurologist.

But it is the loss of sympathy and empathy that especially upsets family and friends. 'She just doesn't care,' they say. Some family tragedy has struck but their mother uncharacteristically ignores the distress, dismisses it, even. Emotionally blunted to the loss, unfeeling and non-reactive. For her family and friends, this loss of warmth, eye contact and engagement seems so *personal*.

---

* Compulsive and ritualistic behaviours characterise FTD: counting, cleaning, collecting, checking, walking the same routes over and over again. Obsessional tendencies lean towards the religious and spiritual.

FTD is an easy diagnosis to miss. Traditional cognitive tests focus on memory but in FTD it is something called executive function that is impaired – those higher-level cognitive processes we use to organise our lives and strategise, plan, problem-solve, pay attention, initiate actions, think in abstract terms, regulate our emotions, exert self-control, make decisions and exercise moral reasoning. Odd behaviour is attributed instead to a primary psychiatric problem, drugs or alcohol. Apathy is put down to depression rather than dementia. Ritualistic cleaning, collecting and hoarding are assumed to represent obsessive-compulsive disorder.

It was Tara, the wistful female friend, and his local GP who filled in the gaps; who spoke of Martin as he was now and Martin as he was then. It took all of us to disentangle the mystery.

In Anita's case, described earlier, her family and friends saw glimpses of the 'old Anita' behind the memory loss of Alzheimer's. But in this disinhibited, hoarding, gesticulating character, there seemed a complete break with Martin's personality.

How important is personality change to your identity, to who you are? If you were to wake up with a new personality tomorrow morning, would you still be you? To understand this, we need to understand what personality is in the first place. To do so, I'd like to start by taking you to Postman's Park.

Selfless

Alice Ayres. Daughter of a bricklayer's labourer who by intrepid conduct saved 3 children from a burning house in

Union Street Borough at the cost of her own young life. 24 April 1885.

Sarah Smith. Pantomime Artist at Prince's Theatre. Died of terrible injuries received when attempting in her inflammable dress to extinguish the flames which had enveloped her companion. 24 January 1863.

William Drake. Lost his life in averting a serious accident to a lady in Hyde Park whose horses were unmanageable through the breaking of the carriage pole. 2 April 1869.

Harry Sisley of Kilburn. Aged 10. Drowned in attempting to save his brother after he himself had just been rescued. 24 May 1878.

David Selves. Aged 12. Off Woolwich supported his drowning playfellow and sank with him clasped in his arms. 12 September 1886.

You'd almost miss the iron gates of Postman's Park in the City of London. Turn south from the Museum of London towards St Paul's and then you'll see a gravel pathway through the gates. Go straight through and scattered around the small garden you'll see gravestones, a sundial, flowerbeds, a fishpond and a few benches where City workers eat lunch. The park opened in 1880 on the site of a former church and burial ground. Its centrepiece today is a monument unveiled in 1900 – G.F. Watts' Memorial to Heroic Self-Sacrifice. It's covered by a terracotta roof around fifty feet long, held up by seven pillars reaching nine feet high. Under the roof is a series of ceramic tablets set against the wall. Each tablet, made up of six or more small tiles, is engraved with a story commemorating someone who committed a selfless act of courage. Alice Ayres, Sarah

Smith, William Drake and many others. Models, the inscription reads, of exemplary behaviour and character.

The Oxford English Dictionary defines personality, one of the key elements of identity, as a 'combination of characteristics or qualities that form an individual's distinctive character'. Their example is 'she had a sunny personality that was very engaging'. One would assume that this sunny and engaging character had the same personality each year, with variations, of course, depending on life circumstances. When she was grieving following a bereavement, her neighbours might say 'She's not herself'. But somehow she always bounced back to her gregarious default state – someone recognisable, *herself.*

Is *Martin* still himself, in any meaningful sense? Perhaps we can separate his personality and behaviour in some way. Personality, after all, is who we are; behaviour is what we do.

But it's hard to preserve these two ideas in isolation for long. Those remembered in Postman's Park behaved in a heroic way. Their personalities, we would imagine by extrapolation, were intrepid and brave – not necessarily just for the selfless moment described on that memorial wall, but perpetually so.

Personality, the sum of one's enduring and predictable characteristics, is now generally considered fixed by the end of adolescence.* This is not to say changes in behaviour

---

* *Adams and Victor's Principles of Neurology* provides a more detailed definition of personality: '(one's) variable place on a scale of energy, capacity for effective work, sensitivity, temperament, emotional responsivity, aggressivity or passivity, risk-taking, ethical sense, flexibility, and tolerance to change and stress. The composite of these qualities constitutes the human personality.'

don't occur over time – of course they do – but personality is heavily influenced early on by genetics and by environmental factors.

Nature *and* nurture shape our personalities, confirmed a 2015 meta-analysis of virtually all twin studies published in the last fifty years: the average variation for human traits and disease correlates to 49% genetic factors and 51% environmental factors. That variation depends on a given trait or disease, so that neurological, ophthalmological and skeletal traits tended to be highly heritable while traits related to values and attitudes – features of identity – have some of the lowest heritability values. Even so, genetic variability has been linked to personality traits such as thrill-seeking, exploration and excitability, anxiety and obsessiveness.

But experience counts, too. Identical twins raised together have differences in personality traits related to their unique experiences and interactions.

In 2013, Julia Freund and her colleagues in Germany published a study that went beyond nature and nurture. They placed genetically identical mice in a common environment and watched for the emergence of behavioural differences over three months. If any differences emerged, the authors speculated, these could not be because of environmental differences (since the mice shared an environment) or simple genetic differences (since these were genetically identical mice).

And indeed as the weeks went by, differences emerged despite sameness. Some mice were more exploratory than others and these exploratory mice reacted to their environment differently. Traits had emerged that could not have been entirely determined by either resources *or* genes. Not only that, but the mice with higher levels of roaming had the most adult-born neuronal proliferation. In other words, more new neurons grew even after their early life and experiences influenced this growth. These changes in turn promoted further individual differences in personality and behaviour, in a sort of feedback loop. Nature and nurture aren't everything: the *way* we live our lives may make us who we are.

Epigenetic changes could contribute to this; experience modifies gene expression,* which in turn influences our paths in life. Pain tolerance, depression, diabetes and breast cancer, and personality traits (such as a propensity for risk-taking, for instance), have been associated with epigenetic changes. Identity follows closely.

And yet FTD had irrevocably altered Martin's premorbid personality – a personality so carefully evolved through his genes and environment, lined by his experiences. Personality is not just a bundle of traits, but the very notion of 'who he is'. His distinctive and characteristic process of thinking and feeling had been thrown off course. With that came a change in how he acted. He spoke differently, ate differently, cared less. He joked differently, too; his sense of humour had changed. Now he was facetious, with a preference for the slapstick rather than satirical. He punned and rhymed his way through the day. He is different, he does differently.

The thing I wanted to understand (Martin's family did too) was whether this shift in personality changed the

---

* Epigenetics refers to the idea that environmental changes alter gene behaviour through the process of DNA methylation at a cellular level.

essence of who he was. Was Martin still the same old Martin, somehow?

You're four years old in this photo. Building a sandcastle, a white sheen of suntan lotion on your forehead, flip-flops just within shot. Another photo: this time it's your first day of school. You look tiny in your school uniform. Tiny and fearless. The shirt collar almost reaches your chin. In these photos you are oblivious to the enormity of this moment, blissfully unaware of the complexities of life that are yet to come. But despite all of this, there is something about you then that is also you now. Other people see it too, this sameness.

'Our old Martin has gone,' Tara told me. There was hardly a trace of his former self; he was a different man now. There is something Cartesian in the colloquialisms we use around dementia and dying, even if we are not especially religious or spiritual. We say that the soul is no longer present, the essence has vanished.

But the Martin of then and the Martin of now must share some of those of overlapping stretches of 'psychological connectedness' I mentioned at the beginning of the book with Anita. Intermediate links carrying his memories, intentions and beliefs to the next link, and the next, and so on. Links from one day to another, one year to another.

But the problem here might be which links had been disrupted. I wonder if a dramatic change in personality implies more of a challenge to identity than a strong shift in memory or physical attributes.

Take the physical form – your body has a spatio-temporal continuity with the one of long ago, even if nowadays there are grey hairs or laughter lines. Let's say I ask you into my laboratory and show you a machine that gives you a new set of fingerprints along with a three-inch increase in height, a nose job, a slightly deeper voice and a new and enlarged set of triceps. You will likely regard yourself as intrinsically the same person even after you leave the laboratory. Physically altered, but the same person nevertheless. But if the machine swaps our personalities instead, you might sense a greater disruption in the continuity of self – you might even feel like a different person. Even sizeable changes to the physical might not impinge upon the perceived 'real' you as much as small changes in personality.

Personality change is the signature of FTD. The unkempt, hostile man in front of me, his personality radically altered, seemed to share little with the 'past Martin' described by Tara and his GP.

But there is more to this than personality change.

Nina Strohminger and Shaun Nichols, from Yale University and the University of Arizona respectively, examined what types of cognitive damage create a stranger, what changes confer fundamental transformation. They spoke to partners and parents of patients with frontotemporal dementia, Alzheimer's disease and amyotrophic lateral sclerosis (ALS, the most common form of motor neuron disease) and discovered that moral faculty plays the primary role in identity discontinuity. It's the disappearance of moral capacities in FTD – empathy, honesty and compassion – that leave patients increasingly unrecognisable to their families and friends. A change in intelligence, memory, physical ability or those personality traits unrelated to moral character (for example, curiosity, creativity, sociability, imagination, artistry, adventurousness and ebullience) did not affect perceived identity in this way.* 'As long as core moral capacities are preserved,' the authors reported in 2015, 'perceived identity will remain largely intact.'

It was Martin's seeming lack of empathy for his family that left them so deeply wounded – his failure to understand Tara's distress about her own mother's cancer diagnosis, his inability to view things from her perspective or to share her feelings. He seemed to lack compassion, unexpectedly so for him. Yes, some personality traits had changed – his wittiness, sociability, adventurousness and decisiveness, for example – but these were not changes that influenced his perceived identity.

Why does a change in moral capacity matter to us more than changes in personality traits unrelated to morality? When forming impressions of others, we place greater emphasis on characteristics associated with morality (e.g., honesty, compassion, cruelty, sincerity, generosity and trustworthiness) than sociability (e.g., friendliness, likeability) or competence (e.g., efficiency and capability). And it is these moral traits that take precedence in deciding whether we like and respect someone, whether someone represents an opportunity or a threat, whether they can be trusted or not. And even how someone will be

---

* The authors divided traits into the fifteen most moralised ('moral') traits – such as honesty, integrity, altruism, justice, mercy, trustworthiness, generosity, loyalty, gratitude, compassion and humility – and the fifteen least moralised ('personality') traits – such as adventurousness, ebullience and humour – representing the idea that personality represents individual-difference traits that are unrelated to moral character.

remembered. A 2014 study from the University of Pennsylvania asked participants to analyse obituaries published in the *New York Times* 'notable deaths' section – 250 obituaries were chosen in all. Moral character information frequently appeared – for study participants, this information was a primary predictor of the impressions they formed of those described despite all the achievements that had put the remembered into the 'notable deaths' section in the first place.

Since the impression we form of others is primarily driven by our assessment of their moral traits, it's not surprising that a change in these moral traits also alters our perception of their identity. It takes our moral emotions – a sense of fairness, empathy and gratitude – to drive social cohesion and cooperation. Will this person help or harm, collaborate or contend? How can we anticipate their behaviour? Values, principles and virtues. When we express these moral emotions, we look for them to be reflected back to us. When there is no reflection, bonds are broken.

It turns out that we perceive a change in moral characteristics as important for our *own* identity, too, not just for the identity or sameness of others. A 2017 University of Chicago study by Sarah Molouki and Daniel Bartels discovered that people are most likely to select morality- and personality-related characteristics as those that they preferred to stay the same in themselves, and experiences and preferences as those they preferred to improve. We see positive changes as being less disruptive to our own continuity than negative ones – perhaps since we already anticipate a journey of self-discovery over our lifetimes. Changes in the right direction mean future-you seems pretty much continuous with current-you; you like the future-you that you encounter – familiar but reassuringly improved, just as you had hoped. Changes in the wrong direction are more likely, we perceive, to create a stranger. 'People define themselves,' say the authors, 'both by who they expect to be and who they want to be, and they will feel less confident in their self-continuity if this trajectory is interrupted.' This means unexpected changes could be particularly disruptive to identity. Let's say you anticipate that you'll age physically over the next few decades. Wrinkles will appear at some stage, knees might ache, there could be a few grey hairs or a receding hairline. If, however, you unexpectedly start to look and feel spontaneously younger and younger with time (not because of cosmetic surgery or knee replacements or hair dye), this would likely cause greater disruption to self-continuity. Expectations matter.

There is no morality centre in the brain, no inevitable causal relationship between brain damage in one region and immorality. Instead there might be a web of morality that, in Martin, has been disrupted – a large functional network that stretches across the brain, one that includes the frontal and temporal lobes, the cingulate cortex and the structures beneath, such as the amygdala, hippocampus and basal ganglia. In a 2011 functional MRI study, neuroscientists reported that we might even draw upon distinct neural systems for different types of moral judgement – one for transgressions involving physical harm, one for dishonesty, one for disgust. And this brain network for moral behaviour is underpinned by genetic, environmental and cultural factors.

People with psychopathic personality disorder have a disturbance in their moral framework but patients with FTD like Martin don't tend to show many of the traits seen in psychopaths – manipulation, deception, grandiosity, calculated moral transgressions or targeted aggression. But there can be similar features in both groups – shallow emotions, a lack of empathy and remorse, a poor ability to learn from punishment and reactive aggression.

Speaking of morals, I have seen far more instances of the moral rights of my patients with FTD being violated, of questionable moral agency (knowing right from wrong) from others, rather than vice versa. Often lacking a concept of overspending, these patients are particularly vulnerable to exploitation. Betting shops turn a blind eye to the demented man who gambles away his life savings in a fortnight. One of my patients bought a car from a local dealer one week and then a second car of exactly the same make and model the following week. The same store manager, who could not possibly have failed to detect a profound behavioural change in the customer, sold him the car anyhow. Then there are the long-lost family members who turn up late in the day to oversee or encourage a change in the will. At times like these, a web of immorality seems to have been spun elsewhere.

The Real Martin?

Tara knew that her uncle was one and the same person over time, in that strictly numerical philosophical sort of sense. But what she cared about was more practical than this. She wanted to know if this was the real Martin, a personality he had concealed from his family all along now unmasked. Or was it his dementia talking, hitting, hating?

It struck me that the reason she asked me this question (and the reason I wanted to answer it so badly) was not just for Martin; it was for us, too. Because if we feel a person has changed, that might alter how we treat them, and how we remember them.

Imagine you're a friend of Martin. If you think the formerly kind and loving Martin is still in that swearing and gesticulating body, you'll feel much worse about crossing the street to avoid him. You even might try to stay on the same side, reach out to him through his violence. If you think the old Martin who cared so much about his appearance is still in there, you might try harder to get him scrubbed up. You might be less hurt by his insults: it's just the dementia talking.

Martin might wonder about these questions, too. But with FTD comes a lack of insight, a denial from very early in the illness of any behavioural and cognitive change and a reticence to seek medical attention. He was not the one looking for answers.

I should emphasise that none of this is to say that Martin was distraught or depressed about this change in his identity in any way. None of this is to say he didn't find meaning in his life as it now stood. Personality change in and of itself is not necessarily a negative development (and indeed it is something we often strive for – a whole industry exists on that premise). And who should decide what a 'good' or 'bad' personality change entails? But it was difficult, for his family and friends at least, to see Martin's personality change as a positive phenomenon. Their perspective might have shifted ever so slightly if these personality changes had arisen as a result of life-saving surgery ('well, at least he's alive', 'it's the price he paid', and so on) or if the personality changes he experienced didn't seem quite so disruptive – for example, if his apathy was more prominent than his disinhibition – or if they did not perceive his moral traits to have altered so significantly.

When I break the diagnosis of frontotemporal dementia, the families are often listening more intently than the patients themselves. I turn the computer screen towards them, show them the MRI scan, the shrivelled frontal and temporal lobes, and I outline the regions that affect personality and behaviour. I describe how damage to this might have caused a change in that. The unspoken translation is that it's not really their loved one's *fault*; they can't help themselves, it's the disease. I see the relief in their eyes. *It's not his fault, it's not him.*

There have been patients of mine with FTD who have gambled away inheritances and alienated long-held friends. There have been more than a few estrangements, separations, divorces. In the days and weeks after the diagnosis 'it's not his fault' is accompanied by questions of 'what if we'd known?' It's sometimes too late for a reconciliation; too much time has passed.

But if this is indeed the real Martin – the bellicose and sarcastic being he concealed from people all these years – their perceptions and memories of him will be tainted. He was a lie all along.

Of course we all display a multifaceted and ever-shifting blend of emotions and tendencies and behaviours that vary over time. The idea of this fluidity is beautifully captured by philosopher John Perry in pondering the imaginary case of a Mr Garrison, who undergoes a neurosurgical procedure called deep brain stimulation for Parkinson's disease. Mr Garrison transforms from a quiet, diligent, Republican family man before the surgery to a talkative, self-absorbed, environmentalist Democrat afterwards. One possibility, Perry suggests, is that until now he was, like the rest of us, 'a disorderly complex of intentional states, held in some sort of equilibrium by external expectations and internal negotiations.' Before the operation, there was always a Democrat-supporting, loquacious environmentalist in there, losing the battle for dominance against the diligent Republican. This Republican character was not a charade or facade either (nor has he necessarily entirely disappeared), Perry thinks, but he just happened to be more prominent because of all the circumstances endured and enjoyed by Mr Garrison. In this case, it was surgery that seemed to liberate a Democrat-supporting, loquacious environmentalist but it could have been religion or alcohol or Hillary Clinton. The new Mr Garrison is authentic, 'a new equilibrium among competing centres. With a little work, maybe his family can get some of the old values and cares to re-emerge.'

This quest to find the 'real person' happens in many sorts of brain injury, not just FTD.

Carol was in her sixties and on probation. During my ward rounds, she referred to her forensic history – multiple prison sentences for public disorder offences – with some degree of pride. She cut a well-known figure in certain parts of Dublin city. She didn't regret the injuries she had inflicted on others – she claimed a good right hook in her younger days. She knew knives and she knew guns.

The blood showed up as bright white circles on an emergency CT brain scan that evening. She had fallen over drunk, cracked her head on the edge of a kerb. Frontal lobes contused, the pressure building in her skull as the swelling shifted her brain to one side.

Within a fortnight the bleeding was beginning to settle, the pressure too. But she was still paralysed on her right side; her speech treacle and words tangled. She thought Princess Diana was alive and that Cyndi Lauper was at number one. 'Girls just want to have fun,' she sang tunelessly during each ward round. Her support worker visited her in hospital later that month and said that Carol was now more courteous and calm than she had ever been before. Perhaps, he ventured, the accident had made her see the error of her ways? But this was no personal revelation, I felt. Carol's frontal lobe damage had instead simply rendered her more placid and apathetic than before. Insight had not propelled catharsis – instead, injury had propelled change.

But his question made me think. When people appear to us to have changed for the better (and that judgement depends on our own beliefs and value system), are we more likely to say they have found themselves? And when they appear to have changed for the worse, are we more likely to suggest that the process involves loss? One study suggests that the direction of change is indeed important in how we perceive personal identity.

Participants read one of two stories. The first told of the protagonist becoming a nicer person after a head injury (he had been cruel and enjoyed harming people before his injury; he became kind and enjoyed helping people afterwards). The second group of participants read that the protagonist became a not-as-nice person after the injury. Participants who read the first story were more inclined to see the man after the accident as 'still the same person' as before. This suggests, thinks author Kevin Tobia, that intuitions about personal identity can depend on the direction of change. But this relates to our intuitions only; it does not explain, Tobia says, whether this direction of change carries relevance to the actual disentanglement of personal identity.

Within weeks, Carol had stolen a pair of scissors from the pocket of one of our nurses and tried to attack her; raw, unbridled anger. Only the paralysis of her right hand limited her assault and somehow the nurse emerged (physically) unscathed. When we did our ward round later, Carol was Cyndi Lauper again, her smile toothless and nothing betrayed of the past few hours. And yet when asked, she admitted to the crime and was unrepentant. She tried to attack another nurse the next day. Was this the old Carol re-emerging? There is no scan, no blood test, to answer this question.

We know that other parts of the brain appear to expose hidden abilities in neurological disorders. As I'll outline in Chapter 6, there is a small subset of patients with FTD who experience a burst of creativity even as their behaviour changes and language decays. They become accomplished painters, photographers, sculptors. As areas towards the front of the brain fade away there seems to be simultaneous release of the inhibition of the visual centres that lie further back in the brain and *de novo* artists emerge from the shadows of an otherwise degenerative disease.

But there is a difference between creativity being exposed as a result of dementia and the exposure of some fundamental or 'true' character. Social decorum and constraints can make us mask all manner of things, but it would be a push to suppose lifelong suppression of a personality formed in adolescence.

Previously held beliefs and values can become more *prominent* as dementia evolves but even this occurs in quite specific circumstances. Patients with semantic dementia (a less common variant of FTD that primarily affects the temporal lobes and causes loss of language abilities) are especially prone to experiencing heightened religious, philosophical and political ideas from their earlier lives. Neurologist Bruce Miller and his colleagues at University of California, San Francisco, discovered that when the dominant anterior temporal lobe in particular is affected (that's usually the left temporal lobe if you're right-handed), although some of these patients 'lose their comprehension' of words like "Catholic" and "Republican", their behaviour remains consistent with their premorbid identity and they continue to attend the same churches and vote for the same political candidates.

This sort of information has been stored quite securely over years, consolidated in a very personal context. It fosters personal identity – these ideas and beliefs make us who we are. Because of how semantic dementia spreads through the brain, these are the ideas and beliefs that linger when others fade.

But the same study found that, in contrast, patients with FTD characterised by predominant involvement of the non-dominant frontal lobe (that's usually the right frontal lobe if you're right-handed) often showed a diminished maintenance of previously learned self-concepts – this is about core values rather than personality per se. They described the case of a seventy-year-old left-handed woman – a mother, wife and office manager. After her husband's death, she described how much she detested him, despite many decades of happy marriage. Raised as a Lutheran, she converted to Catholicism at the age of sixty-nine, donating money to her new church and becoming enamoured of a priest, falsely claiming that they were lovers. She then fell in love with a peripatetic twenty-six-year-old man and announced their impending marriage. Within six months of her conversion to Catholicism, she was severely demented. MRI showed that the non-dominant frontal lobe was primarily involved.

Normal function of the non-dominant frontal lobe is important, the authors conclude, for the maintenance of the self. Other patients in their group with similar brain changes showed profound shifts in self – political orientation, religious conversions, unplanned career changes, sexual deviance and the development of multiple personalities. One woman became newly anti-conservative: 'Republicans should be taken off the earth.' These patients still knew their core attributes and allegiances but that did not stop a dramatic shift as emotionally salient experiences and memories were lost. This was a real contrast to the first group I mentioned (with dementia mainly affecting the dominant temporal lobe), who did not experience this shift in self.

So perhaps our concept of whether we see the 'real you' in dementia has been too naive. It seems instead that where pathology lies dictates whether you lose or find yourself. What and where in the brain is affected can result either in a shift away from existing core values or an increased emphasis on them, with a corresponding change in behaviour. And a change in moral faculty especially informs whether your family and friends still see you as you.

With time though, FTD spares little. I think that overall, Martin's dementia is a destructive process. It ruthlessly annihilates the parts of his brain responsible for social conduct, morals and empathy – the fundamental tenets on which identity is based. It erodes his former identity, the one his friends and family knew. It disassembles the delicate balance we all maintain between impulsivity and restraint, selfishness and selflessness. His disinhibition and his lack of compassion go far beyond a switch in political allegiance or religious affiliation. This is not some sinister being that Martin has kept from us until the end, not some final authentic expression as death draws near.

Grant Gillett, Professor of Medical Ethics at the University of Otago in New Zealand, draws on the metaphor of a tapestry. The colours of the threads contribute to its pattern. What also matters is what is available to the weaver from his or her culture – patterns, combinations of form and colour, and so on. The tapestry he weaves of his life, Gillett says, 'replete with relationships, actions, commitments, myths, incidents, reminiscences, and the rest', will be influenced by his temperament and culture but not solely determined by these things.

'Imagine that the tapestry is attacked by moths. Parts of the tapestry are randomly tangled and obliterated, and the overall pattern is obscured. It would be as mistaken to say that the true self was the degraded self as to say that the true work of art was the mish-mash of disordered threads and fragments of intact weaving left after the moths had done their bit.'

We might imagine ourselves asking the younger Martin what he thinks of his older self. The young Martin who wears cufflinks, reads a broadsheet and takes responsibility for grass verges and fences. His behaviour reflects his personality and his personality reflects his identity. Surely he would be horrified by the maniacal gesticulating man wandering down the high street? Wouldn't he be the first one to say: 'That's not me, that's not who I am?' We don't really know, of course; we're speculating. Who's to say if he knew who he really was? But apply the same logic to yourself as a newly demented person; would you own and endorse the new you?

Martin ended up in a nursing home. He would live for another two years. He would not know that twenty months later we would test a blood sample for a newly discovered genetic mutation. The test would come back as positive. He would not know that the rest of his family would be at high risk of the same disease. He would not know that his niece is terrified that she might face the same fate: that she might live the paradox of surviving her own annihilation.

Picture this. You're walking along the high street and there is Martin, swaying towards you, trousers falling down, urine staining his crotch, agitated. For a moment, he is out of sight as a van passes in between you both. He comes back into view and now he stands upright, wearing braces and cufflinks, broadsheet under his arm. His movements are calm, measured; he places a hand on a friend's shoulder, consoling him about the hurling match lost last week. Martin asks after his family, they chat about the weather, they make plans to meet for a drink next week.

For a few moments, he is himself again.

5
Splintered

He had only gone to the GP to get his travel vaccines, Christopher's wife told me later. But the practice nurse, needle hovering above his arm, had called Dr Ryan in. She had noticed Christopher's triceps muscle was wasted. Just the left one. A bit of poking and prodding and staring.

His arm had felt a bit weak recently, if he were to be honest. He didn't want to be honest.

'Fasciculations,' Dr Ryan said to the nurse. Nobody spoke for a moment.

And then Dr Ryan was putting a hand on his shoulder, gently this time, asking about speech and swallowing and walking and breathing.

Fasciculations are involuntary muscle twitches or contractions, visible under the skin. They are usually entirely benign but one of the first things that came up on Google when she typed in 'fasciculations', remembered his wife, was motor neuron disease. ALS, the most common form is called. The website said life expectancy was three years. Progressive loss of ability to walk, stand, grip, swallow, speak, cough and breathe. They had put bullet points before each verb. Like you had to put a line through each one with the passing of each and every month.

The GP had told Christopher to bring someone along to the neurology appointment. They never said that if it was good news. If it was good news you could just turn up yourself and skip out on your own, close the door behind you thank you very much, your only regret being the price of hospital car parking.

But it wasn't just the fasciculations I heard about when Christopher attended my neurology clinic a few weeks later. Ireland is a small enough place and news travels fast. A nurse recognised Christopher from her hometown. He had been released from prison a year before, she told me. Locked up for sexually abusing a thirteen-year-old boy. Now there were rumours of another victim, another investigation to follow.

Although around 15% of patients with ALS develop dementia, Christopher was spared this. He was however profoundly apathetic, one of the behavioural manifestations frequently seen in the condition – he had no drive or motivation to do much, even if he physically could have.

But he was also kinder now, more thoughtful and empathic, he told me, declaring himself a changed man. He had found God in his last few months. God was his new passion.

I'll tell you more about Christopher later. But really, his story made me wonder about responsibility and retribution and justice. And plain old comeuppance. When someone changes, when their identity shifts, where do reward and punishment lie?

What with his motor neuron disease, Christopher was going to die soon, I said to the nurse. Good riddance, she replied.

Multitudes

> Do I contradict myself?
> Very well then I contradict myself;
> (I am large, I contain multitudes.)
> > Walt Whitman, 'Song of Myself' from
> > *Leaves of Grass* (1855)

In 1979, a psychologist from the University of Montana, John Watkins, hypnotised Kenneth Bianchi. Bianchi was a suspect in the murder of several women and children in California. Here's an account from Watkins' transcript:

Gradually little movements began to appear in one of his [Ken's] fingers during the hand levitation. With much repetition, I secured a complete levitation of the hand to the face. Hypnotic involvement began. Another long deepening procedure, rotating wheels and we had at last achieved a substantial degree of hypnotic depth.

Watkins [JW] asked Bianchi [KB] if there might be another part of Ken that he hadn't yet talked to.

JW: You're not him. Who are you? Do you have a name?
KB: I'm not Ken.
JW: You're not Ken. OK. Who are you? Tell me about yourself . . . Do you have a name I can call you by?
KB: Steve . . .
JW: You're not Ken. Tell me about yourself, Steve. What do you do?

KB: I hate him.

JW: You hate him. You mean Ken?

KB: I hate Ken . . . He tries to be nice.

'Steve' admitted to the murders during the interview on 21 March 1979. 'I fixed him [Ken] up good. He doesn't even have any idea.'

Watkins was convinced:

It was shockingly obvious to me now that I was talking with 'the Hillside Strangler' [this name was used by investigators and the media since several of the victims' bodies were discovered on Californian hillsides]. After getting Steve to describe the details of the killings, both in Bellingham and Los Angeles, I told him he could go where he needed to go and asked to talk to Ken (still under hypnosis). Ken returned. I asked him if he knew about Steve. He replied, 'Who's Steve?' I then told him he would come to know about Steve and what he had done when he, Ken, felt ready to do so.

The following day, Steve re-emerged under hypnosis. Surely, Watkins suggested, Ken must have known about Steve in childhood: 'Shit no, because I [Steve] would stay out until I felt like it. I'd stay out until after everything was done and then I let him come back again, and sit there and think about it. Stupid asshole, ha, ha, ha.' During the trial, Steve knew exactly what he wanted for Ken in court: 'I hope they fucking roast him,' and then 'he would be out of my hair.'

Kenneth Bianchi pleaded not guilty by reason of insanity, claiming that his second personality, Steve Walker, was to blame. The good guy (Ken) had no inkling what the bad guy (Steve) had done.

And so multiple personality disorder would become a battleground where identity, personality and responsibility would be scrutinised far away from philosophical textbooks and thought experiments; instead thrust into a courtroom, dissected on radio phone-in shows and splashed across the front pages of newspapers across the globe. If I wished to understand how Christopher's personality change might inform his responsibility, what better way than to disentangle multiple personality disorder – a condition with the most radical shifts in personality you could imagine?

Kenneth Bianchi was not the only person around that time who drew upon the defence of multiple personality disorder. In 1981, hotel maid Juanita Maxwell claimed that one of her personalities, a nine-year-old, had murdered a seventy-three-year-old woman. On 9 August, the *New York Times* head-lined the case 'Woman with 2 Identities Absolved of Murder':

> After undergoing a startling transformation with the coax-ing of a social worker, the soft-spoken Mrs Maxwell became a giggling, boisterous 'Wanda Weston' who was able to recall details of the crime and admitted beating the woman to death with a lamp in a dispute over a pen.

Maxwell was found not guilty by reason of insanity. Sent to a state mental institution for six years, she robbed two banks after her release, again apportioning blame to 'Wanda Weston'. This time Maxwell spent three years in jail before she was released on probation.

Later, Lee County Circuit Judge Hugh Starnes said: 'It was as bizarre a thing as you would ever see in a courtroom. Here was a very meek lady of humble cultural origins, and she suddenly changed from that type of person to somebody who was going into gales of laughter, who was flirtatious, raucous and ribald, who was calm in talking about the murder. I remember that one of the psychiatrists testified that either she had multiple personality disorder or, if she was faking it, she deserved an Academy Award.'

But before Juanita/Wanda, before Kenneth/Ken/Steve, there was another. Or perhaps, I should say, others.

Sybil, published in 1973, told the story of a woman whose real name was Shirley Mason. The story of Mason's apparent multiple personality disorder and her torturous childhood would sell more than six million copies within four years.

In the inevitable TV movie that followed, Sally Field played Sybil and Joanne Woodward was Dr Cornelia Wilbur, her psychiatrist. Seen by a fifth of all Americans in 1976, it was awarded four Emmys including Sally Field's award for Outstanding Lead Actress in a Drama or Comedy Special.

Sally Field's acting skills were called upon in full force. She played young Peggy Lou, who stood up for Sybil during altercations and who in turn endured protracted abuse by her mother. There was also Peggy Ann, Vicky, Veronica and baby Ruthie. And as Wilbur injected a hypnotised Sybil with barbiturates, other identities (also known as alters) stepped forth – two carpenters named Mike and Sid; the rather religious Mary, resentful Clara, and Marcia, a painter and writer. Vanessa was dramatic, Nancy was paranoid and Helen was timid. Some of the alters had American accents and others English ones.

Both book and film were partly linked to the deluge of multiple personality disorder diagnoses that followed. Before the publication of *Sybil*, there had been fewer than 200 documented cases. Between 1985 and 1995, there were an estimated 40,000.

'Multiple Personality Disorder: The Syndrome of the '90s', went the title of an *Oprah* episode. An episode of *Geraldo* on the subject was headlined 'Investigating Multiple Personalities: Did the Devil Make Them Do It?' Other talk-show hosts – Phil Donahue, Larry King and Sally Jessy Raphael – also lined sufferers up, alters and all. Actress Roseanne Barr described having over twenty alters; their names included Piggy, Bambi and Fucker. Academic papers told of alters who were lobsters, Spock from *Star Trek*, Madonna, and the bride of Satan.

Kenneth Bianchi, it later transpired, had watched *Sybil* in his cell shortly before his psychiatric interviews.

The Construction and Deconstruction of a Diagnosis

A lonely schoolgirl seemingly switches to being an exuberant politician and then an apprehensive army recruit. In one state there might be an abused child, in another the abuser. Ten to fifteen alters per patient are reported in many cases but hundreds and even thousands in others.* The alters within

---

* The official definition from the American Psychiatric Association describes DID as 'presenting with a disruption of identity characterised by the presence of two or more distinct personality states and recurrent gaps in recall of personal information or events. Manifestations of the disorder can include alterations in affect, behaviour, consciousness, perception, cognition and/or sensory-motor functioning.'

each patient often have different ages, genders and sexual orientations. And with each alter, there can be a change in voice, emotional state, posture, talents and handwriting.

Multiple personality disorder, now referred to as dissociative identity disorder (DID), is a defence response, say some mental health specialists, whereby abused children – particularly victims of sexual and physical abuse – dissociate or mentally compartmentalise their experiences. Memories are repressed and distress is relieved. Alters emerge; some never leave.

But here's another possibility. DID is instead simply a socially constructed phenomenon. Patients fall prey to sociocultural expectations of how they should behave. Psychotherapists (perhaps inadvertently, sometimes) generate and reinforce DID in suggestible patients with the media playing a supportive role. One group collaborating across the US and the Netherlands was emphatic: 'Many or most DID patients show few or no clear-cut signs of this condition (e.g., alters) prior to psychotherapy, raising the specter that alters are generated by treatment.'

This idea of hypnotic suggestibility, of *folie à deux*, is evident in Pierre Janet's 1913 description of his patient Lucie. He describes their interaction here (she, hypnotised, replies to his questions in writing):

> 'Do you hear me?'
> [response in writing] 'No.'
> 'But in order to reply you must have heard.'
> 'Yes, surely.'
> 'Very well, how are you?'
> 'I don't know.'

'There must be someone there who hears me.'

'Yes.'

'Who is it?'

'Someone other than Lucie.'

'Ah indeed. Another person. Would you like us to give her a
name?'

'No.'

'Yes, it would be more convenient.'

'All right. Adrienne.'

'Very well, Adrienne. Do you hear me?'

'Yes.'

Compare this to a conversation seven decades later, between
psychologist John Watkins and Kenneth Bianchi:

> I've talked a bit to Ken but I think that perhaps there might be
> another part of Ken that I haven't talked to. And I would like
> to communicate with that part. And I would like that other
> part to come and talk to me . . . And when you are here, lift the
> left hand off the chair to signal to me that you are here. Would
> you please come, Part, so I can talk to you . . . Part, would you
> come and lift Ken's hand to indicate to me that you are
> here? . . . Would you talk to me, Part, by saying 'I'm here.'

At one point, 17% of therapists treating MPD were
themselves patients or former patients diagnosed with
MPD or other dissociative disorders. Psychologist Nicholas
Spanos drew a startling analogy in 1994: 'These therapists,
who help to socialise new patient recruits into the MPD
role, are reminiscent of those in traditional cultures who,
after their own possession, join and sometimes become

leaders of the possession cults that shape and legitimate the spirit possession enactments of new members.'

If we frame DID as a socially constructed phenomenon, it tells us much about how humans interpret flux and instability. Up to two thirds of those diagnosed with DID have borderline personality disorder. Bipolar affective disorder is another common association. When the mood of a predisposed, vulnerable person moves from despondent to elated, when behaviour changes from passive to aggressive, when relationships shift from ambivalent to intense, perhaps all it takes is an encouraging suggestion that these states represent different alters. New personalities can now claim the memories and traits that we would otherwise, for better or worse, be compelled to call our own. A therapist says leadingly, 'I would like that other part to come and talk to me . . .' The stage is set, Part is summoned and christened, it plays its role tentatively at first and then with gusto, its audience applauds and emboldens.

I was in two minds; I didn't know my own mind; I was torn.

The diagnosis of DID remains highly controversial and many who embraced its most dramatic form, with its thousands of alters (and profited from its existence), have now fallen silent, some arguably because of the medico-legal fallout rather than any change in their beliefs. There is no blood test or scan to confirm DID, just a set of diagnostic criteria; bullet points without biomarkers to validate them.

The shift in thinking around DID is reflected in the evolution of *New Scientist* headlines over the years: 'Fractured Minds' in 2003, 'Was Sybil a Psychiatrist's Creation?' in 2011 and 'Multiple Personalities: Takedown of a Diagnosis' in 2013.

I spoke to Steven Jay Lynn, DID expert and Professor of

Psychology at Binghamton University, State University of New York. He believes that people do experience dissociation and this is usually genuine (aside from those few who are malingering to escape imprisonment or gain financially). 'But the full-blown DID presentation – the distinct chaotic multiple personalities who appeared on those chat shows in the 1990s – are very likely the product of social and cultural influences,' he explains. And those influences include media depictions of DID and, he believes, therapists reinforcing the narrative that people house multiple personalities. But he is careful not to dismiss the experience of the patient with DID: 'The point is that even these chaotic, bizarre, and improbable presentations are genuine in the sense that people come to believe in their "multiplicity".' The truth is that they are instead one individual with a distorted sense of identity.

And as the diagnosis has largely lost sway in its most dramatic form of distinct multiple personalities, the careers of its proponents have imploded. A *New York Times* piece in 1988, 'Probing the Enigma of Multiple Personality', explored how different alters within the same patient appeared to have different food allergies. 'We're finding the most graphic demonstrations to date of the power of the mind to affect the body,' said Dr Bennet Braun, a psychiatrist at Rush-Presbyterian-St Luke's Medical Center in Chicago, described as a leading pioneer in the research. 'If the mind can do this in tearing down body tissue, I think it suggests the same potential for healing.'

Some two decades later, Dr Braun would be suspended from practice for two years after one of his patients, Patty Burgus, claimed he had convinced her that she had 300 personalities, partook in satanic rituals and cannibalism and killed babies. She was held in a psychiatric facility for two years. Speaking to the *Chicago Tribune*, she said: 'I began to add a few things up and realised there was no way I could come from a little town in Iowa, be eating 2,000 people a year, and nobody said anything about it.'

She was awarded 10.6 million dollars by Rush-Presbyterian-St Luke's as part of a civil case in which the hospital did not admit wrongdoing.

In the end, even the story of Sybil wasn't all it seemed to be, despite the words of her psychiatrist, Cornelia Wilbur: 'Every psychiatric fact is accurately represented. Sybil's true story provides a rare glimpse into the unconscious mind and opens doorways to new understanding.' In *Sybil Exposed*, author Debbie Nathan suspected otherwise. Sybil had been heavily sedated with barbiturates during therapy. A story of a traumatic tonsillectomy had seemingly been crafted into a story of horrific abuse. And most damning was a letter from Sybil [Shirley Mason] to Wilbur in 1958:

'I am not going to tell you there isn't anything wrong . . . But it is not what I have led you to believe . . . I do not have any multiple personalities . . . I do not even have a "double." . . . I am all of them. I have been essentially lying.' The stories of abuse 'just sort of rolled out from somewhere, and once I had started and found you were interested, I continued . . .'

Wilbur pushed back and insisted that this retraction simply represented Sybil's unwillingness to search deeper into her own soul. Therapy was restarted, heavy-duty drugs were injected, another six personalities emerged – and so did memories of sexual assault, being buried alive, of her mother's orgies with teenage girls. Financial incentives and fame beckoned.

Their therapist–client relationship was unorthodox: Wilbur made regular home visits, Debbie Nathan explains, climbed into Sybil's bed to administer electric shocks, paid her rent, gifted Sybil with her clothes and a cat and offered to get her into medical school. When Wilbur later developed Parkinson's, Sybil moved in to take care of her. Wilbur died in 1992, leaving Sybil $25,000. Sybil died six years later.

But while DID in its old incarnation of countless alters has to some extent faded away in academic and media circles (although it re-emerged briefly in a US comedy drama, *United States of Tara*, which ran between 2009 and 2011; its lead, Toni Collette, won an Emmy and a Golden Globe), it has forced us to confront profound questions about identity and responsibility.

And so we return to the courtroom.

It's Not My/Our Fault

Dissociative identity disorder speaks to the very heart of responsibility. We have, we like to think, a unitary coherent self, with its trials and tribulations, variability and flux. Even on days when I am less like my usual self, I have the same fingerprints and DNA and driving licence and roughly the same moral and ethical footprint as always. I will generally find myself responsible today for what I did yesterday and I have a fair sense that I will assume responsibility, own my actions, for whatever I do tomorrow – irrespective of how my character has changed. If criminal responsibility hinged otherwise, I would rob all the banks I could today, transform my character overnight and then breeze through tomorrow knowing that my new personality guarantees no punishment. Perhaps leniency is awarded for the redeemed character but it does not absolve him or her of guilt.

But as DID cases emerged in the 1970s and 1980s, these assumptions were threatened. Should alters be treated as separate individuals, or is personality just one facet of identity? Why should one alter pay the price for a crime that another committed? Should different alters be sworn in individually, cross-examined separately? These were the questions faced at a Wisconsin rape trial. In June 1990, Mark Peterson, a twenty-nine-year-old grocery store clerk, was charged with second-degree sexual assault of Sarah, a twenty-six-year-old, in the front seat of his car in a municipal park. Or more specifically, he was charged with the sexual assault of one of her twenty-one alters named Jennifer (aged twenty), while another alter, Emily (aged six), watched.

Sarah had been diagnosed with multiple personality disorder, as it was then known, just four months prior. She reported that Peterson had met the alters during a coffee date a few hours before and that he had intentionally summoned the particularly naive Jennifer, who he knew would have sex with him.

'A six-year-old was popping out when I was making love to Jennifer,' Peterson admitted. And later, 'I asked for Jennifer to ask Emily to forget what she saw. Because it was between me and Jennifer.'

Neither Jennifer nor Emily, prosecutors said, was able to consent. They cited a Wisconsin statute that sexual intercourse with a mentally ill person is a crime if the accused is aware of the victim's condition and if the illness renders the victim 'incapable of appraising the [other] person's conduct'. But Peterson denied knowledge of Sarah being mentally ill.

By the time of the trial, forty-six alters had emerged; several seemed to appear repeatedly in court. The judge at Winnebago County Circuit Court told Sarah to take an oath each time a new alter appeared. Lawyers introduced themselves separately to each alter. Testimony was started and restarted with each one. Franny, John, Jamie, Jennifer and Emily all spoke in turn. At one point, the personality of a dog appeared.*

A psychiatrist for the defence questioned the very existence of multiple personality disorder, calling it 'the UFO of psychiatry'.

Peterson was found guilty of second-degree sexual assault but within days, a new trial was ordered on a technicality. The case was never retried and he was freed.

But what happens when it is the accused who claims a diagnosis of DID? When their personality changes drastically, where do innocence and guilt then lie?

It was the dramatic case of Bridget Denny-Shaffer that would be confronted by this very question. In May 1991, Denny-Shaffer posed as a medical student at a New Mexico hospital. Wearing a white coat, the thirty-six-year-old kidnapped one-day-old Kevin Chavez. Leaving his twin behind, she drove to the Texas home of her ex-boyfriend, Jesse Palomares. Denny-Shaffer had had a miscarriage some months previously but, in the months leading up to the abduction, continued to tell her family and Palomares that she was

---

* I'm using the term 'alter' here in some instances because this was the term used during court cases and media coverage at the time. Nowadays, the term of 'identity state' is instead preferred by advocates of DID to emphasise fragmentation or discontinuity of identity in DID rather than simply the dramatic emergence of a succession of different personalities.

pregnant with Palomares's son; she had sent him photos of herself two months before in which she appeared to be pregnant. Palomares arrived home from work to find her lying in bed with a baby in her arms, blood on the sheets and carpet, and a bag with a placenta in it. She had stolen both blood and placenta from the hospital. She asked him to bury the placenta in the garden. He doubted the baby was his. Their relationship was over, he told her. Denny-Shaffer travelled to Minnesota, where she stayed with her mother and teenage daughter. Kevin was her son, she told them. Traced within days by the FBI, Denny-Shaffer was charged with kidnapping. Kevin was unharmed and reunited with his family.

Denny-Shaffer's defence was that her host or dominant personality, Gidget, was unconscious and not aware of the kidnapping for all or part of those weeks and that instead an irresponsible adolescent personality, Rina, and a Mother Superior personality, Bridget, were to blame.*

At trial Denny-Shaffer was found guilty; her insanity defence was rejected. But she successfully appealed her conviction. The appeals court ruled that the trial court should have taken into account that Gidget was not aware of the wrongful conduct of the alters.† Gidget, they

---

* At the time, the host or dominant personality was defined as the personality that has executive control of the body for the greatest percentage of time during a given time period.

† Yet awareness of a crime (which might, in many instances, be synonymous with remembering it) is not necessary to define whether you are continuous with the person who committed the crime. If you were drunk when you stole a traffic cone, you might now not be aware of it (or remember it) until someone confronts you with CCTV footage. Despite your lack of awareness, that was still you who committed the crime and it is you who will face punishment.

concluded, was unable to appreciate the nature, quality or wrongfulness of the conduct controlled by the alters.

The retrial never took place. In 1994, Denny-Shaffer pleaded guilty to interstate kidnapping, and was sentenced to forty-six months at a federal prison for inmates requiring medical or mental healthcare.

Her case acted as an important legal landmark in the history of DID. The fate of the so-called host personality was being decided rather than the alter; nonetheless, the alters were elevated to the status of personhood rather than mental states, memories or perceptions. One defendant sat in the dock to give testimony; several seemed to leave afterwards. But allowing for different 'personalities' within a single defendant cannot serve justice well: it was convenient for Denny-Shaffer that Gidget – the proclaimed innocent host personality – was the one who appeared in court.* Meanwhile the alter who abducted a baby was nowhere to be seen.

Suggesting that alters have entirely disparate personalities and thus identities detracts from assigning responsibility to the person in the dock. Assuming and assigning different personalities to each identity state is as dangerous as naming them, as flawed as christening an emotional state. By allowing personhood to be bestowed upon an identity state, we inflame the fantasy, engage in the conspiracy as we sketch the outline of each avatar.

---

* Circuit Judge Logan observed during the Court of Appeals process that the host personality could have been a participant in planning the abduction that would subject her to liability. She feigned pregnancy, scouted hospitals, checked her ex-boyfriend's blood type, bought baby clothes, altered birth certificates and stole a human placenta.

But let's try another approach. If you accept DID as it was described then, with multiple distinct personalities, would it then be unfair to punish Gidget? It feels unjust to punish this identity state – she (or more correctly it) seemed incapable of committing the crime before or doing so in the future. And punishing Gidget would not result in the rehabilitation of that irresponsible adolescent personality, Rina, or the Mother Superior personality, Bridget; it would not ignite moral enlightenment in Gidget; she cannot reoffend if she did not offend in the first place.* But in a stricter sense, there is still a need to hold Bridget Denny-Shaffer responsible here – in this we observe fairness, pay respect to the victims and their families, deter others who might commit similar crimes. If Gidget is freed, there is nothing to stop the other identity states re-emerging later on, with all their capacity for committing further crimes. Perhaps the identity state labelled as Gidget was even responsible in the first place for letting the others emerge and might do so again. An accessory to the crime.

Jennifer Radden, Professor Emerita of Philosophy at the University of Massachusetts, believes that rather than envisaging an innocent identity state being punished, we could instead reframe this as the so-called innocent identity state, let's say Gidget, bearing the burden of punishment for the greater good. She draws a parallel with what happens when a child's parents are incarcerated. In justifying the burden inflicted on the child, she says, the law appeals to the traditional deontological doctrine of double effect – this is the

---

* This brings to mind the consequentialist view in philosophy – blame or praise would be fitting only if these resulted in the anticipated change in the person and his or her behaviour.

idea that on occasion it is permissible to cause a harm solely as a side (or double) effect of bringing about a good result. In this way, the intent of an action (holding Denny-Shaffer responsible) is distinguished from its actual harmful side effects (Gidget bearing the brunt of the punishment): 'Because the burden suffered by the child is not part of the punitive intent of punishing the parent, the criminal law can avoid the charge of punishing the innocent, insisting that punishment is defined in terms of intent. Thus, the child suffers the burden of punishment, but is not punished.'

The goal of therapy in DID is now to integrate identity states; not to separate them into alters but instead to combine them into one stable non-dissociated unitary being (as much as any of us can be unitary and coherent). Challenging the entity of DID, at least in the form championed by researchers in the 1980s and 1990s, is not to reject the experience of patients who tell us their stories but to reinterpret their dissonance, to move away from partitioning each of their experiences into a personality, to transform chaotic discordance finally into unfaltering harmony.

Kenneth Bianchi: Truth

Back to 1979, when Kenneth Bianchi was watching *Sybil*.

Bit by bit, the truth began to emerge – not at those hypnosis sessions with their rotating wheels but, instead, far beyond the prison walls.

Investigators discovered that he had stolen the identity of 'Steven Walker' in a bid to become accredited as a psychologist. In May 1978, he had placed an advertisement for a psychologist to work with him. Thomas Steven Walker was one of many who applied, forwarding his university transcripts as part of the process. Bianchi then wrote to the universities that Walker had attended, calling himself 'Steve Walker' and requesting new diplomas, enclosing the appropriate fee and a return address of 'Thomas Steven Walker, c/o Mrs K. Bianchi'. He asked that they 'forward the fully completed diplomas EXCEPT for my name . . . I have at an additional expense retained a calligrapher that will print my name in a fancy script of my choice.'

Police found fourteen academic psychological textbooks at his home, including *Handbook of Hypnotic Techniques*; *Dictionary of Behavioral Science*; *Dialogues for Therapists*; *Diagnostic Psychological Testing*; *Annual Review of Behavior Therapy: Theory and Practice*; *Psychoanalysis and Behavior Therapy*; *Modern Clinical Psychology*; and *A Harry Stack Sullivan Case Seminar: Treatment of a Young Male Schizophrenic*.

His story was quickly unravelling. A prosecution psychiatrist told Bianchi that most people with DID had more than three personalities. Within hours, Bianchi duly brought forward another character, 'Billy'.

(Billy Milligan had famously become one of the first people to use the multiple personality disorder defence, two years before, for a series of kidnappings, rape and robbery near Ohio State University.)

Bianchi finally admitted to faking the diagnosis. The sentencing judge said, 'In this Mr Bianchi was unwittingly aided and abetted by most of the psychiatrists who naively swallowed Mr Bianchi's story hook, line and sinker.'

On 21 October 1983, Kenneth Bianchi was sentenced to

life in prison. He is incarcerated at Washington State Penitentiary – Department of Corrections Number 266961. He lost his bid for parole in 2010 and will next be eligible to apply in fifteen years' time.*

In an early hearing, he said, 'I feel like some textbook of psychological disorders. I've been labelled with everything under the sun, and I'm just one person.'

Kenneth Bianchi. Responsible.

By the time police came to question Christopher about a second case of sexual assault, motor neuron disease had almost completely paralysed him. He could move his thumb just a flicker. He could shrug his left shoulder when he wasn't too tired. His speech was slurred, close to incomprehensible. He couldn't swallow without choking and food snaked through a tube in his stomach. The fasciculations were everywhere now. His wife stood beside him, touching a handkerchief to his lips as he dribbled. She had stood by him through his trial, too.

Meanwhile, evidence was mounting that in the past he had assaulted another teenage boy. What would happen next? What should happen when someone, now rendered severely physically disabled and apathetic by a neurological condition, has allegedly committed a crime some years before?

The police should leave Christopher alone, his wife said to me later. He was a different man now – what with his newfound empathy and compassion and his religious awakening.

---

* It transpired that he had committed the murders with his cousin, Angelo Buono Jr. Buono was sentenced to life imprisonment and died in 2002. Bianchi had testified against him.

Agonising over whether someone is 'the same person' seems like a futile exercise when deciding upon credit and blame. We have been asking this same question for centuries, searching desperately for sameness when deciding upon responsibility; memory sameness; physical sameness; psychological connectedness. Instead it might make more sense to suggest that responsibility governs identity; it transcends sameness. If Christopher appears in court today, we deem him to now be the same person as the person who allegedly abused this second teenager *because* he is here in the courtroom to be held responsible.* Christopher, just as we saw in the cases of DID, is still a defendant with agency who acted in certain way at a certain time – claiming a new identity now would not change that. His current state might inform his sentencing, of course, but not his responsibility.

As the website his wife read had predicted, Christopher progressively lost the ability to walk, stand, grip, swallow, speak, cough and breathe. A sentence, of sorts. His wife left him before he died. And he died before the second investigation had been completed. Only God could judge him, he told me in one of our final conversations.

And anyway, he hadn't really done anything wrong, he said. It had all just been a misunderstanding.

Him and Kenneth Bianchi and Juanita Maxwell and Bridget Denny-Shaffer. They told stories of becoming someone else but perhaps they had always just been themselves all along.

* Just as American philosopher David Shoemaker has eloquently outlined, 'moral responsibility presupposes *ownership*: for me to be morally responsible for some action, it must be attributable to me, and this may be true regardless of whether or not I'm identical with the person who performed the action'.

6
Talents

W.H. Auden called it 'the chemical life'. Over the centuries, artists, writers, poets, philosophers and scientists have described creativity surging forth as hallucinogenics and other drugs course through their bloodstreams. Spanish rock art from 4000 BCE featured shamans cradling magic mushrooms. Jean-Paul Sartre hallucinated a group of crabs every day while on mescaline:

'"Good morning, my little ones, how did you sleep?" I would talk to them all the time. I would say, "OK, guys, we're going into class now, so we have to be still and quiet," and they would be there, around my desk, absolutely still, until the bell rang.'

Nobel Prize-winning chemist Dr Kary Mullis, the inventor of the polymerase chain reaction (a method that helps amplify specific DNA sequences), attributed his achievements to psychedelia:

'Would I have invented PCR if I hadn't taken LSD? I seriously doubt it. I could sit on a DNA molecule and watch the polymers go by. I learnt that partly on psychedelic drugs.'

Mind you, the *Washington Post* also called Mullis 'perhaps the weirdest human ever to win the Nobel Prize for chemistry', noting his extra-curricular activities of 'flamboyant philandering ... enlivening his scientific lectures with slides of naked women, advocating the commercial cloning of dead celebrities' DNA, and defending astrology'. Mullis denied a link between HIV and AIDS and claimed that global warming and ozone damage were 'illusions' perpetrated by 'parasites with degrees in economics or sociology.'

But could these drug-addled creatives share anything with the patients who attend my neurology clinic – who have sometimes lost all ability to speak or to walk or to remember?

What might link Jack Kerouac to a woman who begins to compose symphonies only as her dementia evolves? What connects Stone Age artists to someone who draws only in the midst of a seizure?

Neurological conditions and their treatments can transform personality and thinking in such a way that artistry emerges as a by-product of conditions previously defined solely by loss. This might tell us something about how we are all wired for creativity. And whether we should get high to get there.

The Psychotic Painter

Grenoble, 1994.

This is a story about a woman who painted her washing machine.

She had been diagnosed with Parkinson's at the age of forty-one. The nerve cells that make dopamine had begun to degenerate many years before the condition declared itself. Parkinson's has a generally predictable trajectory. It usually starts with a tremor of one hand, and progresses to stiffness of an arm or leg, and then impairs balance. Sometimes the voice softens, dexterity diminishes, there's a shuffling gait, a characteristic blank stare as facial expression is muted. Patients simply slow down – arthritis is blamed, or retirement.

Treatment had gone well, at first. Her symptoms improved dramatically on levodopa – a commonly used Parkinson's drug that is converted by the brain into dopamine. Life resumed some semblance of normality. By 2002, she had transformed her home into an art studio – she had always enjoyed painting in her younger years, painting on the walls of her attic even. Now she rekindled this interest.

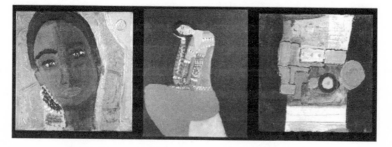

Three works from her first, non-addictive period.

By 2004, her condition had progressed. Her medications were adjusted and the doses ramped up high. She was now also on dopamine agonists, a class of drugs that activates dopamine receptors and so mimics endogenous dopamine. Soon, a keen interest in painting became an unremitting obsession. She began painting all day, sometimes all night: 'I bought huge amounts of materials, and used countless numbers of brushes at a time. I used knives, forks, sponges . . . I would gouge open tubes of paint – it was everywhere . . .'

Addictive period. Photographs of the patient's home.

She painted every available surface: walls, furniture, her washing machine. There was an 'expression wall' – 'I could not stop myself from painting and repainting this wall every night in a trance-like state. My uncontrollable creativity had turned into something destructive.' She began holding parties at her own home, inviting artists, alienating her distraught family and friends.

By 2006, she had been hospitalised, increasingly psychotic because of her escalating dopamine regimen. But her doctors faced a dilemma. Stopping those medications would reignite the very symptoms of Parkinson's those drugs were helping: the relentless trembling and stiffening

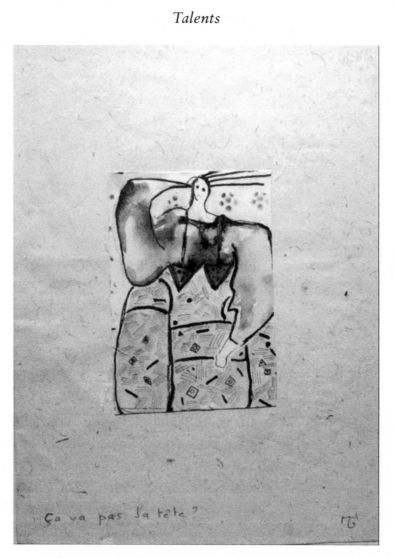

Addictive period. The inscription reads, "Am I going nuts?"

of her arms and legs would return, she would shuffle and sway when she walked.

And so instead they turned to a procedure called deep brain stimulation (DBS). Electrodes were implanted into her brain and connected to a pacemaker-type device, a pulse generator, under the skin around her chest. Electrical stimulation set off from the device towards a brain region called the subthalamic nucleus within the basal ganglia, an area crucial for movement. The procedure was a success – DBS cannot cure Parkinson's but it can help its symptoms in some people and often allows medication doses to be scaled down. This was true in her case – her medications were lowered and she did not turn to stone. She turned her hand to sculpture rather than painting and was all the better for it; her creativity, she explained, was now more tranquil, satisfying and structured. She was herself again.

Created after DBS surgery which allowed dopamine therapy to be decreased. The patient described her creativity as now more tranquil and structured.

It's dopamine-based treatments that drive creative expression, rather than Parkinson's itself. But often that creativity is satisfying and productive, not at all pathological or obsessional. The Grenoble researchers found that eleven of their seventy-six patients on dopamine drugs (all at very high doses) were creative.*

Here were patients with advanced Parkinson's who sculpted, painted, drew and wrote poetry. There were stories of remarkable glass painting, face casting and graphic design. Their creativity had only emerged (or markedly increased) after treatment with dopaminergic drugs. DBS allowed the dose of these drugs to be decreased by almost 70% on average. But there was a price to be paid. Although the procedure improved many symptoms of Parkinson's one year after surgery, creativity also took a hit – only one of the eleven continued to create art in the way they had before.

Actor and writer Joe Narciso wrote about a similar experience following on from his deep brain stimulation procedure:

> I was (am) an actor. When I started taking PD meds, I also started writing. I wrote TV shows and actually sold 4. When I started taking Mirapex [a dopamine agonist] I stopped sleeping, gained 50 pounds and almost ruined my marriage and family I was so compulsive. About everything. EVERYthing. Added levodopa and Comtan and my creativity was in over drive. Still no sleep. I mean, maybe 2 hours a night for 8 years, despite trying every sleeping pill and sleep aid out there. My health was a wreck. Falling down stairs. Breathing issues. Apnea. Choking. Weight.

* As judged by the Ardouin scale – this examines 'hyperdopaminergic' behaviours including excessive eating, creativity, hobbyism, risk-seeking behaviour, compulsive shopping, compulsive use of dopamine drugs, pathological gambling and hypersexuality.

Then I had DBS. Came off meds completely. Lost 40 pounds. No apnea and breathing fine. No choking. No falling. Sleep like a rock EVERY night. Health is way better. Creativity is comparatively non-existent. Obviously I'll take health. But I miss being so creative.

The Novelty Seekers

One original assumption about the emergence of creativity with dopamine treatment was that these medications intensified obsessive tendencies – but this assumption turned out to be flawed. Instead, what matters is the impact of these drugs on personality traits. Dopamine treatment influences Openness to Experience more so than any of the other Big Five Factors of personality (the others being Extraversion, Neuroticism, Agreeableness and Conscientiousness). And in turn, Openness to Experience is crucial to creativity – whether you have Parkinson's or not.[*]

Creativity might seem like an ephemeral, intangible entity. A sort of 'I'll know it when I see it'. But actually a creative response is easily defined: it's novel (or different or innovative), of high quality, and relevant, say the authors of the *Cambridge Handbook of Creativity*. And Openness to Experience predicts creativity more than any of the other Big Five. If you score highly on Openness, write Robert McCrae and David Greenberg in *The Wiley Handbook of Genius*, you'll be willing or enthusiastic

---

[*] You can probably name a whole bunch of personality traits – altruistic, cautious, enthusiastic, original, and so on. But actually researchers have come to realise over several decades that pretty much all of them fall under five overarching and broad categories – the Five Factor Model.

about encountering a wide variety of ideas, situations and feelings. You'll be imaginative and appreciative of art and beauty; your reactions will be rich and deeply emotional – you'll feel goosebumps when confronted by a stunning visual or auditory experience. You'll readily adopt new ways of doing things, have wide intellectual interests and tend to be socially and politically liberal. If this sounds like you, you might be feeling pretty smug right now. But it's not that Openness is better or worse than Closeness; they are simply different ways of approaching the world. Having said that, there *is* such a thing as a creative personality and Openness is the route towards it.

So how does this all link to painting a washing machine? In Parkinson's, dopamine drugs ramp up novelty-seeking, the very trait that correlates strongly with Openness to Experience. And novelty-seekers tend to become bored quickly and extravagant easily. They are impulsive and fickle, quick-tempered and excitable. They avoid routine and repetition and are utterly exasperated by their opposites – the rigid, loyal, stoic, slow-tempered, and frugal.

In 2009, Hungarian and US researchers reported that unmedicated patients who had developed Parkinson's in their forties had markedly reduced novelty-seeking. Conversely, those treated with dopamine agonists displayed increased levels of novelty-seeking. They were ready to embrace new experiences through music, art and travel; ready to seek out people on the very fringes of life. Maybe, indeed, ready to gouge open tubes of paint.

And while novelty-seeking was once linked primarily to antisocial behaviour and substance abuse, more recently it has emerged also as a signature of the curious and creative. Novelty-seekers look for reward and the dopamine that is fundamental to our reward system. Take yourself back, way back, to when Homo sapiens began to migrate out of Africa, some 50,000 years ago. These ancient migratory patterns have recently been associated with variants of a gene called DRD4. This gene codes for dopamine receptors and its variants are found in different numbers in different places: the 4R gene variant is the most common worldwide, the 7R is common in the New World and the 2R is most common in East and South Asia.

The 7R variant makes the receptor less responsive to dopamine – so perhaps people with this variant have to get their novelty hit through the unusual and the intrepid. During the out-of-Africa exodus, rapid migration selected for those with this 7R variant; we know this because it's found more frequently in populations whose ancestors navigated furthest out of Africa. It's not that DRD4-7R is a 'migration gene' as such – rather, that a nomadic lifestyle selects for this variant. This makes sense – these are the very people who will function better in the new ecological and social circumstances that migration brings.

So our dopamine pathways influence Openness to Experience and novelty-seeking, and these in turn are central to creativity. And all of this could lead to a story of a woman painting her washing machine in Grenoble or your ancestors migrating out of Africa. Creativity is ultimately about who you are and what you hope for and how hungry you are to search for it.

A Creativity Prescription?

Should you score some dopamine drugs to modify your personality and enhance your creativity? Your Openness to Experience levels are probably pretty established already at this point – there is a solid heritable component to this Big Five Factor and our tendencies and traits tend to be quite stable after the age of thirty. But there could be a way to beat the odds.

Our brain usually has an innate ability to filter out irrelevant stimuli; this capacity is termed 'latent inhibition'. But creativity thrives when that filter is *muted* – that's when emotions, thoughts and perceptions break through. In a study of Harvard students, the most eminently creative were seven times more likely to have reduced latent inhibition than those who did not score highly on creativity tests. And this is just what dopamine treatment does; it dials down latent inhibition. Combinations ebb and flow. Openness to Experience swells, and associations are loosened. Stimuli are combined in novel ways and the ability to generate multiple solutions to a single problem is enriched. This is a recipe for creative thinking.

But is it a fail-safe recipe? Sure, reduced latent inhibition might point you towards creativity if you also have a high IQ and good working memory (working memory is the skill of holding and processing information for a short amount of time). Otherwise, though, there's a chance you'll be drenched in a waterfall of irrelevant stimuli, a state that's associated with a tendency towards psychosis.

Even if you do decide to steal someone else's Parkinson's drugs, ignoring the perils of psychosis as you do so, there's a catch. External sources of dopamine might rev up novelty-seeking and dial down latent inhibition – but only if your neurons are damaged in the first place. These dopamine receptors only really become sensitive to exogenous sources of dopamine when they are starved of it in the first place, as you might see in Parkinson's. The recipe for creativity goes far deeper than dopamine.

I have one other ingredient for you to consider though: magic mushrooms.

'No poems can please for long or live that are written by water drinkers,' wrote Roman poet Horace (65–8 BCE). Alcohol and drugs have been wrapped in the creativity narrative for thousands of years. And psychedelics like psilocybin (the magic ingredient in magic mushrooms), LSD and mescaline play a starring role.[*]

Shifts in sense of self, time and space, primitive regression, hearing voices, seeing things – the stuff of madness or dreams or religious awakenings. Transformations of perception, mood, emotion and thought.

Psilocybe hispanica is a coprophilous fungus; it loves dung. Specific to the Pyrenees at elevations of between 1,700 and

---

[*] Psychedelic drugs do not mimic the chemistry of dopamine treatments used in Parkinson's, even if some of their effects appear to be similar. All the classic hallucinogens, including psilocybin and mescaline (found in the Peyote cactus), primarily act at serotonin receptors, while LSD also shows high intrinsic activity at dopamine D2 receptors and at alpha-adrenergic receptors.

2,300 metres, it produces small brown mushrooms that contain the psychoactive compound psilocybin. In Spain's Selva Pascuala mural paintings, which date back to 4000 BCE, you'll see a bull pitted against men who stand with bows and arrows. It's a primitive hunting scene that features thirteen mushrooms towards the lower right of the mural; these are now believed to be *Psilocybe hispanica*. It looks like these hallucinogenics primarily had shamanistic ritualistic uses and rock art depicted this way of life. Whether magic mushrooms also inspired the work of these mural artists is unknown.

The fungi theme persists through rock paintings at Tassili in south-east Algeria, some dated to 7,000–9,000 years ago. Bee-headed shamans are covered with mushrooms, dancers hold mushrooms and a humanoid appears to defecate mushrooms. A hallucinogenic mushroom cult of sorts, psychedelics perhaps an intrinsic element of their creative process.

But how might magic mushrooms fuel creativity? UK psychiatrist Ben Sessa, a researcher of psychedelics in psychotherapy, has some ideas. We all have, he thinks, ego-bound restraints that confine us. It's these restraints that allow us to accept preconceived ideas about ourselves and the world around us. Psychedelic drugs challenge those restraints. We let down our guard; barriers tumble and boundaries drift. But there's another, broader feature of the psychedelic experience, Sessa believes. And that's how users discover unique and novel meaning within their experiences. A dawning realisation that they are 'part of a bigger, universal cosmic oneness'.

But whether these experiences lend themselves to creativity is less clear. It's tempting to link dreamlike states to new artistic styles or insights. Echoes of George Bernard Shaw,

'You see things; and you say "Why" but I dream things that never were; and I say "Why not?"'

I'm not convinced that magic mushrooms line the path to creativity. But I don't want to give up on the possibility just yet. Psilocybin could be creeping towards mainstream use and that might allow us to study the relationship between it and creativity in more volunteers using better methodology. It has shown promising – albeit preliminary – results in treatment trials of depression and anxiety. A 2016 study found that in conjunction with psychotherapy, a single dose had an anti-depressant and anti-anxiety effect in patients with cancer-related psychological distress, an effect that was sustained at follow-up over six months later. Seemingly free of addictive potential, psilocybin was also said to increase spiritual well-being and quality of life, and was associated with improved attitudes towards death. Patients described spiritual and mystical experiences and moved towards a dreamlike dimension.

Perhaps this might be a creativity prescription after all. One that I'll be able to write for you. Take one twice a day with meals.

Creativity: Released

> If the doors of perception were cleansed every thing would appear to man as it is, Infinite. For man has closed himself up, till he sees all things thro' narrow chinks of his cavern.
>
> William Blake, *The Marriage*
> *of Heaven and Hell* (1790)

Creativity goes beyond personality traits. It goes beyond one neurotransmitter, one pathway or even one network.

We've always had a sense that there is more to us and more to the world than we can see; that there are hidden depths to be released, talents to be unveiled if only we read the right book or watched the right programme or signed up to the right subscription. If we took the right flight or the right drugs. But sometimes, creativity emerges only from the depths of destruction.

A 1996 *Lancet* report outlined the case of a formerly successful businessman who developed frontotemporal dementia and began to paint for the first time at the age of fifty-six. He developed 'outstanding artistic ability' over the next decade, his neurologists wrote. Even as he changed clothes in public parking lots, shoplifted and insulted strangers, the precision and detail of his paintings evolved. He experimented with colour; his confidence seemed to grow. In his early sixties, as his frontotemporal dementia evolved, as his brain atrophied, he won awards at local art shows. He drew quickly at first, but later took hours to complete even a single line. By the age of sixty-seven, remote and irritable, he only sketched bizarre doll-like figures. But until then, he had defied expectations. As his dementia had progressed, so his artistic expression had flourished.

Other 'never-artists' emerged, their creativity surfacing only as their dementia worsened. One woman was expelled from art class at the age of sixty-six as her behaviour became increasingly erratic; her paintings of rural scenes were exhibited across the state.

A man in his fifties began to paint churches and haciendas remembered from childhood as he lost his speech and searched for coins on the street.

Picture painted by a patient without previous artistic
training, 8 years after onset of frontotemporal dementia.

A seventy-four-year-old woman who had been a brilliant
inventor with exceptional visuospatial abilities began to
lose words with the passage of dementia. She called most
machines 'instruments', unable to distinguish them further.
But she continued to invent, receiving new patents even as
she became paranoid, disinhibited, as she spat and picked
her teeth.

These creatives painted and invented and sculpted, composed and conducted obsessively, feverishly attempting to perfect their art, never happy, never quite finished.

But all had a different type of frontotemporal dementia (FTD) than Martin, who I described earlier in this book. While he had behavioural variant FTD, these new artists had a subtype of FTD called semantic dementia. Affecting the temporal lobes in particular, this variant primarily decimates language. Semantic dementia starts with profound naming difficulties – one of my patients who was a classical music aficionado had difficulty identifying a clarinet when I showed him a picture of one. Later he couldn't name more commonly encountered instruments – a piano and a violin, for example. 'Oh that thing with the sound,' he answered vaguely. As time went on he called all instruments 'music'. Towards the end he just called them 'things'. He also simply lost knowledge of the meaning of words; when I asked him if he watched the rugby match at the weekend, he asked me, 'What's a rugby?' He poured tea into a bowl and put pepper in his coffee. His speech, although saturated with words, was eerily empty – 'that thing', 'da da da', he would say. Eventually, he became entirely mute.

As the anterior temporal lobes fade away in semantic dementia, what happens next can create or perhaps unveil talented artists.

First, there is freedom. Release of the visual centres that lie further back in the brain. Dramatic unfiltered visual experiences can now come to the fore even as language is annihilated. Usually anterior parts of the brain (the anterior temporal and orbital frontal lobes) have an inhibitory influence on the visual areas located more posteriorly. This selective attention suppresses stimuli that are irrelevant to the task at hand. But when these anterior regions are damaged by FTD, they lose their ability to suppress. The governor has exited the building. And so the brain's posterior regions (the posterior temporal and parietal lobes) are released – in contrast, in Alzheimer's these regions fade relatively early on. This process means, current theories go, that cognitive resources in semantic dementia are redirected towards areas that oversee visuoconstructive and visuospatial skills.

Imagine being exquisitely sensitive to the visual features around you and yet not grasping the meaning of what you see – 'what is a forest?', 'what is a kaleidoscope?' This is the disconnect experienced by patients with semantic dementia. Now, only aesthetics matter. One patient was given wooden models of reindeer and painted them with geometric zigzag patterns – red, yellow, white and black stripes. There was no semantic link between this artistry and the object – for him, there didn't need to be.

This sort of release was also seen in a twenty-seven-year-old man whose artistry only emerged when his voice was silenced. Waves would engulf him during attacks, he described. A sense of floating helplessly. During these lost moments, he would draw impulsively and skilfully, all while being unable to speak.

It turned out that he was having seizures during each of these artistic outbursts – this was epilepsy. Fits were triggered from the left frontotemporal lobe, turning off language as they fired. And when this happened, visuospatial skills were released from the right side of his brain. It's the right side of the brain that oversees knowledge of people's faces and their emotions; it is orientated to all of

Drawn by a 27-year-old patient with seizures originating from the left hemisphere of his brain. During the events, he did not speak and sometimes became aggressive. His doctors believed this impulsive creativity represented a "release phenomenon" of the complex visuospatial skills of the brain's right hemisphere.

the things you might think are relevant to the pictures this man created: visuospatial abilities, geometric patterns, mental rotation, imagery, familiar faces and places and realism.* In this man, it took a seizure to release those skills.

What is significant in these different forms of dementia is not just what is released but also what is preserved. Some with semantic dementia still have the capacity to plan, motivate themselves, seek novelty and organise. The brain regions important for these skills – all key for creative output – are spared, at least initially.† Where memory is intact, scenes from an artist's past can colour a canvas, while musicians can call upon previous compositions or patterns.

It's a baffling thought in a way – extensive brain damage can increase our ability to produce unique, novel, even groundbreaking ideas. Professor Simone Shamay-Tsoory and colleagues in Haifa, Israel, assessed patients with head injury, stroke and resected brain tumours and found that damage to the right hemisphere, particularly an area at the front of the brain called the medial prefrontal cortex, was associated with impaired originality.‡ Meanwhile, patients

* Mendez M.F. (2004), 'Dementia as a window to the neurology of art', *Med Hypotheses*, 63, pp.1–7.

† However, because the anterior temporal lobes are devastated, artwork often appears bizarre and distorted, partly since these artists find it difficult to recognise faces and emotions (or, when the right temporal lobe is affected, to understand the meaning of emotions). Although patients with behavioural variant FTD (the type of dementia Martin had) can develop artistic creativity, this is far less common, particularly when apathy predominates and when the ability to plan is impaired since different parts of the brain are affected in behavioural FTD than in semantic dementia.

‡ Originality refers to ideas that are statistically rare and represent an uncommon, unique response. In one creativity subtest, participants in the Haifa study were provided with a list of six common objects (e.g., a stapler, shoe, cardboard box, tyre). They were then asked to list alternate uses for

with damage to the left side of the brain – specifically, the left parietal and temporal cortex – showed elevated levels of originality. Not just that; the larger the lesion in the left parietal and temporal cortex, the greater the originality – only as long, however, as the right side was intact.

As other parts of the frontal lobes shrink in evolving semantic dementia, behavioural inhibition is dampened and impulsivity spirals – sometimes, stable careers are jettisoned for the unpredictable journey of the nomadic artist. Patients leave their families, voyaging abroad to begin their new lives as creatives. There seems to be little fear of the consequences; one man travelled to a remote and dangerous area of Central Africa to embark upon a new career in photography and was promptly arrested by the military. He made it out safely, just.

These stories are not just the substance of isolated case reports. In one series, new or preserved musical or visual abilities were seen in 17% of sixty-nine patients with all types of FTD, most with the semantic variant. It goes beyond the artwork itself, of course, or even its brilliance. This is embodiment and expression. 'Lonely Cowboy's Thoughts' was a case study I read that made me think about how easily that expression might be overlooked. A retired metallurgist developed frontotemporal dementia at the age of sixty-three. He neglected himself and gorged on food. He skipped words in sentences, then lost them altogether. By the age of seventy, he was mute, apathetic, expressed

---

each object. This is a test of divergent thinking – the ability to consciously generate new ideas, then branch out and allow for many possible solutions to a given problem. It correlates with openness to experience.

little emotion and did not seem to understand much of what went on around him. One day, lost for other ideas, his wife put some pencils in front of him. He began to draw. He sketched every day after that, at the same hour, often pictures of women's faces with their hair in braids. Pictures that his doctors at Hôpital de Bellevue, Saint-Étienne, France, described as visual, realistic and symbolic. Despite his silence, his technical skills remained – drawing, colour, details and perspective. Physical features were well defined and proportioned. He drew stereotypical pictures of a cowboy. His relatives confirmed that between the ages of twenty-two and twenty-five, he had worked in a factory and would wear a Stetson. His co-workers had called him 'Cowboy'. On the day he was told his mother had died, the news did not seem to register. Later that day he drew a church and a death's head – figurative and expressionist. Before those pencils were put in front of him, his family had doubted he was 'really there'. When they looked at his pictures, they knew that he was – in some way, at least. All because one day his wife gave him some pencils.

Can creativity be experimentally fostered by drawing upon this concept of 'creativity from destruction'? In 2004, Australian researchers used a technique called repetitive transcranial magnetic stimulation to switch off the fronto-temporal lobe. Seventeen participants were asked to copy a drawing of a horse. A horse was chosen, the authors explained, since they had noticed that typically artistic savants show an interest in horses and other hooved animals. Participants were then zapped with repetitive transcranial magnetic stimulation to the left motor cortex (as a control condition) or the left frontotemporal cortex (the experimental condition). Some received no magnetic stimulation at all. It was stimulation of the frontotemporal lobe that led, the authors reported, to striking improvements in one participant's creative ability.

This improvement – specifically in representational accuracy and artistic merit – lasted just minutes and only persisted while the magnetic stimulation was being actively applied. The result was not replicated in other participants – perhaps because the experimental procedure needs to be refined in some way, or because they didn't have nascent creativity in the first place, or because the success of one participant was a fluke. Wearing a magnetic stimulation device and being zapped every time you lift your paintbrush sounds like a cumbersome and possibly ineffective route to creativity. But would you prefer it to taking an acid trip? To help you answer this, I'd like to tell you about Robert Crumb.

High

The walls flap in the breeze like tapestries. They run like melted wax. The floor flows like a river. The folds and textures of cloth become rich and wonderful to look at. Lights seem to change gradually. The air seems to have become textured, coloured or with structure, particularly near the corners of objects.

Stories of visual release are common to those with semantic dementia and to those on an acid trip.

In the late 1950s, the psychiatrist Oscar Janiger studied the effects of LSD (lysergic acid diethylamide), then legal, on hundreds of volunteers including Cary Grant and Aldous Huxley. The quote above about walls flapping and floors flowing is from one of the artists who participated in those studies.

But there is no systematic research supporting the idea that LSD truly enhances creativity. Most examples from the 1950s and 1960s revolve around those people who were already keen artists, who, having taken acid, experienced a change in style or form. Which invites the question: do drugs drive creativity or are the people taking them already creative?

Take the US comic artist Robert Crumb. You might well recognise his work, if not his name. Fritz the Cat, Mr Natural, The Old Pooperoo, Angelfood McSpade and The Snoid: his characters initially inhabited the underground comic scene in the late 60s before entering mainstream popular culture. His illustrated slogans are legion, 'Keep on Truckin'' being one, and his album artwork is celebrated. The album cover for Janis Joplin's *Cheap Thrills* in 1968 was his creation and made it to number nine in *Rolling Stone*'s Greatest Album Covers of all time. Crumb refused payment from Columbia Records for the *Cheap Thrills* cover: 'I don't want Columbia's filthy lucre.'

The influence of LSD on Crumb's work was explored in a 2011 piece for the *Journal of Psychoactive Drugs* by Matthew Jones of Temple University in Philadelphia.

In the mid-1960s Crumb experienced a trip on LSD that he called his 'fuzzy acid' experience. It started with 'the usual trippy sensations, the visual effects, and expanding consciousness into infinity – like WOW.' But then, 'all of a sudden everything went, like, fuzzy – like the reception went bad – lost the picture, the sound, everything – it was so weird, but not particularly frightening. For the next couple of months, I felt like the guy in *Eraserhead* . . . everything was dreamlike and unreal.'

And it was during this dreamlike phase between March and April 1966 that Crumb let go, he said later, of trying to have any fixed idea about what he was doing and instead created stream-of-consciousness comic strips. Perceptions were heightened and associations were loosened. 'A grotesque kaleidoscope, a tawdry carnival of disassociated images kept sputtering to the surface . . . especially if I was sitting and staring, which I often did. It was difficult to function in this condition, I was certifiably crazy, I sat staring on the couch at Marty's apartment, or on long aimless bus rides around Chicago. These jerky animated cartoons in my mind were not beautiful, poetic or spiritual, they were like an out-of-tune player piano that you couldn't shut off . . . pretty disturbing . . . And what a boon to my art! It was during that fuzzy period that I recorded in my sketchbook all the main characters I would be using in my comics for the next ten years; Mr Natural, Flakey Foont, Schuman The Human, The Snoid, Eggs Ackley, The Vulture Demoness . . . It was a once-in-a-lifetime experience, like a religious vision that changes someone's life, but in my case it was the psychotic manifestation of some grimy part of America's collective unconscious.'*

* 'Crumb on Crumb. *Minds are Made to be Blown*' http://www.crumb-products.com/pages/about/minds.html. Originally featured in *The Complete Crumb Comics, Vol. 4: Mr. Sixties!*, p.viii.

Since altered perception and expanded consciousness drive creativity, Jones suggests that this was a ripe period for gathering ideas and inspirations.

Panel from Crumb's autobiographical
Dumb: The R. Crumb Story, 1994.

But effecting these harvested ideas and inspirations creatively requires emerging from the psychedelic *Eraserhead* experience itself – only then are the powers of conceptualisation restored. The same idea is seen in semantic dementia – visual release can only be realised as artistry if other faculties – planning and multitasking and judgement and motivation, for example – are relatively intact.

Jones set out to compare Crumb's LSD-inspired work to his non-LSD-inspired work and predicted that the former might show more perceptual alteration techniques than the latter.

He analysed and coded 308 pages of Crumb's comic text from 1958 (before Crumb had experimented with psychedelics); 1965, when he first started experimenting with LSD; 1967 and 1968, following on from his 'fuzzy acid experience' the year before; and then his later work in 1977 and 1978, after he had stopped using LSD.

Crumb's pre-LSD work had the lowest degree of 'perceptual alteration', a term that incorporates measures of boundary loss, intensity, disorganisation, distortion, abstraction and fragmentation. In fact, there wasn't even a hint of fragmentation, disorganisation or distortion in the very early days but of course this likely represents the fact that Crumb's artistry was just taking off. There was a dramatic increase in perceptual alteration scores following Crumb's 'fuzzy acid' experience, with 127 instances of 'disorganisation' coded for in 1967 but none in 1965 – the work just after his 'fuzzy acid' experience is perceived by many to be his best creative output. These perceptual alterations decreased but still persisted even two years after he had given up psychedelics. So, Jones argues, the fluidity of consciousness and perceptual chaos that had marked Crumb's fuzzy acid trip filtered into his artistry afterwards.

It's worth mentioning that this was hardly a controlled, rigorous study and that there are confounding factors, not least Crumb's use of other drugs such as marijuana. But Crumb's story suggests that creativity requires more than a loosening of associations, visual release and altered perceptions. His time as 'Eraserhead' was not his most fruitful or critically acclaimed artistic period; at the height of an LSD trip, other faculties can take a hit – attention, memory, motor performance, learning and intelligence – and creative expression then suffers, too.

It was only in the months afterwards that Crumb's creativity flourished. This was when his resurgent technical skills re-emerged, when his concentration returned, allowing him to reproduce the images that had dominated his 'fuzzy acid' trip.

Crumb later explained in a BBC documentary that stopping LSD and marijuana transformed his work: 'I finally felt my head clear and I started to get more serious about drawing again and more interested in the technical aspects of drawing and I began to really enjoy being able to concentrate in this way that I'd forgotten how to do from being stoned all the time.'

The stories of artists on LSD and those with semantic dementia tell us much about the creative potential we might all hold. That visual release and perceptual chaos are crucial for creativity. But that often creativity follows only if other skills are preserved.

Not everyone with semantic dementia becomes artistically expressive. Not everyone who takes LSD does either. And it wasn't just LSD that made Crumb think outside the box: 'I was always a contrarian,' he told the *Guardian* newspaper in 2016. 'My wife says sometimes I'm too much so – born weird. I always felt there's something odd and off about my nervous system. If everybody's walking forward, I want to walk backwards.'

Some people have always walked backwards. With or without drugs or dementia.

The Incubation of Daydreams

Picture Jack Kerouac on amphetamines, furiously typing an early draft of *On the Road* in 1951. 'Benny has made me see a lot,' he later wrote to Allen Ginsberg. 'Benny' was Benzedrine, his amphetamine of choice. 'New material wells up like water forming its proper level, and makes itself evident at the brim of consciousness.' It took just three weeks and a continuous 120-foot-long scroll that he had taped together from rolls of architect's paper. Most stories, however, conveniently omit that *On the Road* was not born of a spontaneous three weeks of labour but instead pains-takingly crafted for some years beforehand in Kerouac's mind and in journals, followed by many drafts until 1957. The original conclusion of the story from that scroll remains unknown, the edges chewed by a cocker spaniel – 'Ate by Patchkee, a dog', wrote Kerouac. Whether amphet-amines helped things along was a matter of opinion. Truman Capote concluded, 'That's not writing. That's typing.'

W.H. Auden also espoused the use of amphetamines, starting off each morning with Benzedrine for twenty years. Writing for the *New Yorker*, John Lanchester remembers that Auden 'took a pragmatic attitude toward amphet-amines, regarding them as a 'labor-saving device' in the 'mental kitchen', with the important proviso that 'these mechanisms are very crude, liable to injure the cook, and constantly breaking down'.

Originally marketed as an over-the-counter nasal decongestant in 1932, Benzedrine didn't become a prescription-only drug until more than twenty-five years later. Amphetamines enhance dopamine signalling in the brain and were advertised heavily in the 1960s as energy boosters, optimism enhancers and slimming aids – they were known as 'Mother's little helper'. Before that, they had been used throughout the Second World War. During Blitzkrieg, for instance, German soldiers used an estimated 35 million amphetamine tablets over a three-month period. Their popularity has not waned: in 2016, they were the fourth most popular illegal drug in England and Wales and globally the second most commonly used illicit drug (cannabis took prime position). They are popular today as performance enhancers in athletes, and among college students looking for an extra kick as cognitive enhancers or just to make it through a cycle of studying and partying.

And amphetamines are still prescribed legally in various forms to treat ADHD and occasionally narcolepsy.

The obsessive focus that characterises amphetamine use in some is also a signature of certain conditions that I see at my neurology clinic – some with semantic dementia, for example, strokes (very much depending on what region of the brain is affected and how extensively), and others on very high doses of dopamine drugs for Parkinson's. Autistic savants frequently have obsessional behaviour that is directed towards a solitary field of interest. Prolific artistic output ensues, skills develop but creativity does not always follow from repetition, restriction and compulsion.

Obsessive behaviour can dial up attention and processing speed but can hamper existing talent. Take the use of amphetamines in creative people. In a 2016 study in Israel, thirty-six healthy adults were given either methylphenidate (also known as Adderall) or placebo. Intriguingly, the researchers excluded one participant because of his ornithophobia – his fear of birds. Little more is said about the issue or what became of this man. The rest, the non-ornithophobics, were then tested on their creative abilities. Verbal creativity was increased in those with lower novelty-seeker tendencies but reduced in those with high novelty-seeking, the latter being associated with creativity. Kerouac might not, on this basis, have benefitted creatively from amphetamines even if they did help his focus. Cognitive enhancers with a caveat.

To make things worse, creative novelty-seeker types – the very group that is least likely to benefit from amphetamines creatively – end up having greater drug-wanting behaviour. That's likely since pre-existing high levels of novelty-seeking predict greater release of dopamine in an area called the ventral striatum. This suggests that novelty-seeking creatives are particularly susceptible to substance abuse, a high price not even worth paying for their art.

In any case, there is something to be said for letting the mind run free, for imagination and daydreaming and distraction. Ask Newton and Einstein. Or the French mathematician Poincaré, whose geometry eureka moment emerged when he stepped onto a bus: 'At the moment when I put my foot on the step the idea came to me, without anything in my former thoughts seeming to have paved the way for it, that the transformation that I had used to define the Fuchsian functions were identical with those of non-Euclidean geometry.' He described his ideas as rising in crowds, colliding, interlocking, stabilising. It was his 'unconscious work', he said, that led him to his best discoveries.

Think of all those times you've desperately tried to come up with solutions or concepts to no avail, only for them to drift into view when least expected. The difficulty with obsession is that there might be focus without ideas.

This has been tested experimentally in various ways. In one study, 'Inspired by distraction. Mind wandering facilitates creative incubation', psychologists Benjamin Baird and Jonathan Schooler at the University of California, Santa Barbara, asked 145 undergraduate students to generate as many alternate uses as they could think of for common objects – a brick, a stapler, and so on – within two minutes. This is a well-validated and established test of creative thinking. It was followed by an incubation period where participants either engaged in a demanding task (a timed memory test that required high levels of focus), an undemanding task that maximised mind wandering (this required less focus and only infrequent responses), a twelve-minute interval rest or no break at all. All four groups then had to repeat the alternate-uses task. The students in the mind-wandering groups scored an average of 41% better on the follow-up tasks. So if you're trying to creatively solve a problem, you're best off taking some time out and engaging in a different but not too taxing task that allows your mind to wander before returning to the same challenge.

Why does this happen? Well, the explanation may be that it allows two special networks that normally antagonise one other to instead work in tandem. The first, the brain's default-mode network, becomes active during mind wandering. This network is associated with imagining the future, remembering the past, generating novel ideas and reflecting on our own emotions and the emotions of others. Recent functional MRI research suggests that it works synergistically with another brain network, the executive control network, which springs into action for tasks of working memory and when we try to keep thoughts on track, organise them, evaluate outcomes and follow rules. Here's where synergy comes into its own: the executive control network selects and assesses ideas that were in turn generated through spontaneous thinking during mind wandering. Studies that placed jazz musicians and rappers (separately, that is) in functional MRI scanners have demonstrated that this synergy is crucial when musicians improvise and freestyle. Creativity arises from collaboration.

Creativity Consent

As doctors, we tell our patients about the potential side effects of the medications we prescribe. When we consent a patient for surgery, we outline the possible risks. But not many of us consent to loss of creativity. Joe Narciso, the actor I mentioned before, felt that he lost his creativity after his DBS operation. Not that he regretted having DBS; it transformed his well-being. But might he have held off the operation for a bit longer to write a few more screenplays if he'd known? Likewise, a few antidepressants induce apathy, with consequent effects on the motivation to create. There have been almost thirty case reports of altered pitch perception in musicians who are taking the anti-seizure drug carbamazepine.

The priority is of course to treat debilitating forms of psychosis and depression– the presence of any disorder is hardly useful for creativity if it's very severe. But it's worth thinking about which drugs we choose. There is a range of medications available for seizures and for mental health disorders, and if creativity is a crucial part of our patients' lives, then our choice and timing of treatment needs to reflect that.

Discovered

> The bloom, whose petals nipp'd before they blew
> Died on the promise of the fruit, is waste;
> The broken lily lies – the storm is overpast.

Percy Bysshe Shelley, 'Adonaïs: An Elegy
on the Death of John Keats' (1821)

Creativity is a soup of heritability and environment and experience, of neurotransmitters and networks. Of focused attention and mind wandering. Of openness and of novelty-seeking.

There are parallels in the lessons learned from the stories of the patients I've told you about and from the users of magic mushrooms and LSD and amphetamines. The visual release of semantic dementia unveils hidden talents, potential we all harbour to a greater or lesser extent. The LSD experiences of Robert Crumb tell us that creativity is not always realised in the moments of extreme perceptual chaos and sensory overload, but instead can follow unobtrusively afterwards. In both, the abilities that are preserved are as important as the ones that are lost. The stories of obsession, with drugs and in dementia, expose the truth: that creativity lies in the incubation of daydreams.

There is a danger to romanticising illness for the creativity it is said to bring – the *spes phthisica* that was John Keats' TB; the consumption that ravaged his fragile twenty-six-year-old body was thought by some at the time to release creative passion and genius. Poetry emerged only from physical devastation. Théophile Gautier, nineteenth-century poet, novelist and critic, wrote, 'I could not have accepted as a lyrical poet anyone weighing more than ninety-nine pounds.'

But undeniably the stories you've read have been of those with neurological conditions who saw things they were blind to before. Who achieved things they never had before. Neurodegeneration is a high price to pay for creativity – too high for most of us. But to see these conditions framed only by loss, only as neurons fading and networks dying, is to deny what still lives.

Part III

Consciousness

This is our journey as awareness ebbs and flows.

Disembodiment in the dead of night that will disintegrate, levitate and duplicate you. And perhaps ultimately enhance you, if you allow for it. Body swaps and immersive illusions. The architecture of self, constructed and disassembled. Here are encounters with floating climbers and somersaulting astronauts, angel stuff and astral matter.

Next, the consciousness of sleep infiltrated by fantastical dreams and ephemeral visions. Nightmares realised and circuits that brighten and fade as savage violence pervades deep slumber. Is this the true self in sleep or instead a perpetual stranger?

And finally, as consciousness fades further, we shall meet the awake yet unaware. A search for sameness when, at first glance, there is none to find. An exploration of rewiring and rerouting and resurrection.

And who we become when we're not ourselves.

7
Disintegration

A stocky red-faced 5 foot 8 inches of a man. If he was scared, he didn't show it too often. The faded blue letters of 'LOVE' tattooed onto the knuckles of his left hand, 'HATE' on the right.

Telling me that his spirit had left his body wasn't what he had wanted to do this morning. But he was scared that it would happen again. And that fear had brought Kevin here.

Have I gone mad, Doctor?

He had woken in the middle of the night, drifting mid-air. There he was, staring downwards at his own physical body – motionless, still lying in bed. Its eyes closed. Or perhaps, Kevin realised, *his* eyes closed?

He and I sat in the twenty-first century in a windowless clinic room with its prison-blue walls, its stacked boxes of white latex gloves and its perpetually dripping tap. But I could have heard these Cartesian tales, these stories of body and soul divided, across cultures and times.

Over the years I would see other patients who declared themselves disembodied, in some manner no longer anchored in their physical form.

Our sense of sameness over time is deeply embedded in embodiment, even if the physical form changes with each passing year. With disembodiment, we drift away from the moorings that previously secured our sense of self. As we float above our physical bodies, our identities can shift, too.

I wanted to understand how Kevin found himself floating by the ceiling. And perhaps through understanding how he had lost his sense of self, I might understand how we construct ours.

Out-of-body experiences like Kevin's can now be artificially generated in you or me in a research laboratory within minutes. And as jarring as this sensation might be, it's also one where a profound threat to identity could become a force for good.

'I've lost the run of myself,' we say sometimes in Ireland. A sort of 'I've gone a bit mad.' Losing a sense of self speaks to insanity. Or to religion.

Sherlock Holmes, or perhaps some part of him, once took a trip to Devonshire. 'My body has remained in this arm-chair and has, I regret to observe, consumed in my absence two large pots of coffee and an incredible amount of tobacco,' he told Watson. 'After you left I sent down to Stamford's for the ordnance map of this portion of the moor, and my spirit has hovered over it all day. I flatter myself that I could find my way about.'

Normally, our centre of awareness is located behind our eyes and inside our own bodies. I have a 'real me' that seems to live within 'my' body – the 'I' or subject of experience and thought. In self-consciousness lies the feeling that 'I' experiences are bound to the self.[*] This stable sense of self,

* Blanke, O. (2012), 'Multisensory brain mechanisms of bodily self-consciousness', *Nature Reviews Neuroscience*, 13.8, pp.556–71.

this embodiment, allows me to believe that I am the same person over time. All of these elements were imperilled when Sherlock Holmes departed his armchair to drift over a Devonshire moor.

A range of autoscopic* phenomena can disrupt this centre of awareness. There's the out-of-body experience as Kevin had described – more of that later. And then inner heautoscopy, whereby you see your inner organs visually hallucinated in a space outside your body; a sort of fish tank of shiny bobbing viscera. There's the less dramatic and fairly common 'feeling of presence' – the sense of someone near your own body. In negative heautoscopy, you are unable to perceive your own body as you stare down at it or as you face a mirror. A reflection, unseen. And lastly, the doppelgänger, central to many a journal report and Gothic novel. Take the 1937 report of a French man with four of them – his own corpse in bed, another wandering around the room, a third himself as a young man dressed in rags and the fourth a double assisting at his own burial.

The self flits between one and the other or exists within both, a nomadic existence.

Kevin's was an out-of-body experience: he saw his own body, described a sensation of being disembodied (he located his self outside his body) and he looked upon the world from a distant and elevated perspective.

He had disintegrated. Or, more specifically, his sensory integration had gone awry; an incongruence between what he saw and what he sensed. 'Mine' became 'Mine?'

---

* Greek: *autos* –'self', *skopeo* – 'looking at'.

Usually, like the rest of us, Kevin could look at his own body from his *own* eyes in his *own* head. But not that night.

Out-of-body experiences, which have an incidence of around 5%, have traditionally been explained in paranormal and religious terms. But times have changed. Today, I wouldn't be distilling Kevin's experiences into the stuff of astral journeys or spirits or phantoms.

I didn't yet know whether he had a neurological or psychiatric disorder – out-of-body experiences have been described by patients with schizophrenia, severe depression or anxiety, post-traumatic stress disorder, migraine and epilepsy, for example. They're reported in patients with sleep disorders such as narcolepsy and sleep paralysis. Drugs like ketamine also seem to act as a trigger. Out-of-body phenomena have been later recalled by those who have been put under general anaesthesia or survived a cardiac arrest. Occasionally, these events occur with no obvious cause or precipitant at all. And to disentangle these, we need to look to the sky.

Floating Climbers, Giant Pilots and Somersaulting Astronauts

To understand how the bodily self is deconstructed is to understand how it is constructed. And one thing that matters in this architectural feat is our so-called sixth sense: proprioception. That's position sense – cemented through signals from receptors throughout muscles, skin, tendons and joints. So if I ask you to stand in the dark and then touch your nose with your index finger, you'll be able to do this because proprioceptive input provides continuous information about the position and movement of the body and its parts. Interrupt those signals and it's difficult to tell where our bodies and each body part are in space. Finger misses nose and pokes eye.

And that's probably why abrupt positional changes feature in many an out-of-body experience. Extreme-altitude climbers are especially prone to curious perceptual happenings, particularly above 6,000 metres. Here, hypoxia, social deprivation and stress likely play a role, too. The body floats, these climbers report, or moves like an automaton. An imaginary person lingers close by, the mind and body dissociate.

In a study of eight world-class mountaineers, five had felt separated from their own body at one time or another and viewed it from afar. Life-threatening danger (falls or avalanches) frequently factored into these experiences.

After a walk of eighty kilometres at an altitude of about 5,000 metres, one climber remembered: 'I could no longer feel myself walking. Instead, I felt my body floating up and down to the rhythm of the waves meeting the shore.'

And this was an account from another climber after solitary bivouacking at an altitude of 7,500 metres:

'For several minutes, it seemed to me as if the tent were at least five times as large as I knew it to be. The strangest thing, however, was that my own body felt five times as large as well, although as judged by my eyes I could not make out any changes, neither concerning my own body nor concerning my own environment.'

Pilots have these sorts of tales to tell, too. The 'break-off phenomenon' describes a feeling of physical separation from the earth at high altitude. A 1957 survey of aviators

(137 navy and marine pilots flying above 13,000 feet) found that 48% reported the phenomenon, particularly pilots of single-seat aircrafts. There were stories of detachment, dreamlike twilight states and spatial disorientation. For some, this brought exhilaration and exalted power. 'I feel like I . . . have broken the bonds from the terrestrial sphere'; 'I feel like a giant'; 'I feel something like a king.' Three pilots reported that they felt closer to God. Others, however, only remembered feelings of loneliness, anxiety and bewilderment.

Pilots who experience break-off phenomenon at its most extreme have the sense that they exist outside their bodies and even outside the aircraft itself. Sometimes this sensation dissipates when they redirect attention to a cockpit check or a radio message or a clear visual reference outside – the terrain below, for example.

Add to this proprioceptive entropy a hint of vestibular chaos and you're well on your way to hovering by a ceiling lightbulb. The organs of the inner ear serve the vestibular system. They sense accelerations, angular and linear, that occur with each movement you make. This generates movement of your eyes, head and body so that your gaze and posture are stabilised in three-dimensional space. And it's the interaction of the vestibular system with other sensory ones that allows you to figure out your body orientation, sense the speed and direction of movement and stop you from keeling over.

And that's why damage to part of the vestibular system of the inner ear or its central brain connections can result in the room-tilt illusion, where there's a transient tilt perception of the visual surrounding so it appears to be on its side or, occasionally, upside down. Meanwhile, pilots describe the inversion illusion (particularly in high-performance aircrafts) during the sudden change from a fast climb to levelling out. The vestibular organs of the inner ear are then overstimulated and pilots develop a terrifying impression that the aircraft is in inverted flight or tumbling backwards. The temptation is to lower the nose of the aircraft, which only intensifies the illusion further.

Astronauts, often just after experiencing weightlessness, also describe usually short-lived sensations of feeling continuously inverted in zero gravity, even though they're in a 'visually upright' orientation in the cabin. Cosmonaut Gherman Titov was the first to report this in 1961: 'The weight vanished as quickly as *Vostok* separated from the booster . . . and I felt suddenly as though I were turning a somersault and then flying with my legs up!'

So, we've learned from these pilots and climbers and astronauts that visual, proprioceptive and vestibular function are all crucial to our sense of bodily consciousness.* And all of these can be disrupted as we depart from ground level.

But why do people have out-of-body experiences back on earth, even in the absence of a vestibular disorder or epilepsy or ketamine – all things that might provoke the sort of multisensory disintegration I've just described?

The answer to this might lie in brain differences rather than disorders. One UK study suggests that cortical

---

* Signals from inside the body and the visceral organs (interoceptive signals) are also important. Various studies have presented participants with a virtual body that illuminates synchronously or asynchronously with their breathing or heartbeat. Synchronous illumination shifts self-location and self-identification towards the virtual body.

hyperexcitability plays a role; an inbuilt neural vulnerability. We know that this sort of hyperexcitability occurs in patients with the visual aura of migraine, for example – when transcranial magnetic stimulation is applied to the visual cortex, there's a lower threshold for inducing phosphenes (flashes of light) than in those without migrainous aura. So it's conceivable that those who have had out-of-body experiences without any neurological condition have a general increase in this baseline cortical excitability. In turn, neural processing is disrupted, not to a point where it reaches the threshold for the aura of migraine or epilepsy but enough to trigger hallucinations with a strong visual component.

But I wonder if we could recreate this disembodiment here on earth in all of us?

'I do not have the possibility of distancing myself from my body, nor it from me,' wrote German philosopher Edmund Husserl a century too early.

He hadn't visited one London research laboratory in 2007.

Sitting Behind Yourself

I'm going to run an experiment on you. You're in a research centre in Queen Square in Bloomsbury. There's a lot of history around here. King George III, later in his life, was treated for 'madness' in one of the houses just a few doors down. And the National Hospital for the Paralysed and Epileptic opened in spring 1860. Starting with a house at 24 Queen Square leased at £110 a year, it was the first specialist Neurology hospital in the world. During the First World

War, as the hospital expanded, 1,200 sailors and soldiers were admitted to its wards. Much later, having been rebuilt after being bombed in the Blitz, the hospital was renamed the National Hospital for Neurology and Neurosurgery – its current incarnation.

Here you are, several decades on. Welcome to the laboratory. Have a seat. Put on this pair of head-mounted displays – essentially elaborate goggles connected to two video cameras one and a half metres behind you. This means you're viewing stereoscopic images* of your own back through a real-time video feed – as if you are sitting behind yourself.

Now you can feel me tapping your chest with a plastic rod but I'm out of your sight – remember that all you're seeing through your contemporary goggles is the view from the cameras behind you, of your back. At the same time, I'm stretching behind (the real) you and synchronously tapping another rod in the space at chest height just below the cameras. You can see my arm moving in that space, thanks to the view through your goggles, so now you *think* you're seeing the chest of an 'illusionary body' being tapped.

I keep tapping. Two minutes go by.

If you're like most of the other participants, you're now utterly convinced that you are sitting behind yourself – one and a half metres behind your real body. This is where your real self, you sense, is now located. And as your centre of awareness shifts, you lose self-identification with your real body.

---

* Images from the left and right video cameras are presented on the left and right eye displays, respectively.

If all of this isn't disconcerting enough, I'm now swinging a hammer towards you. Or rather I'm swinging a hammer towards the camera (the virtual body). Chances are that your threat response has just skyrocketed. I measure this through your evoked skin conductance, in essence your sweatiness. In the 'fight or flight' response, your sweat activity increases and consequently skin conductance, too. And so I see that you have emotionally responded just as if you are located behind your physical body.

At Queen Square on this day, the spatial unity between body and self was suspended within 120 seconds.

'Everywhere in the world, self starts with body,' wrote psychologist Roy Baumeister. Until it does not.

Neuroscientist Henrik Ehrsson conducted the experiments I've described in a 2007 study with the Wellcome Trust Centre for Neuroimaging at University College London, collaborating with his Swedish colleagues. In later experiments he and his team at Stockholm's Karolinska Institute went on to show that the seen physical body is even disowned: when participants observed their own body being threatened with a knife, there was a significantly lower threat response compared to an impending assault on the virtual body.

A whole range of perceptual processes provide the sense that we are located within our physical bodies. Get these things aligned in synchrony and we are ourselves and feel like ourselves.

But Ehrsson's experiments and others like them manipulate the visual first-person perspective (the extent to which you experience the outside world from your own body) while carefully keeping visuo-tactile stimulation correlated. And it's the synchronous part of the experiment that's key – a continuous match between visual and sensory information about the state of the body. The out-of-body illusion only works if the taps on your chest and in front of the camera are delivered synchronously rather than asynchronously and if there is no delay between the seeing and the tapping. That day in Queen Square, a multisensory conflict arose; the seen (the virtual body being tapped with a rod) did not match the felt (your own chest being tapped). Your brain then tried to reconcile all these disparate signals and left you seemingly departing your own body – your centre of experience shifted outside of it, the 'real you' displaced.

In Kevin's out-of-body experience, two representations of the body were formed but only one could be selected to anchor the self. Perspective became extra-corporeal.

Critics suggested that these experiments weren't precisely out-of-body experiences – not quite Kevin floating by the ceiling or Sherlock's spirit above Devonshire. But Ehrsson and his team were undeterred. By 2008, they had performed a body swapping experiment. This time, two cameras were attached to a mannequin's helmet. Participants tilted their heads downwards as if looking down at their bodies and saw the mannequin's body rather than their own. A rod was used to stroke their own abdomen (which was out of view) in synchrony with strokes to the mannequin's abdomen (in view). And again with this shift in visual first-person perspective, body ownership drifted towards the mannequin body. The experiment even worked when another person was used instead of a mannequin. And by 2011, a group of Swiss researchers led by neuroscientist Olaf

Blanke created perspective shifts that led participants to believe they were drifting above their own bodies.

The stories were sounding more like Kevin's than ever.

Influential German philosopher Thomas Metzinger now discarded previous paranormal and religious explanations for out-of-body experiences. The idea of a 'subtle body' had formed the core of some of these interpretations – an ethereal breath of life that sustains the physical body only to depart silently during altered consciousness and after death – the Hebrew *ruach*, the Arabic *ruh*, the Latin *spiritus*, the Greek *pneuma* and the Sanskrit *prana*. But, concluded Metzinger, 'research now makes it an empirically plausible assumption that this subtle body does indeed exist, but it is not made of "angel stuff" or "astral matter". It is made of pure information, flowing in the brain.'

We frequently view shifts in sameness and self as ominous, or at least as perturbing. Yes, Kevin had been euphoric to begin with as he drifted effortlessly towards the ceiling. But this dissipated swiftly.

Rather as Swiss biochemist Ernst Waelti described it in 1983:

The process of detachment started at the fingertips, in a way that could be clearly felt, almost with a perceptible sound, a kind of crackling. It was precisely the movement which I actually intended to carry out with my physical hands. With this movement, I detached from my body and floated out of it with the head leading. I gained an upright position, as if I was now almost weightless. Nevertheless, I had a body consisting of real limbs. You have certainly seen how elegantly a jellyfish moves through the water. I could now move around with the same ease. I lay down horizontally in the air and floated across the bed, like a swimmer, who has pushed himself from the edge of a swimming pool. A delightful feeling of liberation arose within me. But soon I was seized by the ancient fear common to all living creatures, the fear of losing my physical body. It sufficed to drive me back into my body.

There are echoes here of 'The Stolen Body', an 1898 short story by H.G. Wells. Mr Bessel leaves his own body only for an evil spirit to replace him: 'All through those hours the persuasion was overwhelming in Mr Bessel's mind that presently his body would be killed by its furious tenant, and he would have to remain in this shadow-land for evermore.'

But what if the experience of disembodiment could be leveraged in some positive way, the fear of losing one's physical body simultaneously extinguished? I believe that if we could linger a little longer in the shadow-land, we might just revel in its existence and reap its rich rewards.

Thinking Yourself Thinner and Chiller and Pain-Free

She was a thirty-seven-year-old Italian woman with a body mass index of 62.2 kg/m2. 'Super-super obese' is the technical term for this nowadays. Her weight had rapidly spiralled after a year of marriage. With a sedentary lifestyle and nightmarish in-laws, she had started to binge-eat. So obese was she now that she sometimes stopped breathing at night.

But here was a chance for change. She had been offered a place on an intervention programme to lose weight. Yes, she would be happy to sign up. But there was one barrier standing in the way of success. And that was the phenomenon of body-size distortion.

Those seeking inspiration to lose weight might stick a photograph on the fridge of a slim person (either a previous version of themselves or perhaps a celebrity they aspire to resemble). I want to look like that. I *could* look like that. Their ability to estimate their own body size seems to influence their inner dialogue.

Yet this patient in Italy, super-super obese as she was, had profound body-size distortion – she underestimated her width by about 50%. And she overestimated her body circumference by almost 20%. This, the researchers suggested, represented a multisensory impairment of body perception.

Virtual reality programmes have influenced eating behaviours before but a body-swapping illusion would provide the chance to switch to a first-person perspective, to intensify presence beyond conventional virtual reality. In this way, this Italian patient would not just view an avatar but instead could deeply experience the illusory ownership of a non-obese virtual body. Then, the researchers reasoned, her own body perception might also shift. And so they performed an illusory swap that switched her sense of bodily self to a slim body. A body that could breathe without gasping and sleep without drowning.

Afterwards, she was better able to estimate her own body size and went on to successfully complete a programme of physical and psychological intervention. Her motivation had improved after the body-swap illusion, she reported. By the end of the programme she had lost 3.7% of her initial weight. True, this report of improved motivation was simply a subjective one and a one-off at that and the duration of the programme is unclear. The intensive psychological therapy she received must have enhanced her motivation, too, and yet isn't even mentioned in the published paper. So I wouldn't read too much into that aspect of the research. But what's truly intriguing here is how a switch in body ownership could lead to a decrease in body-size distortion.

Similar findings have been reported in women with anorexia: an experiment using a body-ownership illusion (a swap to a body with a healthy body mass index) found that they were less likely to overestimate their real-life body size.

The next step will be to see if these body-swap experiments effect change and improve prognosis in eating disorders – those with more severe, refractory presentations of anorexia have a mortality rate anywhere between four and fourteen times the general population. New treatment approaches are desperately needed.

Here's another possible application of body-swap experiments in an entirely different sphere. I'd like you to imagine that you're standing in front of an audience. Eleven scientists are looking directly at you, their faces supremely stern and serious. Not a hint of warmth or welcome here. The room is hot, the stakes are high, your heart beats fast. At this moment, what sort of illusory body would you select to dial down your anxiety?

A 2015 experiment provided participants with the option of an entirely invisible one. This was created with the head-mounted display set-up I've mentioned before – but instead of a mannequin being synchronously stroked with a rod to create the illusion, those strokes were applied for sixty seconds to an area of empty space that represented an invisible body. Having an invisible body in front of those stern and serious scientists reduced social anxiety, measured both by heart rate and by subjective response. Leave your body, leave your fear. As usual, the experiment didn't work if the stroking was asynchronous; in other words, it wasn't just the illusion itself that was responsible but instead a transfer of body ownership that was a condition for success.

It's all very well being invisible for two minutes, but how can this be translated into any meaningful and lasting treatment for social anxiety? Virtual reality exposure therapy provided in this way might, suggest the researchers, be the answer. One step at a time, the solidness of the virtual body is incrementally increased as it navigates anxiety-provoking situations within a virtual world. A shift in self that is therapeutic rather than threatening.

Ahead lies the possibility of melding these techniques with brain computer interfaces (BCIs). With BCIs, the brain's electrical signals are analysed and used to control external devices.

Imagine if this technology could be harnessed for those who are paralysed after brain or spinal cord trauma – creating a full body illusion accompanied by BCI might mean they could take ownership and control of a virtual body within a simulated environment. One where they could develop navigational skills, and practise and perfect fine motor control alongside conventional physical rehabilitation.

This does require tempering of expectations though, not least because of the technical and financial barriers of using BCI to control an illusory body that functions effectively in a virtual world.

Initial excitement around more basic virtual reality technology has been dialled down. A recent *Lancet* study found that in stroke rehabilitation, simple, low-cost and widely available recreational activities (cards, bingo, Jenga or ball games) seemed to be as effective as non-immersive virtual reality technologies – the Nintendo Wii gaming system in this case. Imagine, shiny virtual reality was only as good as plain old bingo.

But the shortcoming of those earlier virtual reality interventions was that they were non-immersive. They did not shift body ownership. The aim of illusory body experiments is to do just that, to elevate presence. And that might, just might, make a difference.

In My Shoes and Your Shoes

How can we put ourselves in the shoes of others when we insist on only wearing our own? Catapulting ourselves out of our bodies, living the perspective and identity of another through body illusions, could allow us to do just that.

We're far less likely to mentally simulate the actions of those of another race. In one Canadian study, there was activation of the motor cortex when thirty white participants watched an action performed by a member of their own race on a video screen. But this activation was significantly reduced when an action was performed by a member of a racial out-group (e.g., East Asian, South Asian and

African-Canadian members). This was more so the case when participants watched the actions of groups they disliked, and the effect was most marked for people with higher levels of prejudice to begin with.

The idea behind the mirror neuron system is that we activate motor cells in our brains when we see the same movements in others, a phenomenon first seen in macaques. Neurons in the premotor cortex (the area for planning and executing movements) are active not just when the macaque performs an action but also when each sees the same goal-directed action being performed by another macaque or person. How much this relates to empathy, social understanding and imitation is contentious, particularly when even the mere presence of mirror neurons in humans is controversial. Perhaps the system instead just reflects how we choose and control motor tasks. Either way, initial overblown claims have been somewhat retracted. But the concept is helpful for breaking down illusory body experiments – a broad mirroring effect is influenced by various factors, race included.

Take the results of a Chinese study from a few years ago: when participants saw others of the same race experiencing pain, there was recruitment of the same neural network as would have been seen if they were in pain themselves. However, there was decreased neural activation of pain circuits (and, by extrapolation, *possibly* empathy) if they watched ethnic out-group members in pain relative to in-group members. In other words, a reduced activation of bodily representations.

And here's where full body illusions might play a part. Even illusory ownership of a dark-skinned rubber hand reduces implicit racial bias. In fact, the more intense the participants' illusion of ownership over a dark-skinned rubber hand, the more positive their implicit racial attitudes became.

A 2017 study delved deeper. Of thirty-two white Caucasian females, half were embodied through a full body illusion in a White virtual body and the remainder in a Black virtual body [the researchers' categorisations, capitals included]. Visualise the levels of presence here – the virtual body was programmed to move synchronously with the participant and the virtual body's movement corresponded with real body movements. Each embodied female interacted in two different sessions, lasting six minutes apiece, with a White and a Black virtual partner. The key measure here was mimicry of actions – we tend to automatically mimic the behaviours of in-group members, a marker of interpersonal sensitivity and empathy.

White participants, when embodied as a Black participant for those six minutes, treated a Black virtual partner as if she was a member of their in-group (as analysed by mimicry). They then treated their White virtual partner like an out-group member (as seen by decreased mimicry). In other words, their *virtual* body rather than their real body influenced who they mimicked more. Imagine if this potential empathy could be extended beyond six minutes, beyond this setting with its awkward head-mounted displays and video cameras. The possibilities to overcome implicit biases are as infinite as the challenges.

Sometimes in neurology we find answers and treat disorders and this next paragraph comfortably wraps up the ones that came before. Not all of the time, though, and not with Kevin. I arranged some tests for him, a brain scan and an EEG, and we talked that day about what sorts of things might be causing these episodes and what sorts of things weren't. But he never turned up for those investigations or for his next appointment at my Queen Square clinic.

I walked home that evening from Queen Square. Past the house where King George III stayed during his bouts of madness. Through Bloomsbury by the local ghosts of Darwin and Dickens and Woolf and Yeats. Down Euston Road where Mr Bessel's evil spirit had roamed 'flourishing a can of burning colza oil and jerking splashes of flame therefrom at the windows of the houses he passed'. By Madame Tussauds where queues formed every day to see dead doubles. Up along Baker Street where Sherlock Holmes once was and wasn't at the same time.

That whole walk I was the 'real me' within my body, the 'I' of my experiences and my thoughts. And although light was fading and darkness was falling as I walked through Regent's Park, I felt safe and secure and entirely myself. I hoped Kevin did, too.

And yet I realised that a profound experience of disembodiment need not invariably speak to the ominous, need not forever bear the haunting theme of a Gothic novel. Instead it might be the stuff of recovery and rehabilitation, of empathy and compassion. In losing ourselves, we have the potential to find something better and to be someone better.

8

Slumber

It was 1845. Wealthy Massachusetts man Albert J. Tirrell walked into a brothel on Cedar Lane near Beacon Hill. He slit the throat of twenty-one-year-old Maria Bickford, the woman he had been having an affair with. Then he set the building ablaze and fled.

Investigators later described the scene:

The dead woman's jugular vein and windpipe had been completely severed, her hair had been partly consumed by fire, and her face had been charred and blackened by flames. A number of fires had been set in the room where the body was discovered, the walls of the room were splattered with blood, a nearby washbowl contained a quantity of bloody water, and a bloodstained razor was found at the foot of her bed. Some articles of men's clothing were found in the room, along with a letter initialled A.J. T. to M.A.B.

It was several months before the twenty-two-year-old was captured in New Orleans and then returned to Boston to stand trial.

There were no witnesses, his defence argued. Bickford had probably taken her own life. And even if Tirrell had committed the crime in his sleep it was in, his lawyer Rufus Choate insisted, 'an unconscious trance or under the influence of a nightmare'. Walter Channing, former Dean of Harvard Medical School, testified that it was possible to commit murder while sleepwalking.

It was a brazen defence and Choate was a convincing orator. In his six-hour closing speech, he cited Tirrell's long history of sleepwalking – in this state he had previously broken a glass window, tried to knife his cousin, kicked a door while in pursuit of an imaginary horse and had once almost smothered his wife.

The jury deliberated for two hours. Tirrell was acquitted. He was, however, sentenced to three years in prison for adultery.*

You are drifting into sleep. The movements of your eyes slow, they roll a little, your muscles relax. Perhaps a falling sensation or a momentary jerk of an arm or leg. Your awareness of your surroundings begins to fade. Now, your muscles become even looser. Your detachment from the waking world grows. Soon, you descend into deep sleep. Eye movements disappear. If I try to wake you now, you'll probably be confused and disorientated. Rapid eye movement sleep follows next – you lose muscle tone throughout most of your body. Your pupils constrict – the fight or flight response is not needed here. This REM stage is the home of your most vibrant, intense dreams – a virtual imaginary world is created without all the stimuli of the real one.

And on it goes. This sleep cycle, the stages I've just described, lasts around 100 minutes and happens four or

---

* After the trial he wrote to Choate insisting that half his legal fees be returned – he had been so obviously innocent of murder that Choate hardly deserved the full amount. Choate's response to this goes unrecorded.

five times in a night. As the night unfolds, the REM stage lasts longer and longer. Your brain is active in different ways throughout.

If I bring you into a sleep laboratory and wake you during REM sleep, there's a high chance you'll tell me about a dream (80% of the time), perhaps with its own scene changes, surround sound, immersive convoluted plots, intrigue and intricacy.

But even if I wake you from non-REM (NREM) sleep, the chance you'll tell me about a dream experience of some sort is 60% – even if only subtle ephemeral imagery, unadorned thoughts and perceptual snapshots.

Consciousness in sleep fades at times but dreamlike experiences, whether in REM or NREM sleep, whether cinematic or prosaic, speak to conscious experience in sleep. The same cortical area seems crucial to dreaming in both states – a characteristic 'hot zone' towards the back of the brain (in the parieto-occipital region). Here lies the neural correlate of dreaming in all its forms.

The theme of violence in sleep is as contentious as it is complex. When it does occur, it relates to the very nature of consciousness and in turn to identity. Who are we when we dream or sleepwalk? If not ourselves, who do we become?

Although centuries of research have explored consciousness in our waking hours, it's consciousness as we dream that might tell us more about ourselves.

But since the plots of dreams can be bizarre, the landscape unfamiliar, the characters curious, is there anything of the self in our dreams? Or do we lose ourselves entirely?

The Dream Director

The consciousness states of your waking hours and of your dream world share so much that it's hard to argue that you're anyone else as you dream. As you describe your dreams to others, you depict how *you* felt or what *you* did. You describe these dreams as yours, not somebody else's. And if someone stole your dream away from you – well, that would feel intrusive, you would take it personally.

There is a sense of continuity of self in dreams even as there are radical differences in your experiences or ethics or capabilities. You are usually the protagonist, located within the body you inhabit during wakefulness, assuming a first-person point of view just the same. Even if you are not represented in the dream, you are its gatekeeper.

Just as in wakefulness, dreams – particularly in REM sleep – are frequently infused with a vibrant multisensory experience – sometimes animated enough that we awaken and wonder if those events really happened. The frustrations of your daily life seep into dreams, the antagonists of your waking consciousness arrive to do battle at night. The dialogue of your dreams often reflects the narrative of your day. Speech usually makes sense; grammar is preserved even where content is fantastical. You see faces, people and places. Motion and shape and colour and structure. Plots and themes.

Since waking consciousness and dreaming consciousness seem so similar, you might anticipate that the same structures and functions activate during both states. A 2013 Japanese study published in *Science* found just that.

Researchers compared brain activity during dreaming to that of waking consciousness – for the latter, participants viewed images that corresponded to their dreams. The same neural substrate was activated in each.

That's not to neglect the incongruity that pervades dreams – features that deviate from what would be expected in the real world. Even then, in one early study the dream self only deviated from the real self in 8% of reports. The dream self being the subject who acts in or observes the dream world; the dream is experienced from its point of view.

Sometimes a younger self appears, just occasionally other characteristics shift. Here is one dream report from a twenty-five-year-old blond-haired female Finnish student:

'It's the Second World War and I am a dark-haired, strongly built, Finnish male soldier. The enemies are probably German . . . [Later in same dream]: I could see myself in a mirror. Now I was a blond, strongly built woman.'

And yet she still saw herself as the dreamer, the protagonist, the embodied 'I'.

Meanwhile other characters in dreams show incongruous features around twice as frequently as those in the dream self. Thinking and language (spoken and written) seem to be particularly inconsistent – a pattern seen in just under a third of reports.

The content of dreams can change even if the self does not. Reverie is sprinkled with amnesia; we meet others forgetting they are estranged or no longer alive. Emotions are heightened – the structures that drive them are highly activated during REM sleep, no longer stifled by others.

We are passive spectators in dream consciousness.* Intent, analysis, reason and rationality and logic fade as the frontal lobes and their connections are dialled down. In the more intricate dreams of REM sleep, we accept the fantastical, the impossible, a sort of magic realism infused with mysticism. Old men grow young, we reach the horizon without crossing the ocean, a magic carpet hovers above us as we buy a pint of milk, a trail of blood passes along the Street of the Turks to inform a mother that her son has died.

This is an immersive cinematic experience. You are a director unconstrained by a budget or by health and safety laws. There no rules to be followed and no limits to be exercised.

Perhaps this allows you to cast yourself as a heroic protagonist with capabilities that evade you during your waking hours – you scale impossibly tall skyscrapers, swim through rip tides and walk across quicksand to save others. You might instead become ruthless or malevolent in your starring role, qualities absent from your more pedestrian daytime existence – you rob a bank at gunpoint or cheat on your partner without compunction. But these actions could simply reflect the editorial freedom of a dream director rather than any sort of Freudian revelation of your unconscious base desires. For many years, enigmatic and cryptic qualities were attached to dream states. Dreams, as ancient beliefs had it, bleakly foreshadowed or brightly reflected divinity, exposed dark passions and unspeakable truths.

---

* The exception being lucid dreaming, where we are aware that we are dreaming and report an element of control over our dreams.

But this is a narrative as unsubstantiated as the stories of your liberally edited dreams.

As Erin Wamsley, cognitive neuroscientist, writes:

'Despite thousands of years of dream interpretation, and the proliferation of dream symbol dictionaries on bookstore shelves, there is no systematic empirical evidence that dreams contain symbols to any greater degree than our typical waking thoughts, let alone has there been any empirical support for a particular system to "decode" these symbols.'

All the same, there are parallels between dream states and wakefulness – particularly the resting wakefulness of daydreaming.

As Wamsley describes, vivid hallucinatory perceptual imagery can be the stuff of daydreams and waking mental activity as well as of dreams. And perhaps dreams are no more bizarre than our waking thoughts – if we measure bizarreness by sudden discontinuous shifts, then the number of these are greater in reports of waking fantasy than in dreaming. Finally, there's some overlap, albeit by no means complete, between brain activity patterns in restful wakefulness and in sleep – common signatures in the default mode network that generate conscious thought and imagery in wakefulness. Conscious experience in each seems to be generated in comparable ways and there are commonalities in their neural origin. More binds than divides.

And so the consciousness of sleep has as much to tell us about ourselves as the consciousness of our waking hours. Even as the set changes and its characters revolve and centuries turn, the self in your dreams is, for the most part, an embodiment of your waking self. Amnestic and lacking self-reflection at times yet bearing the essence of you. The self who levitates within your dreams is generally the same self who walks through your day.

It's a serene thought. You remain you even as the tides of consciousness wash in and out on the shore of sleep.

That's all well and good when your dreams are confined to a typical dream state – one of significant muscle paralysis. Your body remains still as you scale those skyscrapers, immobile as you rob that bank. But imagine physically acting out these dreams in a state of apparent sleep – eyes closed but limbs liberated. Would you own yourself then? How might this threaten your identity, your sense of sameness, when you awaken?

Sleeping with the Enemy

> ... he was thrusting his sword in all directions, speaking out loud as if he were actually fighting a giant. And the strange thing was that he did not have his eyes open, because he was asleep and dreaming that he was battling the giant ... He had stabbed the wine skins so many times, believing that he was stabbing the giant, that the entire room was filled with wine ...
>
> Miguel de Cervantes, *Don Quixote*
> *de La Mancha* (1605)

A few years ago, Dilip and his wife, Kathleen, arrived at my clinic. They were both in their late sixties. The sort of couple long enough together that each looks to the other as their sentences trail off. They wore matching spectacles and fleece jackets.

'He keeps trying to kill me, Doctor,' she said.

And then a sort of nervous laughter between them both.

Dreams are just dreams until they're not.

During the day Dilip was enjoying his retirement, visiting his allotment and tidying up the attic. Generally making a nuisance of himself at home, Kathleen added. But at night-time, he dreamed that he was being chased by armed robbers or stalked by wild animals. Last night he had watched Kathleen being pursued by a shadowy figure down an alleyway. More violent dreams in the past year than he had ever had before. And Dilip heroically attacked them all – he swung a right hook towards the burglar, crushed the neck of a rhino, karate kicked the shadowy figure to the cobblestones.

But really it was Kathleen, sleeping beside him, who was being punched and half-choked and karate kicked.

During all of it, in Dilip's mind he was only saving himself or gallantly defending her.

No matter how fantastical our dreams are, we are usually immobile during them – the muscle paralysis we experience during REM sleep means we cannot act those dreams out. But in Dilip's case, the brakes had been released. No longer the standby actor waiting in the wings; he had been called on stage to perform. When he woke in the morning, he would remember some of the elements of the performance – the chase and the escape, the brutality of it all. But each time he was horrified to hear that Kathleen had borne the brunt of his ferocity.

Dilip, I realised, had REM sleep behaviour disorder – RBD. Unlike many other sleep disorders, which tend to happen in childhood (sleepwalking and sleep terrors, for example), RBD is usually seen in adults, especially in men over the age of fifty.

If Dilip had come to my clinic a few decades earlier, he might well have been committed to a psychiatric institution. Or prison. But RBD was identified in the mid-60s and formally named around twenty years later. Now we know it occurs in about 2% of older adults.

Each attack might last only sixty seconds or so but can recur during the night. Round after round for Kathleen in the boxing ring.

Sleep studies proved Dilip's violence was limited to REM sleep – his brainwaves showed its classic highly active characteristics as his arms thrashed about. The usual muscle atonia (loss of muscle tone) that should have rendered him immobile had vanished.

It's the brainstem, particularly a region called the pons and its projections, that is crucial for paralysing skeletal muscle during REM sleep. In the 1960s, French researchers discovered that previously amiable cats with lesions created in these areas seemed to act out their dreams during REM sleep – 'violent and abrupt jerks involving all of the muscles, vertical leaps so intense that the animal collides with the ceiling of the cage, aggressive attack, with emotion, against an imaginary enemy, fear, with retreating behavior culminating in a defensive posture'.

So if the region or its connections are damaged in some way, REM sleep behaviour disorder can follow – muscle atonia is eliminated but not just that; locomotor activity is ramped up.

Kathleen had been left bruised more than once as Dilip valiantly defended her – injuries are seen in two thirds of the bed partners of those with RBD.

Researchers described the actions of one man who developed the condition aged seventy:

'On one occasion he held his wife's head in a headlock and, while moving his legs as if running, exclaimed, "I'm gonna make that touchdown!" He then attempted to throw her head down toward the foot of the bed. When awakened, he recalled a dream in which he was running for a touchdown, and he spiked the football in the end zone.'

His wife survived, somehow.

In about a third of cases, patients are themselves injured at some point. Case reports describe lacerations, bruising, fractures and even brain haemorrhages. 'She jumped out of bed and fractured a hip while enacting a dream in which she was escaping from "grotesque men with hands like claws and swarms of bees who were attacking me".'

Dilip had moved a bedside lamp in case he lashed out; there was a rug on his side in case he fell out of bed. But the attacks were becoming even more forceful and Kathleen found it increasingly difficult to wake him up as she came under attack.

Patients with RBD have tried all manner of measures to contain their violence – tethering themselves to their beds with a dog leash, wearing oven gloves or sleeping on a padded waterbed. Others have constructed plywood barriers or removed every single piece of furniture from the bedroom. One long-suffering spouse kept a broom under her side of the bed as a 'wake up' poker, 'yet on occasion this would be grabbed by her husband and used as a sword'.

Now Dilip was thinking of sleeping in the next room for the first time in their forty-year marriage.

At least I could offer him treatment for his RBD though, and I was optimistic that it would help. About 90% of patients have some response, often a complete one, to a benzodiazepine called clonazepam. Others respond well to melatonin.

But there was another statistic I needed to tell Dilip about. As more patients have been identified with RBD and successfully treated over the years, we've begun to realise that many develop a consistent pattern of symptoms – a tremor, a shuffling gait, stiffness in the arms or legs. It turns out that 50% or more of patients with RBD will go on to develop Parkinson's or one of its variants. In these conditions, the brainstem also seems vulnerable in some way. But it can take ten years or more for Parkinson's to evolve after the first episode of RBD.

For Dilip, it was going to be a long wait to find out if Parkinson's lay ahead.

In the dreams of his RBD, Dilip saw himself as the protagonist. But even when the dreams were certainly his and the actions were undeniably his, the brutality he simply could not own.

For Kathleen, there was no doubt that the ferocious behaviour of her husband during sleep was inherently at odds with the calmness of his character during the day. Then again, she said, he was trying to gallantly defend her the way he might in his waking hours. In a way, through the brutality he was just being himself.

Eyes Open, Sense Shut

[Enter LADY MACBETH, *with a taper*]

GENTLEWOMAN [continuing]: Lo you, here she comes! This

is her very guise; and, upon my life, fast asleep. Observe her; stand close.

[. . .]

DOCTOR: You see, her eyes are open.

GENTLEWOMAN: Ay, but their sense is shut.

William Shakespeare, *Macbeth* (1606), Act 5, Scene 1

Toronto, May 1987. Twenty-three-year-old Kenneth Parks had fallen asleep watching TV that Saturday night. At some point, nobody knows exactly what time, he put on his shoes and jacket and drove fourteen miles across town to his in-laws' house in Scarborough. Afterwards, he arrived at a police station covered in blood:

'I just killed someone with my bare hands; oh my God, I just killed someone; I've just killed two people; my God, I've just killed two people with my hands; my God, I've just killed two people. My hands; I just killed two people. I killed them; I just killed two people; I've just killed my mother- and father-in-law. I stabbed and beat them to death. It's all my fault.'

Parks had beaten his mother-in-law with a tyre iron he had taken from his car and then stabbed her to death. He stabbed and strangled his father-in-law, who survived. He pleaded not guilty to charges of first-degree murder and attempted murder – his defence: sleepwalking.

Parks, it seemed, had become a different person as he drove across town. A gentle giant, his mother-in-law had described him as in the early days, long before the events of that Toronto night. It seems unfathomable, perhaps scarcely believable, that a simple short circuit in his sleep cycle could unleash such inhumanity. His sleepwalking defence was met with widespread scepticism. But we know more about consciousness now than we did then. And so I wonder if we might explain what happened that night through this newfound understanding of how consciousness shifts in sleep; through the neuroscientific developments that surfaced long after Ken Parks took that tyre iron from his car over thirty years ago.

Sleepwalkers are silent for the most part, occasionally uttering just a few intelligible words as they meander, blundering initially with eyes open, their navigation then becoming more precise. They exist, zombie-like, typically for around ten minutes in a mental state between wakefulness and sleep.

Sometimes they become agitated and complex behaviours arise: nocturnal eating, sexual acts, cooking or driving. Seventeenth-century scholar Pierre Gassendi described a man who crossed a swollen river on stilts. There was the eighteenth-century Italian nobleman Augustin Forari, who during bouts of sleepwalking would get dressed, ride his horse and practise the harpsichord. And the wonderfully titled but entirely unverifiable 1814 case report: 'Publication of Surprising Case of Rachel Baker, Who Prays and Preaches in Her Sleep: With Specimens of her Extraordinary Performances Taken Down Accurately in Short Hand at the Time; and Showing the Unparalleled Powers She Possesses to Pray, Exhort, and Answer Questions, During Her Unconscious State.'

Violence towards others tends to occur in adults (it's exceedingly rare in children)* and is inflicted without intent – perhaps

---

* The prevalence of sleepwalking reaches around 10–15% in children aged eight to twelve but persists after the age of ten in a quarter of cases. The prevalence in adults is around 2–4%.

the sleepwalker is woken and becomes combative in this disorientated and perplexed state. Or else they just happen upon someone else – wrong place, wrong time.

But most sleepwalkers are not violent in any way towards others, despite repeated episodes over many years. Instead, there are likely other genetic and environmental factors that raise the risks.

Ken Parks' savagery did not reflect the behaviour of the typical somnambulist; it saw him become one of the most notorious sleepwalkers in legal history.

It had been a tumultuous time in Parks' life. He had embezzled $30,000 at work to cover betting debts. He hid the truth from his wife initially and their marriage endured the strain. He lost sleep, his levels of stress escalated. He rarely saw his in-laws despite their previously close relationship.

Eventually, his deceit was uncovered at work and he was fired. There was no choice but to put the family home up for sale.

After a Gamblers Anonymous meeting, he decided it was time to come clean – he planned to tell his grandmother on Saturday 23 May and his in-laws the following day.

But that Saturday morning, Parks changed his mind – he and his wife argued and he went out to play rugby with friends. He returned home only for another quarrel to unfold. At 8.30 p.m., he put his daughter, five months old, to bed. His wife joined him downstairs for a bit and then she went to bed around midnight. Parks fell asleep watching *Saturday Night Live*.

What happened next was described in a case report some years later.

The next thing Ken reports being able to recall after falling asleep was looking down at his mother-in-law's face. Her mouth and eyes were open and she had a 'frightened "help-me"' look. He did not recall seeing marks or blood on her face. His next remembrance was hearing the younger children of the in-laws yelling upstairs. Following this, there is a period of patchy recall for isolated events with amnesia for others in between. For instance, Ken recalled subsequently being at the top of the stairs attempting to reassure the children by yelling 'kids, kids' (they were hiding behind a door and later reported only 'animal noises'), being back downstairs, starting his car and it lurching forwards, realising in the car that he had a knife in his hands, shaking the knife onto the floor and subsequently saying at the police station upon questioning 'I think I have killed some people . . . my hands'. It was only at this time that Ken felt the hand pain related to his severe and multiple severed flexor tendons.

To understand how Parks might be capable of such extreme barbarity is to understand how consciousness shifts as slumber emerges. We know now that in moments of NREM sleep (the stage where sleepwalking occurs), complex motor behaviours and altered consciousness can coexist. It's a phenomenon not exclusive to humans.

The bottle-nose dolphin might appear to be asleep but occasionally has one eye open – in this state, the electrical activity from one half of the dolphin's brain is that of NREM slow-wave sleep. Unexpectedly, though, from the other half emerges a clear wake pattern. This is a state of dissociation – where rest and vigilance coexist and where dolphins can float and swim and, crucially, can surface in order to breathe. This unihemispheric slow-wave sleep is also a trait of porpoises, toothed whales, certain types of eared seal and several species of bird (even in flight), from the peregrine falcon to the mallard, the domestic chicken to the blackbird. And a similar form of dissociation – coexisting NREM sleep states with episodic wakefulness – is seen in hibernating animals.

This dissociation is characteristic of sleepwalking – there are not only signatures of wakefulness but also characteristics of NREM sleep.

Boundaries blur. And so the sleepwalker rambles around rooms, tumbles down stairs, leaps out of windows, all while ensconced in the deepest stage of non-REM sleep.

Our understanding of the dissociation of consciousness between sleep and waking today allows for profoundly different assumptions and decisions in the courtroom relative to decades or even centuries ago. Take the May 1853 case of seventeen-year-old nursemaid Sarah Minchin, who was tried at the Old Bailey for 'feloniously cutting and wounding Frederick Smith, with intent to murder him'. Minchin claimed to have been sleepwalking, had a childhood history of same and had little memory of the attack on her thirteen-year-old charge, who suffered superficial injuries.

A surgeon, Mr Bullock, who attended to Frederick, was cross-examined about menstrual cycles rather than sleep cycles.

MR RIBTON *to* MR BULLOCK

Q. If a girl of the age of the prisoner, about seventeen, was suffering from a disordered state of the menstruation, would that be liable to affect her head?

A. No; there is a disease called nymphomania. But that would not be likely to do it – persons often have pains in the head, caused by a disordered state, or a temporary suppression of the menses, but never to be mad, or out of their minds through it – I do not know that it frequently makes them delirious.

Minchin's sleepwalking defence was rejected. She was found guilty and sentenced to three months in prison.

There is a contemporary hypothesis, though, for violence committed in a state of seemingly deep sleep.

Certain pathways are selectively activated and others hypoactivated in sleepwalking. Those selectively activated pathways are normally drawn upon for complex motor and emotional behaviour in wakefulness. This is how that seventeenth-century sleepwalker might have been able to cross a swollen river on stilts or how that eighteenth-century Italian nobleman could ride a horse and practise the harpsichord. And yes, how some could stab or strangle when apparently asleep.

But what's also crucial is the pathways that seem to become hypoactive during sleepwalking – those projecting to the frontal lobes. These areas, particularly around the prefrontal cortex, are crucial for judgement, insight, inhibition of emotional responses, self-reflection, planning and attention. When they are dialled down, all those functions are compromised. This happens to all of us in slow-wave sleep without collateral damage – it's a time when judgement or insight or inhibition are not required. But in sleepwalkers, these hypoactive pathways now can't suppress the unexpectedly activated ones – those for motor and emotional behaviours. As the sleepwalker wanders, structures that are normally kept in check are liberated. The amygdala, for example, modulates our response to threat. But when it is no longer moderated by the frontal lobes, unwarranted aggressive behaviour surges forth.

Parks underwent laboratory sleep studies and was found to have unusually high levels of slow-wave sleep, typical of the deep sleep of sleepwalkers. There were other electrical signatures of sleepwalking, too. Of course this did not prove he was sleepwalking at the time of the crime, but it did strengthen his case.

In 1988, Ken Parks was acquitted of the first-degree murder of his mother-in-law and the attempted murder of his father-in-law.

I doubt that Parks would have been freed if he had stood at the Old Bailey in 1853. But I wonder whether Sarah Minchin might have been acquitted if she had ended up at Ontario Supreme Court in 1988.

The Dream Defence

As the popularity of the sleepwalking defence strategy rises, there is a danger of being blinded by sleep science, by talk of hyperactive and hypoactive brain regions and their electrical signatures. What if perpetrators of serious crimes are being freed by facts that don't apply to them? It's a strategy increasingly being used for other crimes, often successfully – twelve of eighteen UK rape cases in which sexsomnia was used as a defence (between 1996 and 2011) resulted in acquittal. The stakes are high.

There are recommendations published by forensic sleep

experts to guide courtroom decisions – these work to establish whether a sleep disorder might be relevant to a crime.

Violent acts committed during sleep are typically of abrupt onset, one set of recent guidelines suggests.* Usually impulsive, senseless and without motive. Afterwards, the sleepwalker is perplexed and horrified by his or her actions, without any attempt to escape or conceal what they have done (contrast this with Albert Tirrell, who I mentioned at the opening of this chapter – Bickford's room was set alight after the murder and Tirrell fled the city). In sleep-related violence, there is usually some degree of amnesia for the event although most sleepwalkers remember fragments – perceptual elements, images, thoughts or emotions. All of these elements seem to apply to Parks. No motive could be found for his crime either – there was nothing as far as anyone could tell to be gained personally or financially.

There also needs to be an underlying bona fide sleep disorder. Parks had a personal and family history of sleep-walking, and later sleep studies – electrical recordings of his brainwaves, muscle activity, eye movements and breathing – supported his tendency to sleepwalk. This sort of evidence strengthens, might even seal, a defendant's case.

But these guidelines also suggest that in cases of sleep-related violence, the victim will have been coincidentally present or else the victim approached or even provoked them. And yet, Ken Parks instead drove right across town,

* Bornemann, M.A.C., and Schenck, C.H. (2017), 'Sleep, Violence, and Forensic Implications' in *Sleep Disorders Medicine*, New York: Springer, pp.1175–85.

independently, without incitement. Driving during presumed sleepwalking has been reported in other instances where there was no harmful intent but it is certainly not typical. Most cases of sleepwalking last seconds or minutes; Parks' lasted far longer.

Even if there is dissociation in sleep, how deep does this run? Parks would have been enveloped by the petrified screams of his in-laws as he brutally stabbed, bludgeoned and strangled them. Yet, he claimed that he was almost entirely unaware throughout.

The truth is that there is no way to reconstruct the crime. Nothing that definitively tells us whether a defendant was sleepwalking on the night in question or, even if they were, whether this relates to the crime itself. At most, the results of sleep studies will speak to tendency rather than responsibility.

Even if sleepwalking were to be somehow confirmed at the time of a crime, should it allow for exoneration? If you are a sleepwalker and know that you have a tendency to become violent, shouldn't you remove sharp objects from reach at night-time, avoid alcohol or drugs that might trigger these episodes, seek medical advice, perhaps have someone hide the car keys before you turn in for the night? Shouldn't you accept responsibility not just for who you are but also who you might become?

Light fades and our muscles relax and our eyelids flicker. In sleep, consciousness ebbs and flows. In dreaming, conscious experience persists. And so, for the most part, there is continuity of self – even as the set is reconstructed and the actors are recast.

Ken Parks has kept a low profile since his acquittal. In more recent years, he ran for the position of trustee at a local school in Durham but immediately faced a backlash when his history came to light. An email circulated: 'Fellow candidate is bad news . . .' it started.

'The issues that have been brought up were 20 years ago,' Parks told one newspaper, 'and yes, are a matter of public record. Now, 20 years later, I am just a concerned parent that is trying to make sure the children of our community get the best education possible. Nothing more, nothing less.'

But Parks might always be judged for his actions that night in May 1987. Perhaps because we suspect that in sleep, something of ourselves persists. A sameness of sorts. And no matter how neuroscientific advances disentangle consciousness in sleep, that suspicion might never shift.

9
Calling Time

Charlotte had been studying English Literature at university. One Tuesday evening, her mother found her unconscious on the bathroom floor. Her lips were blue. There was no note.

Her mother had performed mouth to mouth. And the paramedics had arrived quickly and of course had known exactly what to do. The emergency room team kept her alive. All of those people fighting the fate that Charlotte had planned out for herself that morning.

Forty-eight hours passed. I was asked to see her in Intensive Care; to determine her prognosis. For a moment, it did not feel as if Charlotte had been saved. She was severely brain-injured, unresponsive. I looked at her brain scan, searching for the normally clear boundaries between grey and white matter; preserved boundaries signal cause for optimism, evidence of preserved function. But no, those boundaries were blurred, almost indistinguishable.

The ventilator hummed and infusions ran and monitors beeped; the functions of Charlotte had been outsourced.

At the foot of the bed there was a slanted desk and across it was stretched a large sheet of paper. A graph plotted the rise and fall of her blood pressure, temperature, oxygen levels and pulse. On the top right was a list of her medications and infusions. Below this, the nurse had written the plan for the day – replace catheter, chase chest X-ray result, supplement magnesium, neurology team review. The entirety of Charlotte's day, what had happened that morning, what would happen later, existed on this page.

Consciousness is an intrinsic part of identity. And since the moment Charlotte ended up on the bathroom floor with an empty bottle of pills next to her, her life and the lives of those around her had irrevocably changed.

I wonder what happens to Charlotte's identity when she is unable to respond to her surroundings, when she is unable to have experience of 'I' or self or knowledge of existing, unable to impart memories or present her personality to us? What remains? First for Charlotte's family and friends. Then for Charlotte herself. And finally, what does this mean for the rest of us?

I step closer to Charlotte's bedside. Here is what I see.

There's a white identification band on her wrist with her name and a seven-digit hospital number – the number is in larger print than her name. A ventilator pushes air through a tube inserted into her windpipe. There's a small grey pulse oximeter on her finger measuring oxygen saturations in her blood. A bag of saline hangs high above her bed with an infusion pump running its fluids into her veins. There is a central line tunnelled into the skin on the right side of her neck; through it flows medications that stabilise her blood pressure. A catheter snakes its way from her bladder to a bag that is hooked to the railings at the side of the bed. There are dark blue compression stockings on her legs to stop blood clots from forming.

On her forearms, scars. She used to wear long-sleeved tops, her mother said. They didn't know for months.

Through all of this, though, there is a recognisable face, a recognisable body. Yes, her skin is pale and there's some swelling of her hands and a laceration around her left temple. But even in this comatose state, this looks like Charlotte. Just like all of us when we go through physical changes – we are still our bodies. Cells dividing, hair greying and knees wearing, our body is still stable enough that others recognise us and we recognise ourselves. For those who know her, in this likeness she remains Charlotte. Body swollen, bruised, still.*

And so when Charlotte's family and friends visit her in Intensive Care, they'll walk past each bed until they say 'that's her'. If someone dies in a car crash, his family will be asked to identify him in the morgue and they'll say 'that's him'. There'll be an outpouring of emotion for all the things he said and did and was. A line-up at a police station – the witness points: 'She did it, it was her.' Her shadow, her fingerprints, her in the mirror, her. There is recognition. But this seems more a case of identification – being exactly alike – and less a case of identity – being one and the same over time.

Perhaps Charlotte's loved ones have little other choice than to try to ground her identity in the physical. Yet if they could somehow salvage her memories and personality and

---

* There are variations on this theme of the brute physical approach. Take the bodily criterion as described by philosopher Harold Noonan. Artefacts, let's say an oak tree or a ship, persist over time. Their persistence, he explains, does not consist in their retention of the same matter since objects can be patched up. Instead it lies in the retention of form in the face of their matter undergoing gradual replacement. Just as living things are 'necessarily involved in a constant exchange of matter with their environment'.

narrative and moral agency and transplant them into someone else who had a radically different physical appearance, then surely that someone else would be Charlotte.

But for now, they see her past and her potential future and the rich complexity of what was and might be her life. Identification and identity collide.

Then again, I am only here to formulate Charlotte's prognosis, to figure out whether the ventilator should stay on or be turned off.

I shine a light in her eyes – her pupils dilate. I gently touch the edge of her cornea with a wisp of cotton wool – her eyes blink; the reflex is intact. On I go, checking other reflexes, examining the potential for recovery.

The ventilator stays on.

The Face of Sameness

The face – there's something different about the face. This is where Charlotte's family and friends, when there is little else to connect to, will see *her*. Her face brings a sense of sameness where there is little else to secure it. Where we come from and who we are is written there. Ancestry, parentage, race, ethnicity, age, emotion, expression and communication.

I wonder what this means though for an unconscious person whose face bears little or no resemblance, perhaps because of facial trauma, to the face in framed photographs at the bedside – the face at a graduation ceremony or a twenty-first birthday party. The face in the thoughts and hopes of others.

Imagine Charlotte's face was horrifically disfigured in a car crash – would that mean she was any less *her*? When

her memories and narrative and personality are inaccessible to her family and friends, at least her face brings some
sense of sameness. What would it mean now if her face was
entirely unrecognisable?

For that, I'll lead you into the world of face transplants.

In June 2007, Carmen Blandin Tarleton was battered by her
estranged husband with a baseball bat and soaked with indus-
trial lye. She sustained burns to over 80% of her body including her eyelids, upper lip and left ear. News reports issued
graphic content warnings before showing Tarleton's injuries.

Facial transplants are not performed simply for aesthetic
purposes; there are functional goals, too – the renewed
ability to breathe and chew and speak and blink and smile.
But the potential impact on identity was a key concern for
the Royal College of Surgeons in England in 2004. It
would be unwise to proceed with facial transplantation,
their report concluded, without further research:

> Disruption to one's facial appearance, especially the inabil-
> ity to recognise oneself, represents a profound disruption
> of body image and may constitute a major life crisis. The
> response to a dramatic change in facial appearance can be
> akin to a bereavement reaction and can result in grieving
> followed by a slow process of adaptation.

Facial expressions affect our interaction with others,
they noted, but also how we ourselves feel, each expression potentially modulating our mood rather than exclu-
sively the other way round.

Tarleton told the *New Scientist* that after her transplant (once she regained her vision – she had been blind

for the first two years after the attack), she felt that she had lost herself in some way, that she had borrowed someone's face: 'I couldn't see who I was before. Even my eye colour had changed. I couldn't see me in there. It was disturbing.'

For some who are severely disfigured, a sense of loss of identity is felt keenly, even if transiently so (this is not inevitable of course; each experience is unique). But here Tarleton was, coming to terms not only with her previous disfigurement but now with a new identity, an assimilation of her own self and of someone who no longer existed.

Facial transplant recipients have a different bone structure to the donor and so Tarleton wasn't quite wearing the face of somebody else. Instead she saw the face of her former self and her donor's – Cheryl Denelli Righter, who had died of a stroke. Two faces created one reflection. Since the characteristics of the donor face can fade over time, even this reflection might shift.

'After seeing my old reflection for forty years it is going to take a while to look in the mirror and not think, "Hey, this doesn't really look like me." I've sort of gotten used to it. It's not stressful – being disfigured was a lot more stressful.'

Meanwhile her donor's daughter, Miranda, saw her late mother: she later told Tarleton, 'I get to feel my mother's skin again, I get to see my mother's freckles, and through you, I get to see my mother live on.'

Almost forty facial transplants followed in the decade after the first was performed in 2005. Tarleton did eventually come to accept her new self and she and other recipients have reported improvements in body image, mood, sense of self, quality of life and social reintegration. These positive outcomes are of course predicated on selecting patients who are appropriate for this complex surgery and on psychological and psychiatric support throughout.[*]

A facial transplant is a unique transformation – a transplant of perpetually visible expressions, a shift in recognisability and familiarity.

What does this mean for Charlotte's family and friends? Her face looks familiar, in contrast to Tarleton's after her original injury and her transplant, and to some extent I think that maintains her identity for her family, specifically in this very early aftermath of her hospital admission. Charlotte seems a bit like Charlotte when everything else has changed. Her identity in some way salvaged. She remains, to them, one and the same person.

A change in facial appearance after facial trauma or a transplant can be dramatic enough that the person will be unrecognisable at passport control. So that's about identification. But there is no doubt that sometimes it's about identity, too.

Rewiring and Renewal

I graduated from medical school in 2003, in that naive state of still not knowing what I didn't know.

---

[*] That support is needed not just for the surgery itself but for the multiple revision operations that frequently follow, possible rejection of the transplant, and the potential complications of immunosuppressive drugs – these include life-threatening infections and cancer. To date, the mortality rate for facial transplants is 11.5%.

A month later, news broke worldwide that a man in Arkansas named Terry Wallis had woken up after nineteen years.

On 13 July 1984, near Stone County, a white Chevy truck had plunged through a guard rail into the dry riverbed below. Terry, then nineteen years old, was discovered only the next day. The driver, his friend, was killed instantly.

Terry's daughter, Amber, had been born just six weeks earlier.

For nineteen years the former mechanic lay seemingly unresponsive. First in a coma, then, doctors told his family, in a vegetative state. In a nursing home in the town of Mountain View, his parents visited him each day. They took him home every second weekend for almost two decades.

But over the years, they noticed sporadic signs – occasionally a smile that seemed to be directed at them, an almost imperceptible nod of agreement. But were these true signs of awareness? The rest of the time, week after week, month after month, there were little more than grunts and grimaces.

On 11 June 2003, his mother, Angilee, came to visit. Just like any other day. The nurse's aide asked Terry if he knew who had walked into the room.

'Mom,' he answered.

After that the words kept coming, slurred and slow as they were. 'Pepsi' and then 'milk' and then whole sentences. Terry thought he was still nineteen years old. In his mind, Ronald Reagan was President. His memories were fractured, his limbs weakened, he needed round-the-clock care to be fed and washed and turned. But he could speak, haltingly, and could recognise his family. Over time some recollections of his childhood and teenage years were reignited and gained clarity.

What had been going on in Terry's brain for the last nineteen years? In Terry and others like him, are those grunts and grimaces an indication of something more?

Nicholas Schiff and research colleagues at Weill Medical College of Cornell University looked deep into Terry's brain through a technique called diffuse tensor imaging (DTI). DTI tracks water molecules to show the brain's white matter tracts – essentially its wiring. They combined this with PET scanning to uncover his brain's metabolic activity and found that around the time Terry had said 'Mom', there was still significant damage, as you might expect – the sort of destruction where, at first glance, reasonable recovery would be considered unlikely. There was atrophy throughout the brain and brainstem and severe widespread axonal injury; in other words, both the volume and wiring of the brain had been compromised. But what caught the attention of the researchers was that there seemed to be large regions of increased connectivity posteriorly in the brain; this pattern wasn't seen in control participants. There was increased metabolic activity in this region that would fit in with the neuronal regrowth that accompanied his recovery. In those two decades, it seemed that new pathways and circuits were being formed through every grunt and grimace. Pathways that led Terry towards 'Mom' and 'Pepsi' and 'milk'.

But this was not the sort of axonal regrowth that would happen in most other people who had suffered such severe brain damage – these posterior regions, linked to awareness, happened to be among the least affected during Terry's original injury. Here were relatively intact regions where rewiring could perhaps begin – some networks still firing even where others had been silenced. Providing every barely responsive patient with the most intensive rehabilitation would not lead them to this point after two decades. Terry's case was exceptional.

Eighteen months passed and now Terry's condition had improved a little more. He could count to twenty-five. He had a bit of movement in his arms and legs. This time a scan showed that those large regions of white matter posteriorly in the brain had normalised and now connectivity changes were surging through the middle of the cerebellum. Axons were sprouting, the authors suggested, from those posterior regions towards other targets. This large-scale rewiring seemed to correlate with the improvement in Terry's speech and motor function – a dynamic process of regrowth and rerouting. Some new networks regressed while others gained prominence.

While novel slip roads and sidewalks had coursed their way through Terry's brain, the Berlin Wall had fallen, the Soviet Union had disintegrated, the internet had risen up. The world had seen the Lockerbie bombing, and the space shuttle *Challenger* and Chernobyl nuclear disasters. Princess Diana had died. Ronald Reagan, the President he remembered from two decades before, had Alzheimer's.

And in the Ozark Mountains of Arkansas, Terry's wife had moved on to another relationship. She'd had three more children.

In that nursing home soon after he finally came to life, Terry met his daughter, Amber. She was now nineteen, the same age as her father had been at the time of the crash. Later, he would meet his newborn granddaughter.

New connections continued to form.

Around three months later, I visited Charlotte again. She seemed unaware and unresponsive when I arrived. But so had Terry Wallis, for the most part. And yet on 11 June 2003, he had said 'Mom'. Might Charlotte turn the corner in this way? And if so, would it take another nineteen years?

Consciousness is easy to define in medical terms even as it is difficult to understand in philosophical ones – there is wakefulness (typically with eyes open) and awareness of oneself and the environment. Both states are a function of deeper brain structures such as the thalamus and the brain-stem, but also of the connections of these structures to and from a cerebral cortex that has structural and functional integrity.

Charlotte had initially been in a coma – a usually eyes-closed transient state after, for example, a cardiac arrest or trauma, which can drift towards very different outcomes. In between brainstem death and recovery, there are hinterland disorders of consciousness. And it was my job to find out where Charlotte belonged.

A mention of brainstem death first though – this is where the functions of the brainstem completely and irreversibly fail. As described rather bluntly in a 1996 book published in the UK: 'If the brainstem is dead, the brain is dead, and if the brain is dead, the person is dead.' The controversial consciousness cases that reach media attention are hardly ever about brainstem death because for most of us – professionals and the public alike – there is little that is contentious about the diagnosis.* It is an irreversible state: eyes never open, breathing ceases without support, basic reflexes disappear. Care is withdrawn.

Terry Wallis was initially diagnosed as being in a vegetative state, a term developed some forty years ago to reflect an existence where so-called vegetative functions persist – intact (without needing support from machines) blood pressure and temperature regulation, digestion, breathing and secretion of hormones. Like patients in a coma, patients in a vegetative state do not respond and are unarousable. But their eyes open spontaneously even though there is no awareness of self or environment and no ability to interact with others. The brainstem is intact but higher functions are not. Awake but not aware.

When I examine patients in a vegetative state, there is no purposeful or voluntary behavioural response to any sort of stimulus – nothing when I wave something in front of their eyes, nothing when a loved one speaks to them. No gestures towards communication, no sign of understanding and no response to pain. The only responses are reflex ones – yawning and grunting, for example – since the higher functions of the brain lie dormant. But, perhaps tortuously for some families, the deeper structures of the brain (the hypothalamus and brainstem) work well enough to ensure that life

---

* In the US and some European countries, for example, the term 'brain death' is used and requires that entire brain function has irreversibly ceased rather than just the brainstem. Nonetheless, there are many parallels in how the final confirmatory assessment is conducted. Organ transplant can be considered once brainstem death has been confirmed. Some recent cases that did reach the media's attention were related to religious objections around the concept.

persists if medical and nursing care are provided. Artificial hydration and nutrition sustain existence, drop by drop. The heart beats strongly. The lungs draw in air and expel it vigorously – life of the most basic sort embedded profoundly in unconsciousness.

At some point, Terry Wallis had departed the vegetative state and reached the minimally conscious state (MCS) – one step up the ladder and a term only introduced in 2002. These patients show signs of voluntary behaviour, at least occasionally – those sporadic signs of life that Terry's parents had seen. Inconsistent but reproducible and purposeful. It wasn't around as a term at the time of his crash but it described his condition precisely – a place of fluctuating awareness of self and environment. A fragile knowing of the world but unequivocally so.

And so my job was to distinguish whether Charlotte was in a vegetative state or a minimally conscious one. It mattered. I knew that of those who reach a minimally conscious state within the first three months of coma onset (rather than remaining in a vegetative one), 70% or more will emerge. But even if she did get to this point, this liberation from the minimally conscious state, how might Charlotte's future look?

A 2010 French study tracked patients who were initially comatose and then entered either a vegetative state (twelve patients) or a minimally conscious one (thirty-nine patients). By the time five years had passed, a third of the patients in a minimally conscious state emerged from it. But even those thirteen were left with severe disabilities: all had cognitive impairment and twelve were totally or almost entirely dependent on others to help with the daily tasks of feeding, bathing and dressing. Half still needed full-time nursing home care. (As for the rest of the thirty-nine, fourteen died, nine remained in a minimally conscious state and three were lost to follow-up[*].)

The prognosis for the twelve patients in a vegetative state was decidedly more grim. Nine died, and two remained in a vegetative state. One patient was lost to follow-up. This and other studies confirm that the chance of recovery from a chronic vegetative state is close to zero one year after traumatic and three months after non-traumatic brain damage. And in these patients, it is fair to consider the futility of treatment, carefully so, and to consider whether it is ethical to continue artificial hydration and nutritional support.

Based on this key study, if Charlotte was in a vegetative state at this three-month stage, the future lay bleak. If I diagnosed her as being in a minimally conscious state, her prognosis just might shine brighter. But the longer she remained in that minimally conscious state, the worse the outlook: if she only emerged from it six months down the line rather than now, there was a high chance she would be entirely dependent on others and institutionalised for the rest of her life.

---

[*] Some studies specifically carried out in brain rehabilitation units for patients with traumatic brain injuries are more optimistic about the prognosis of MCS. They have reported that moderate disability rather than severe disability is the more common outcome and that this level of recovery is seen in about half of patients. About a fifth of the patients who eventually emerged from MCS in one of these studies even returned to work or school, albeit not necessarily with the same capacity as before. These various studies differ in the age and medical complexity of patients and their prognosis to begin with and so it's difficult to reach a one-size-fits-all interpretation.

Distinguishing between a minimally conscious state and vegetative state is difficult as it is crucial. Wait for sedatives to wear off and for that pneumonia to be treated. Watch every movement – a purposeful flicker of effort or just a reflex? Check every response to auditory and visual stimuli – is there a hint of a reaction to loud noises, do her eyes fixate on a moving mirror? Can she reach out for this comb, can she kick this ball, can she look at the ceiling when asked, can she stick out her tongue? Or are there only the most basic of responses – blinking or fluttering of the eyelids when I clap loudly? Yawning and moaning instead of intelligible speech? Assess and reassess. Add up the score. Return the next day and the next week and the week after.

But even then around a third of patients said to be in a vegetative state are misdiagnosed. And this means sometimes the ventilator is switched off too early or a feeding tube is withdrawn prematurely or subtle signs of pain are missed. Someone who might benefit from rehabilitation is denied it. (It's important to emphasise that these decisions *can* be made early if brainstem death is diagnosed, since this is an absolutely irreversible state – the issue I'm talking about here is assuming a diagnosis of a vegetative state and missing a diagnosis of a minimally conscious one.)

I assessed Charlotte that day. Others did, too, when she was later transferred to a brain injury unit. Doctors, nurses, occupational therapists and physiotherapists – we all recognised that Charlotte was in a minimally conscious state. She could, just sporadically, visually track the movement of family members and doctors around the room. She had cried once, the nurses told me, when her mother showed her a family photograph. And at least twice she had seemed to reach out for her father's hand when he reached out for hers. These responses were fleeting. Much of the time, she lay with her eyes open, grimacing and blinking, Days or weeks might pass, her family said, without any meaningful response at all. And although this diagnosis of a minimally conscious state gave her a sliver of a better prognosis, I wondered if this was what she would have wanted. What had she been thinking that summer morning many months ago when she hadn't left a note? She could hardly have imagined this.

Discovered by Magic

I had gazed beneath the surface. Seen glimpses of Charlotte beyond the face that her family recognised, beyond the scars and tubes and infusions. But my methods of assessing Charlotte's consciousness, having heard about Terry Wallis' case, seemed quite simplistic now. I was looking for what was missing as much as searching for what was present.

Some of the rudimentary diagnostic tools we use as neurologists are as valuable as they are archaic. The first reflex hammer was introduced by a Philadelphia neurologist, John Madison Taylor, in 1888 (a similar percussion technique of the chest, abdomen and back had been introduced in 1761 based on how wine-growers thumped wine casks to determine the levels of liquid). The ophthalmoscope – a torch-like instrument we use to view the inside of the eye – was invented by a German physiologist, Hermann von Helmholtz, in 1851; a prototype of sorts had been designed in England four years earlier by Charles Babbage. Yes, we complement these techniques with plenty of contemporary ones but even then, the first patient CT scan was performed in 1971 in Wimbledon; EEGs were first used on patients in the 1920s and 1930s; and MRI scanners reached our hospitals in the early 1980s.

That these diagnostic tools were invented long ago need not undermine their utility. For many a patient in a comatose or vegetative state, shining a pen torch into their eyes and tapping their reflexes has given me precious information that would not necessarily be bettered by emerging research techniques. But as search tools on a voyage to discover awareness? When I ask these patients to follow an instruction, and they can't, is this just because they can't recall the instruction or comprehend it or hear it, rather than them lacking awareness?

There are detailed coma scales we perform at the bedside that aim to disentangle these complexities, but I was beginning to realise that these methods might be inadequate to detect hidden signatures of consciousness such as those missed in Terry Wallis and in others who lay motionless and seemingly unaware.

There must be another way, I thought.

And there was.

Schoolteacher Kate Bainbridge was twenty-six years old when she developed a form of encephalitis. Inflammatory lesions were scattered throughout her brain – in the deeper brain structures (the thalami and brainstem) and higher up in the cortex. Four months later, her eyes opened intermittently but did not consistently focus on anyone or anything. Her arms and legs remained still.

Adrian Owen, a neuroscientist at Cambridge, and his research team searched for further signs of life. Kate was placed in a positron emission tomography scanner and shown photographs of familiar faces as well as control pictures of unfamiliar ones. And when she was shown those familiar faces, an area called the fusiform face area lit up on her scan. This is exactly the area that lights up, when we are fully conscious and well, when we recognise a familiar face. Here Kate was, ostensibly without any awareness, and yet she had this seemingly complex reaction beyond all expectations. Propelled by this finding, the intensity of her rehabilitation was stepped up. Two months later she was more responsive. Eight months after she had first developed encephalitis, she could clearly recognise faces and speak in short sentences: 'Don't like physiotherapy.' She was later able to use a wheelchair but it was several years before she was able to speak.

This study was published in the *Lancet* in 1998. The authors admitted it didn't prove much about consciousness or awareness – it just showed that her brain was able to perceive and process visual stimuli. And perhaps Kate's recovery might have evolved spontaneously even without intensive rehabilitation. Even her diagnosis was controversial – some critics suggested she was in a minimally conscious state rather than a vegetative one.

But later, she wrote to Adrian Owen thanking him for performing the brain scan: 'It scares me to think of what might have happened to me if I had not had mine,' she wrote. 'It was like magic, it found me.'

Adrian Owen and his team persisted, their 2006 *Science* paper winning over some of their critics.

This patient was twenty-three years old. She had sustained a severe traumatic brain injury in a road traffic accident. Five months later, she was still unresponsive.

Owen asked her to imagine when she was in the scanner that she was playing tennis. This is a motor imagery task – in healthy conscious people the supplementary motor area (SMA) – a region involved in planning complex movements – lights up when they imagine swinging a tennis racket towards a ball. And this is exactly what happened to her. The SMA shone brightly.

Then she was asked to imagine that she was walking around her house and to visualise all that she would see. This is a spatial imagery task and the parahippocampal gyrus and nearby regions* light up when we imagine this sort of activity. And once again, these areas lit up on her scan, just as is seen in healthy volunteers.

It seemed that she could understand spoken commands and was responding to them through brain activity. This, Owen and his team concluded, showed that she was consciously aware.

But critics insisted this was just some sort of purposeless reflex action, a tantalising step away from clear consciousness with its unequivocal wakefulness and awareness.

All of this eventually led to a *New England Journal of Medicine* study in 2010. This time the team used the same motor imagery and spatial imagery tasks but added a 'yes' or 'no' component. So when patients in a vegetative or minimally conscious state were asked 'Do you have any brothers?' they had to imagine playing tennis for 'yes' or navigating around the house for 'no'. The investigators were blinded – they didn't know the answers to these questions. Out of all the fifty-four patients, they

---

* Including the premotor cortex and the posterior parietal cortex.

identified five who could wilfully modulate their brain activity – until then four had been deemed to be in a vegetative state by clinical assessment, without a hint of behavioural responsiveness. All five had suffered traumatic brain injury. Once again, there was substantial activation in the supplementary motor area (just as for healthy volunteers) with accurate responses. In four out of the five, the scans associated with spatial imagery showed activation in the parahippocampal gyrus, just as in healthy conscious people.

Here was a suggestion that they could think and feel even when no medical bedside tests had unearthed these capabilities.

But these patients who seem to have these signatures of consciousness are likely an atypical gathering. They have somehow preserved functional integrity of key structures despite severe brain injury.* And there is a crucial difference between Charlotte and this group. The recovery rate from a brain injury caused by hypoxia (decreased oxygen supply, as happened after her overdose) is much worse than a brain injury caused by trauma. So even those occasional optimistic figures I mentioned earlier were less likely to apply to her.

These approaches from Owen and other groups are just being used in a research setting right now. They haven't been validated in larger studies in any way and they have only been trialled in a handful of participants. They remain

---

* Those structures being the anterior forebrain mesocircuit and the closely linked frontal parietal network. Schiff, N.D. and Fins, J.J. (2016), 'Brain death and disorders of consciousness,' *Current Biology*, 26(13), pp.R572–R576.

difficult to perform in routine practice although lower-cost and mobile options are being researched.

But Owen thinks that there is awareness in up to 20% of patients previously diagnosed as being in a vegetative state.

As tempting as it is to roll out this new technology, it's worth considering the implications for Charlotte and her family.

Let's say I put Charlotte in a scanner. I've seen her a couple of months ago and didn't find any signals of awareness at the bedside. I'm also remembering that her hypoxic brain injury has a worse prognosis than a traumatic one. Her parents and sister wait outside the scanning room, pacing, desperate. Charlotte's future, their future, will be determined within the next hour. If her scan shows areas that remain resolutely silent, should I really step outside that room, ask her family to sit down, tell them that there is no hope? True, when those brain regions fail to light up that might well tell us that Charlotte is not aware, not responsive. But perhaps the only reason I haven't detected awareness in Charlotte is because I happened to test her as she was flitting in and out of awareness – that's the nature of a minimally conscious state. Clouds lifting and then settling once again. Secondly, being able to imagine playing tennis or wandering around the house requires a whole host of cognitive functions – working memory, decision-making, language, sensory and executive function. In many ways, these are tests of the ability to make a choice and to communicate, not catch-all tests of awareness. If Charlotte has difficulty with any single one of these cognitive functions, she might have difficulty with visualising herself hitting a tennis ball or looking into her kitchen; I might then assume she has no awareness when in fact she does. And finally, perhaps I'm using the wrong investigations for *her*; maybe she would respond if I used a different type of scan or different research techniques.

Conversely, since this technique hasn't been tried and tested on a widespread basis, the results could hint at awareness when there is nothing of the sort. And if so, Charlotte could be kept alive for years, given intensive rehabilitation and nursing care, in the vanishingly rare hope that she might one day awaken and ask for her mother. A firing premotor cortex that imagines playing tennis is not the same as being out there on court. It's not the same as perception, comprehension, memory, personality, speech, morality agency, decision-making or rationality. And yet the feeding tube stays in and the infusions keep running, all for outcomes that can't possibly be realised. Futility and false promises collide.

And then the most contentious question of all. Let's say we think she has some level of awareness. Should we ask her if she wants to be kept alive?

'Charlotte: imagine playing tennis for "yes". Imagine walking around your house for "no".'

A binary option. Who in this room will ask this question and who will enact her wishes?

The truth is that we're not at a point where we can reliably make decisions based on these techniques, no matter how intriguing they are. But that does not mean that I don't want to. As I stand there with my reflex hammer and my ophthalmoscope, as useful as they are, I am a doctor woefully ill-equipped.

Lazarus

In 1994, Louis Viljoen was working as a hospital switchboard operator when he was hit by a truck in his hometown of Springs, fifty kilometres east of Johannesburg. He was thrown from his BMX bike. His injuries were catastrophic. At the hospital, doctors shone a light into his eyes and saw his pupils dilate. But his brain scan showed haemorrhages everywhere – especially in its deeper structures – in the left lentiform nucleus, the thalamus, brainstem and cerebellum. The ventricles were filled with blood. It's true that traumatic brain injury carries a better prognosis overall than hypoxic injury but here that hardly seemed to matter.

By the time Louis was moved to a rehabilitation centre, his eyes opened spontaneously. But he did not respond to the voices of his family or staff. He showed no reaction when they looked into his eyes or stroked his arm. Sometimes the left side of his body twitched involuntarily. He had no control of his bowel or bladder.

His mother visited each day. Five years passed. Contractures developed in his limbs. Throughout, there were none of the subtle signs of awareness that Terry Wallis' parents had seen. Louis remained silent.

Local family doctor, Dr Wally Nel, had known Louis since he was a baby, sat him on his knee back then, administered his vaccinations and seen him for coughs and colds. He still looked after him now even though Louis's healthy childhood was a distant memory. One day in 1999, Dr Nel prescribed a sleeping tablet – zolpidem. Louis had been restless that morning, clawing at his bedsheets. His mother crushed up the pill for him. She watched and waited and hoped that it would settle her son.

And then this:

'After about 25 minutes, I heard him making a sound like "mmm". Then he turned his head in my direction. I said, "Louis, can you hear me?" And he said, "Yes." I said, "Say hello, Louis," and he said, "Hello, Mummy." I couldn't believe it. I just cried and cried.'

He could answer simple arithmetic questions and could pick up food and put it into his mouth. He was able to remember the name of his favourite rugby player. He could swallow and speak by telephone and make jokes. His mother and staff asked him to write down words they spoke to him. And Louis could do it.

Louis received the drug daily from then on and even though it wore off after around four hours, returning him to a state of little responsiveness, his overall levels of awareness began to improve even in between doses. The jerking movements settled. And then the effect lasted longer and longer until he didn't need to take the tablet at all. He remains in a wheelchair today and is still cognitively impaired. But Louis Viljoen had been woken up after five years by a sleeping pill. One that costs around £1.50 in the UK for a month's supply.

Nel and his colleagues entitled their paper about Louis 'Extraordinary arousal from semi-comatose state on zolpidem'. The hype did not seem misplaced.

Later, he and colleagues performed SPECT (single-photon emission computed tomography) scans, first before giving Louis the sleeping tablet and then after. The before-zolpidem scan predictably showed that large areas of his brain were underactive. But after zolpidem, there was not just generalised activation of the cortex relative to the cerebellum but also a marked activation of the areas that had been underactive before – in both the cortex and the brain's deeper structures.

How could a sleeping tablet wake people up? Probably by resetting the circuit. But there's a catch – the circuit has to be in good enough shape to be switched on in the first place. And for most people in a minimally conscious state, this isn't an option.

Zolpidem seems to shift the balance of inhibition and stimulation of brain networks. If enough neurons in the prefrontal cortex are functioning despite a catastrophic injury, then modulation of subterranean brain structures could reset the circuit. And it's the thalamus, a structure deep within the brain, that plays a key role in arousal of the cortex. It is zolpidem's effect on the thalamus that seems to be the answer here. The drug enhances the activity of GABA, which is one of the brain's inhibitory transmitters; in other words, zolpidem inhibits inhibition. This has knock-on effects on various loops of excitation and inhibition (these feedback effects are radically different in people without brain damage – so for them, zolpidem really does act as a sleeping pill).* Ultimately, in

---

* Normally in healthy individuals, there are excitatory projections from the cortex to a deeper subcortical structure called the striatum. The striatum then usually inhibits the globus pallidus interna (GPi) but this inhibitory pathway can be affected in brain injury. The mesocircuit hypothesis suggests that when damage to the cortex in turn affects the striatum's usual output, the GPi can now inhibit the thalamus unopposed. There is thus a shutdown of loop systems, which circle from the cortex (which has excitatory projections) to the striatum and the thalamus and back to the cortex again. And so zolpidem through its direct inhibition of the GPi might help rebalance these parts of the circuit – in a way, substituting the effect of the

patients like Louis, it seems that zolpidem frees the thalamus to excite the cortex. Cognition and motor function and speech are reactivated. Alertness is reignited.

But when we wake patients in this way, are we reigniting the person who lived before? A previous identity resurrected or at least a sense of sameness restored? The level of recovery in other patients has varied.

There was the case of a thirty-one-year-old who had suffered a traumatic brain injury after a road traffic accident three years previously. Diagnosed as being in a vegetative state, he screamed relentlessly and could not interact with family or staff. For four hours or so after taking zolpidem he could state his name and age, albeit with much effort. He managed to focus on TV progammes and laugh at the funny scenes. And his SPECT scans showed the same improvement as Louis's, particularly in areas towards the front of his brain. Five years later, he was still responding to zolpidem. Another soul awoken.

In Israel, a fifty-year-old woman had suffered a cardiac arrest and severe anoxic brain injury eighteen months previously. Now she lay in a minimally conscious state – awake but with only random involuntary writhing movements of her limbs. She was silent for the most part. Thirty minutes after zolpidem, she was alert. She spoke. The twisting movements settled a little. After another fifteen minutes, she began to answer simple questions. She read, wrote and managed simple calculations. She recognised family members and showed affection towards them and laughed in context. She remembered some events from her past. She fed herself with

---

striatum, ultimately allowing the thalamus to kick-start the cortex.

a spoon and moved her arms and legs voluntarily. And then she stood, taking a few steps, with one person holding her on either side.

Within four hours, the elixir had worn off. Her minimally conscious state re-emerged. But the next dose of zolpidem brought her round again.

Despite great excitement around zolpidem, only one of fifteen patients responded to it in a 2009 placebo-controlled trial in Pennsylvania. Researchers reported a shift from a vegetative state to a minimally conscious one in a man with traumatic brain injury.

Another study that examined sixty patients (around half had sustained a traumatic brain injury) failed to show any significant improvement with zolpidem. And a third study the following year discovered that of eighty-four patients, four had some response but this lasted only one or two hours. These responses included turning towards the sound of a voice even if inconsistently so, answering a yes-or-no question, an occasional thumbs-up a couple of times in an hour or reaching towards or using an object. One patient fell into a deep sleep; another became so restless that padding was added to their wheelchair to prevent injury.

Here's an account for Patient 22:

After placebo: 'The family reports that he blinks once for yes and 2 or more times for no. The examiner found "no" to be inconsistent and difficult to determine vs. spontaneous blinking. During the hour 3 assessment, P22 opened his mouth to command on 3 of 4 trials.'

After medication: 'P22 displayed increased alertness (one instance of fixed gaze; increased attempt to move right arm/hand and right thumb). He was noted to pull head upright, reach for objects, play "thumb war", and hug mother and girlfriend.'

The truth is that for every Louis Viljoen there might be hundreds of thousands, possibly more, who will never respond to the drug. But the tablet is cheap, takes moments to crush, can be given at low doses and as a one-off trial should have few side effects. Imagine the moment when a previously unresponsive patient hugs her daughter or plays 'thumb war' or tries to walk – isn't it worth giving the tablet a chance? But in trying to resurrect patients in this way, in a search to establish some sort of sameness, zolpidem might only leave them painfully aware of their existence – one where no major improvement is likely. These were the fears of one family in the UK.

J was a fifty-three-year-old woman who had a brain haemorrhage on a family holiday in the Lake District in August 2003. She now existed in a vegetative state. A former community health worker herself, she needed twenty-four-hour care in a nursing home. In 2006, her hospital trust applied to discontinue and withhold life-sustaining treatment and medical support including nutrition and hydration. Then, they argued, she would retain 'the greatest dignity until such time as her life comes to an end'. The court was swayed by expert medical advice and ordered a three-day trial of zolpidem. J's family (her husband, two children and her mother), felt that she would never have wished her life to be prolonged in this 'unbearably cruel' way. What would happen, they asked, if she awoke and realised what had happened to her and the state she was in?

As it happened, the drug caused J only to become more somnolent. And so the original wishes of her family and the hospital trust were eventually respected. Artificial nutrition and hydration were withdrawn.

Her husband later spoke to the *Daily Telegraph*:

'Somewhere along the line people have forgotten that just because you can perform a particular medical treatment doesn't necessarily mean that you should. In J's case she was given a drug that she wouldn't have wanted.'

Calling for an inquiry, he asked, 'What level would count as beneficial? If she had been capable of scrabbling her hands, would that mean, "We've got to keep her alive"?'

It's not just zolpidem. There are other interventions under investigation as I write this that aim to resurrect these patients – surgical procedures and both novel and old medications among them. But I wonder how ethical it is to revive someone who can then only sporadically make eye contact with a family member or move their right leg or play 'thumb war' before disappearing into the depths of oblivion once again? To force them to realise what state they have ended up in when further sustained recovery is impossible. To tantalisingly offer a window of hope right before shutting the blinds so abruptly.

Of course there are good reasons for heroic neurosurgical measures to ease brain swelling after trauma, for drilling into skulls and inserting shunts. For CPR and defibrillators and helicopters that get brain-injured patients to hospital as quickly as possible. Because these measures could be the difference between life and death, could be the key to a meaningful recovery. There is no room for nihilism in these situations. But some of those saved will be consigned to these hinterland states of consciousness – a pyrrhic victory of sorts. Although a miracle sleeping pill might wake them, it's worth thinking about what they're waking up to. And how we might bear responsibility for the life that greets them.

Charlotte ended up at a rehabilitation unit for young brain-injured patients. Last I heard she was still in a minimally conscious state. And nothing transformed that – not the newest of scans or the most experimental of techniques.

As I've learned more about neurology over the years, I've thought that perhaps prognostication might become easier. But I think the more I know (and there's always yet more to learn), the more difficult it has become.

With stories like those of Louis and Kate, the world of prediction gets murkier. With each groundbreaking discovery in consciousness, the further certainty drifts away. As those ventilators hum and infusions run and monitors beep, as those pupils dilate, as that blood pressure soars, information outweighs insight.

What really lies beneath the surface is still at times intangible, unreachable, incomprehensible.

I said before that when I graduated from medical school I naively didn't know what I didn't know. Now I'm better at knowing what I don't know. And I'm not sure if that's a good thing.

I want to end by telling you about what happened to Terry Wallis.

He was the Arkansas man I mentioned before whose car crash landed him in a ravine. Who had been left in a vegetative state, then a minimally conscious one, eventually waking up after nineteen years to say 'Mom' and then 'Pepsi' and then 'milk'.

Terry now lives with his family in Round Mountain in Faulkner County, Arkansas. When visited by Jordan Hickey, writing for *Arkansas Life*, in 2014, Terry still needed full-time care. He had to be turned every two hours to prevent bedsores. He had to be fed and his drinks were thickened to stop him choking. He could remember the date and sometimes names. He could answer questions but was less likely to initiate conversations. He still watched *Gilligan's Island* and *The Beverly Hillbillies*. A Hollywood studio was going to make a movie of his miraculous recovery but they never did. Perhaps it wasn't quite miraculous enough.

His personality had now changed, his mother said. More mild-mannered and softer than before his accident. Less stubborn and obstinate. Angilee saw glimpses of her son, but sometimes she imagined how things might have been had he not been in a crash, had he not been 'wrecked', as she and her family termed it:

'When you get to thinking . . . well, I don't really anymore, but I used to – I was real bad about thinking about, "Well, I wonder how he would be if he had not been wrecked?"' Angilee says. 'And that person is gone . . . That person that he was before is gone.'

And yet somehow, Terry Wallis is still alive. Terry and the others I've told you about have proved that many of our assumptions about consciousness were deeply flawed. Somehow, that should give us hope.

Epilogue

I wrote this book because of a question I was asked some years ago by my friend Anna. Her mother had just been diagnosed with a brain tumour. Previously aloof, indifferent, uncaring, she had now become affectionate and compassionate, frequently telling Anna and the rest of the family that she loved them.

Was this her real mother, Anna asked me?

It was, I answered. This expression of love was more than just a side effect of her cancer; it was authentic. This idea settled us both in a way. But afterwards I wondered if I had been evading a disconcerting truth – that her maternal declaration of love was solely the result of a cancerous mass pressing upon her brain's frontal lobe. Perhaps this was nothing more than simulated empathy created through sinister pathology.

In these chapters, I have taken a journey through who we become when memories evaporate and personality shifts and consciousness ebbs and flows. And I've realised that how we see identity in ourselves and in others is often shaped by the lens we choose. Despite getting lost along those cliffs above a fishing village and despite leaving her handbag in the fridge next to the cream cheese, something of Anita still remained through the disrupted syntax of her speech, the abnormal proteins clumping within her brain and the bleak atrophy of Alzheimer's on her scan. She was embodied at least until the more advanced stages – resolutely interacting, engaging, embedded in the world – and yet our medical model of dementia had at times sought to diminish her existence, to refuse her determination to be. That is not for a moment to dismiss the inexorable neurodegeneration that marks Alzheimer's, or how patients might mourn for their past, or the immense challenges faced by their families. But it does speak to searching for sameness in all its guises instead of assuming its inevitable loss.

In Charlie's confabulations of purple trampolines and egg and spoon races, he grounded and validated himself in the memories that were true to him, a chronicle of self. And as Charlotte's family sat by her bedside in the early days after her overdose, they chose to direct that identity lens towards her physical recognisability – in her face they saw sameness where it was otherwise impossible to find.

That lens can bring identity into sharp focus but wilfully twist it the wrong way, and there are stark consequences. In dissociative identity disorder, those with a fractured sense of identity were coaxed to summon up multiple personalities from the depths of their distress. And so emerged, in a frantic media climate that celebrated this alluring chaos, patients with hundreds of alters, convinced they had partaken in satanic rituals and cannibalism. Criminals like Kenneth Bianchi jumped on the defence bandwagon that was multiple personality disorder – and almost managed to escape.

But there are times when a threat to identity is irrefutable, irrespective of which way you twist the lens.

Connections and continuity are essential in establishing sameness over time. When certain links are annihilated – autobiographical memory or moral character for example – identity is difficult to secure.

Think back to Benjaman Kyle waking up by a dumpster behind a Burger King in Richmond, Georgia. Bewildered, his personal history decimated, unable to time-travel to his personal past, he was found yet still missing. Likewise, when Martin's personality changed radically and he lost those moral traits we value so highly in one another, it was difficult to detect the Martin of years gone by. That is not to say that this hostile, gesticulating, unkempt man was now the 'real' Martin, though – he should not be defined by the merciless erasure of social conduct, morals and empathy that characterises frontotemporal dementia. He should not be defined by destruction.

And so when Anna dug deep in search of connections and continuity, in a sense she felt that there were echoes of her mother still. True, she had never been particularly tactile; she was sometimes stand-offish, resentful even. The pregnancy in 1980 had been a surprise – unwelcome then, the marriage necessary. A successful career jettisoned against her will because those were different times. As the months went by, Anna saw her mother's former remoteness as a function of her upbringing and events from her child-hood, concealed until conversations over those last few months. But had Anna doubted inherently that her mother loved her, all these years? Not really – there had been expressions of love in many of the things she had done for her family, if not in the words she had spoken to them. There were still some connections from her mother then to her mother now, memories and traits and gestures, enough to allow for a sense of sameness, enough to allow that this expression of love was more than a pronouncement of pathology.

We can't help but search for the best version of ourselves and others sometimes. Because then we can see that Anita is more than the fog of her amnesia, Dilip is more than the violence of his sleep, Charlotte is more than the blurred boundaries of white and grey matter on her brain scan. We cannot easily let disease and disorder erase personhood.

Looking for absolute sameness, for the real you, is of course in many ways impossible – we all live in a state of constant flux, what with our memories under permanent reconstruction, our personalities evolving and our consciousness fading and brightening. But I think it is right, imperative even, to seek out those subtle signs of sameness, to listen for the echoes of connectedness and continuity. Because that's when we finally see what lies beneath. If we had not searched so deeply for sameness, we might otherwise have missed Anita's embodiment or those signatures of awareness in the apparently unconscious, or the artistry freed solely through neuronal destruction.

Sometimes there, in the depths of loss, lies profound promise.

Notes

PART I
Chapter 1: *Missing*

. . . identity is steeped in connectedness. Parfit, Derek (1984), *Reasons and Persons*, Oxford: Oxford University Press.

. . . a sense of personal identity across time and hence they lack person-hood. Brock, Dan W. (1988), 'Justice and the severely demented elderly', *The Journal of Medicine and Philosophy*, 13.1, pp.73–99.

Does it matter what we call it – spirit, soul, inner self, essence, identity – so long as we have experienced it? Pointon, Barbara (2007), 'Who am I?: The search for spirituality in dementia. A family carer's perspective', *Spirituality, Values and Mental Health: Jewels for the Journey*, p.114.

A body is to be clothed in easily wipeable fabrics . . . Lee-Treweek, Geraldine (2008), 'Bedroom abuse: The hidden work in a nursing home' in Johnson, J., and De Souza, Corinne (eds.), *Understanding Health and Social Care: An Introductory Reader, 2nd ed.*, London: Sage Publications, pp.107–111.

Despite advancing dementia, 'Iris remains her old self in many ways.' Bayley, John (1999), *Elegy for Iris*, London: Macmillan.

. . . the unconscious motives and the self-deceptions that each of us has in considerable measure. Mathews, Debra J.H., Bok, Hilary, and Rabins, Peter V. (eds.) (2009), *Personal Identity and Fractured Selves: Perspectives from Philosophy, Ethics, and Neuroscience*, Baltimore: JHU Press, p.170.

Permission for re-use has been granted by the Guarantors of Brain. Garrard, P., Maloney, L.M., Hodges, J.R., and Patterson, K. (2004), 'The effects of very early Alzheimer's disease on the characteristics of writing by a renowned author', *Brain*, 128.2, pp.250–60.

This project is a sort of scientific thing. Sabat, Steven R., and Harré, Rom (1992), 'The construction and deconstruction of self in Alzheimer's disease', *Ageing & Society*, 12.4, pp.443–61.

... *strategies now used internationally to provide patient-centred care and to empower families.* Kitwood, T. M. (1997), *Dementia Reconsidered: The Person Comes First*, Maidenhead: Open University Press.

Chapter 2: *The Honest Liars*

... *in Finland people always eat lamb and the inhabitants are Tatars.* Korsakoff, S. S. (1955), 'Psychic disorder in conjunction with multiple Neuritis (Psychosis polyneuritica s. cerebropathia psychica toxaemica)', *Neurology*, 5.6, pp.396–406.

Confabulation removed, surgical success. Dalla Barba, Gianfranco, et al. (2016), 'Recovery from confabulation after normotensive hydrocephalus shunting', *Cortex*, 75, pp.82–6.

... *past memories floating into the present even though they are not pertinent to the reality of now.* 'Spontaneous confabulation and the adaptation of thought to ongoing reality', *Nature Reviews Neuroscience*, 4.8, p.662.

The Swiss authors of the chronological theory later circled back to Pavlov ... Nahum, Louis, et al. (2009), 'Disorientation, confabulation, and extinction capacity: Clues on how the brain creates reality', *Biological Psychiatry*, 65.11, pp.966–72.

... *the memory of a woman with a bee's head could not.* Turner, Martha S., Cipolotti, Lisa, and Shallice, Tim (2010), 'Spontaneous confabulation, temporal context confusion and reality monitoring: A study of three patients with anterior communicating artery aneurysms', *Journal of the International Neuropsychological Society*, 16.6, pp.984–94.

Flashbulb memories were described by psychologists Roger Brown and James Kulik ... Brown, Roger, and Kulik, James (1977), 'Flashbulb memories', *Cognition*, 5.1, pp.73–99.

'... *so exciting emotionally as almost to leave a scar upon the cerebral tissues.*' James, William (1890), *The Principles of Psychology*, New York: Henry Holt.

Their study recruited 3,000 adults from seven US cities. Hirst, William, et al. (2009), 'Long-term memory for the terrorist attack of September 11: Flashbulb memories, event memories, and the factors that influence their retention', *Journal of Experimental Psychology: General*, 138.2, p.161.

Notes

... the rich, subjective experience of recollection that occurs with emotion allows for faster decision-making. Phelps, Elizabeth A., and Sharot, Tali (2008), 'How (and why) emotion enhances the subjective sense of recollection', *Current Directions in Psychological Science*, 17.2, pp.147–52.

We grow ever more confident in our memories as they develop blurred edges. Talarico, Jennifer M., and Rubin, David C. (2007), 'Flashbulb memories are special after all; in phenomenology, not accuracy', *Applied Cognitive Psychology*, 21.5, pp.557–78.

... conventional understanding of what happens when memories are reignited. Nader, Karim, Schafe, Glenn E., and Le Doux, Joseph E. (2000), 'Fear memories require protein synthesis in the amygdala for reconsolidation after retrieval', *Nature*, 406.6797, p.722.

... nor does it allow for the extent and depth of trauma or how remote that trauma was. Hardwicke, Tom E., Taqi, Mahdi, and Shanks, David R. (2016), 'Postretrieval new learning does not reliably induce human memory updating via reconsolidation', *Proceedings of the National Academy of Sciences*, 113.19, pp.5206–11.

... lost in a shopping mall as a child even though they had not been. Loftus, Elizabeth F., and Pickrell, Jacqueline E. (1995), 'The formation of false memories', *Psychiatric Annals*, 25.12, pp.720–25.

... suggestive memory techniques to convince undergraduate students that they had a criminal history. Shaw, Julia, and Porter, Stephen (2015), 'Constructing rich false memories of committing crime', *Psychological Science* 26.3, pp.291–301.

Lawrence Patihis and his colleagues tested HSAM participants in a 2013 study. Patihis, Lawrence, et al. (2013), 'False memories in highly superior autobiographical memory individuals', *Proceedings of the National Academy of Sciences*, 110.52 pp.20947–52.

... one patient with a ruptured aneurysm was convinced that she had to go home to feed her baby ... Schnider, Armin, von Däniken, Christine, and Gutbrod, Klemens (1996), 'The mechanisms of spontaneous and provoked confabulations', *Brain*, 119.4, pp.1365–75.

Some patients with ruptured brain aneurysms, for example, initially have so-called spontaneous confabulation ... DeLuca J., and Cicerone, K.D. (1991), 'Confabulation following aneurysm of the anterior communicating artery', *Cortex*, 27, pp.417–23.

In 2013, Elizabeth Loftus examined case evidence as part of the post-conviction review. Loftus, Elizabeth F. (2013), 'Eyewitness testimony in the Lockerbie bombing case', *Memory*, 21.5, pp.584–90.

If your mugshot is seen before a line-up, the chances of being falsely identified as a criminal rises to 20% . . . Brown, Evan, Deffenbacher Kenneth, and Sturgill, William (1977), 'Memory for faces and the circumstances of encounter', *Journal of Applied Psychology*, 62.3, p.311.

Almost 80% of US judges in a 2004 survey acknowledged this mugshot-induced bias phenomenon to be true. Wise, Richard A., and Safer, Martin A. (2004), 'What US judges know and believe about eyewitness testimony', *Applied Cognitive Psychology*, 18.4, pp.427–43.

. . . wearing clothes similar to those of the suspect viewed by the eyewitness. Lindsay, R. C. L., Wallbridge, Harold, and Drennan, Daphne (1987), 'Do the clothes make the man? An exploration of the effect of lineup attire on eyewitness identification accuracy', *Canadian Journal of Behavioural Science/Revue canadienne des sciences du comportement*, 19.4, pp.

'. . . *even if they must rely on more than one story to do so.*' McAdams, Dan P. (2001), 'The psychology of life stories', *Review of General Psychology*, 5.2, p.100.

'. . . *and are potentially destructive in psychotherapeutic contexts.*' Strawson, Galen (2004), 'Against narrativity', *Ratio*, 17.4, pp.428–52.

Chapter 3: *Mugshots*

'. . . *over 50% of all subjects went on the merry-go-round and the Tea cup ride.*' Hamond, Nina R., and Fivush, Robyn (1991), 'Memories of Mickey Mouse: Young children recount their trip to Disneyworld', *Cognitive Development*, 6.4, pp.433–48.

Eight-year-olds remembered only 36% of these past events. Van Abbema, Dana, and Bauer, Patricia (2005), 'Autobiographical memory in middle childhood: Recollections of the recent and distant past', *Memory*, 13.8, pp.829–45.

. . . running-wheel mice (who had more neurogenesis) were more likely than sedentary mice to forget experiences. Akers, Katherine G., et al. (2014), 'Hippocampal neurogenesis regulates forgetting during adulthood and infancy', *Science*, 344.6184, pp.598–602.

Harvard psychologists, Roger Brown and David McNeill, described the experience in 1966 Brown, Roger, and McNeill, David (1966), 'The "tip of the tongue" phenomenon', *Journal of Verbal Learning and Verbal Behavior*, 5.4, pp.325–37.

Notes

. . . identified in about 90% of native speakers of fifty-one languages.
Schwartz, Bennett L. (1999), 'Sparkling at the end of the tongue: The
etiology of tip-of-the-tongue phenomenology', *Psychonomic Bulletin &
Review*, 6.3, pp.379–93.

This cue familiarity triggers the TOT. And hopefully the sneeze. Metcalfe,
Janet, Schwartz, Bennett L., and Joaquim, Scott G. (1993), 'The cue-
familiarity heuristic in metacognition', *Journal of Experimental
Psychology: Learning, Memory, and Cognition*, 19.4, p.851.

*. . . impaired retrieval of thoughts that were formulated only a few feet
away, through a doorway in another room.* Radvansky, Gabriel A.,
Krawietz, Sabine A., and Tamplin, Andrea K. (2011), 'Walking through
doorways causes forgetting: Further explorations', *The Quarterly
Journal of Experimental Psychology*, 64.8, pp.1632–45.

*. . . labels absent-mindedness as one of these sins, which occurs either when
encoding memories or retrieving them.* Schacter, Daniel L. (2002), *The
Seven Sins of Memory: How the Mind Forgets and Remembers*, New
York: Houghton Mifflin Harcourt.

*In one study of memory failure in pilots, seventy-four of seventy-five self-
reported errors were prospective ones* . . . Nowinski, Jessica Lang,
Holbrook, Jon B., and Dismukes, R. Key (2003), 'Human memory and
cockpit operations: An ASRS study', *Proceedings of the 12th
International Symposium on Aviation Psychology*.

Prompts to remember to remember. Dismukes, R. Key (2006), 'Concurrent
task management and prospective memory: Pilot error as a model
for the vulnerability of experts', *Proceedings of the Human Factors
and Ergonomics Society Annual Meeting*, 50. 9, Los Angeles: Sage
Publications.

'*. . . severe headaches, anxiety, sweats, insomnia, masturbation five or six
times a night . . .*' Hacking, Ian (1998), *Mad Travelers: Reflections on the
Reality of Transient Mental Illnesses*, Virginia: University of Virginia
Press.

*. . . hysterical amnesia, as it was then labelled, was a mechanism of evasion,
a form of psychological defence.* Abeles, Milton, and Schilder, Paul
(1935), 'Psychogenic loss of personal identity: amnesia', *Archives of
Neurology & Psychiatry*, 34.3, pp.587–604.

Psychological trauma, say supporters of one of these theories . . .
Markowitsch, Hans J., et al. (2000), 'Neuroimaging and behavioral
correlates of recovery from mnestic block syndrome and other cognitive
deteriorations', *Cognitive and Behavioral Neurology*, 13.1, pp.60–66.

We are captivated by the theatre of it all. Lynn, Steven Jay, et al. (2012) 'Dissociation and dissociative disorders: Challenging conventional wisdom', *Current Directions in Psychological Science*, 21.1, pp.48–53.

. . . *approximately 8% of perpetrators of other violent crimes and a small percentage of non-violent offenders.* Kopelman, Michael D. (2003), 'Psychogenic amnesia' in Baddeley, Alan D., Kopelman, Michael D., and Wilson, Barbara A. (eds.), *The Handbook of Memory Disorders*, New Jersey: John Wiley & Sons.

In the end, there was no doubt. His was wilful deception. Tombaugh, Tom N. (1996), *Test of memory malingering: TOMM*, North Tonawanda, New York: Multi-Health Systems, Inc.

'All these people, all over the country, trying to solve this case? That's a hell of a drug.' Wolfe, Matt, 'The Last Unknown Man', *New Republic*, 21 November 2016.

They live only in the present; their past is experienced in the absence of recollection. Palombo, Daniela J., et al. (2015), 'Severely deficient auto-biographical memory (SDAM) in healthy adults: A new mnemonic syndrome', *Neuropsychologia*, 72, pp.105–18.

'. . . *by using the unplugged electrical cable of a lamp.'* Markowitsch, Hans J., and Staniloiu, Angelica (2013), 'The impairment of recollection in functional amnesic states', *Cortex*, 49.6, pp.1494–1510.

'. . . *we have to have a notion of how we have become, and of where we are going.'* Taylor, C. (1989), *Sources of the Self: The Making of the Modern Identity*, Cambridge: Cambridge University Press, p.47.

'. . . *protracted existence across subjective time.'* Wheeler, M.A., Stuss, D.T., Tulving, E. (1997), 'Toward a theory of episodic memory: The frontal lobes and autonoetic consciousness', *Psychological Bulletin*, 121, pp.331–54.

Establishing a continuum of sameness is not an option. Markowitsch, Hans J., et al. (1997), 'A PET study of persistent psychogenic amnesia covering the whole life span', *Cognitive Neuropsychiatry*, 2.2, pp.135–58.

'I felt like I should be in my forties, and here I'm looking at an old man in the mirror.' Schechtman, Marya (2015), 'Interview by Simon Cushing', *Journal of Cognition and Neuroethics* (Philosophical Profiles), pp.1–31.

Notes

PART II
Chapter 4: *The Stranger*

The composite of these qualities constitutes the human personality.' Ropper, Allan H. (2005), *Adams and Victor's Principles of Neurology*, 179, New York: McGraw-Hill Medical Publishing Division.

'Even so, genetic variability has been linked to personality traits such as thrillseeking, exploration and excitability, anxiety and obsessiveness.' Ebstein, R.P., Novick, O., Umansky, R., Priel, B., Osher, Y., Blaine, D., Bennett, E.R., Nemanov, L., Katz, M. and Belmaker, R.H. (1996), 'Dopamine D4 receptor (D4DR) exon III polymorphism associated with the human personality trait of novelty seeking', *Nature Genetics*, 12(1), pp.78–80.

. . . confirmed a 2015 meta-analysis. Polderman, Tinca J.C., et al. (2015), 'Meta-analysis of the heritability of human traits based on fifty years of twin studies', *Nature Genetics*, 47.7, pp.702–9.

In 2013, Julia Freund and her colleagues in Germany published a study that went beyond nature and nurture. Freund, Julia, et al. (2013), 'Emergence of individuality in genetically identical mice', *Science*, 340.6133, pp.756–9.

. . . have been associated with epigenetic changes. Identity follows closely. Kaminsky, Zachary, et al. (2008), 'Epigenetics of personality traits: An illustrative study of identical twins discordant for risk-taking behavior', *Twin Research and Human Genetics*, 11.1, pp.1–11.

As long as core moral capacities are preserved [. . .] perceived identity will remain largely intact.' Strohminger, Nina, and Nichols, Shaun (2015), 'Neurodegeneration and identity', *Psychological Science*, 26.9, pp.1469–79.

When forming impressions of others, we place greater emphasis on characteristics associated with morality . . . Brambilla Marco, et al. (2012), 'You want to give a good impression? Be honest! Moral traits dominate group impression formation', *British Journal of Social Psychology*, 51.1, pp.149–66.

A 2014 study from the University of Pennsylvania asked participants to analyse obituaries . . . Goodwin, Geoffrey P., Piazza, Jared, and Rozin, Paul (2014), 'Moral character predominates in person perception and evaluation', *Journal of Personality and Social Psychology*, 106.1, p.148.

A 2017 University of Chicago study by Sarah Molouki and Daniel Bartels . . . Molouki, Sarah, and Bartels, Daniel M. (2017), 'Personal change and the continuity of the self', *Cognitive Psychology*, 93, pp.1–17.

. . . and the structures beneath such as the amygdala, hippocampus and basal ganglia. Fumagalli, Manuela, and Priori, Alberto (2012), 'Functional and clinical neuroanatomy of morality', *Brain*, 135.7, pp.2006–21.

. . . one for transgressions involving physical harm, one for dishonesty, one for disgust. Parkinson, Carolyn, et al (2011), 'Is morality unified? Evidence that distinct neural systems underlie moral judgments of harm, dishonesty, and disgust', *Journal of Cognitive Neuroscience*, 23.10, pp.3162–80.

. . . a poor ability to learn from punishment and reactive aggression. Mendez, Mario F., Shapira, Jill S., and Saul, Ronald E. (2011), 'The spectrum of sociopathy in dementia', *The Journal of Neuropsychiatry and Clinical Neurosciences*, 23.2, pp.132–140.

. . . it does not explain, Tobia says, whether this direction of change carries relevance to the actual disentanglement of personal identity. Tobia, Kevin Patrick (2016), 'Personal identity, direction of change, and neuroethics', *Neuroethics*, 9.1, pp.37–43.

. . . they continue to attend the same churches and vote for the same political candidates. Miller, Bruce L., et al. (2001), 'Neuroanatomy of the self: Evidence from patients with frontotemporal dementia', *Neurology*, 57.5, pp.817–21.

'. . . fragments of intact weaving left after the moths had done their bit.' Gillett, Grant (2002), 'You always were a bastard', *Hastings Center Report*, 32.6, pp.23–8.

Chapter 5: Splintered

Here's an account from Watkins' transcript. Watkins, John G. (1984), 'The Bianchi (LA hillside strangler) case: Sociopath or multiple personality?', *International Journal of Clinical and Experimental Hypnosis*, 32.2, pp.67–101.

'. . . either she had multiple personality disorder or, if she was faking it, she deserved an Academy Award.' McLeod, Michael, 'What Ever Happened to Juanita Maxwell?', *Orlando Sentinel*, 19 May 1991.

'. . . the possession cults that shape and legitimate the spirit possession enactments of new members.' Spanos, Nicholas P. (1994), 'Multiple identity enactments and multiple personality disorder: A sociocognitive perspective', *Psychological Bulletin*, 116, p.143.

Would you talk to me Part by saying "I'm here." Schwarz, Ted (1981), *The Hillside Strangler: A Murderer's Mind*, New York: New American Library.

'. . . there was no way I could come from a little town in Iowa, be eating 2,000 people a year, and nobody said anything about it.' Hanson, Cynthia, 'Dangerous Therapy: The Story of Patricia Burgus and Multiple Personality Disorder', *Chicago Magazine*, 1 June 1998.

'. . . once I had started and found you were interested, I continued . . .' Nathan, Debbie (2011), *Sybil Exposed: The Extraordinary Story behind the Famous Multiple Personality Case*, London: Simon and Schuster.

Thus, the child suffers the burden of punishment, but is not punished. Radden, Jennifer (2002), 'Multiple personality disorder and responsibility', *Southern California Interdisciplinary Law Journal*, 7. 2, pp.253–66.

The goal of therapy in DID is now to integrate identity states. Gallagher, Shaun (ed.) (2011), *The Oxford Handbook of the Self*, Oxford: Oxford University Press.

Chapter 6: *Talents*

'. . . and they would be there, around my desk, absolutely still, until the bell rang.' Gerassi, John (ed.) (2009), *Talking with Sartre: Conversations and Debates*, London: Yale University Press.

'. . . I learnt that partly on psychedelic drugs.' Nutt, David (2012), *Drugs – Without the Hot Air: Minimising the Harms of Legal and Illegal Drugs*, Cambridge: UIT Cambridge.

global warming and ozone damage were 'illusions' perpetrated by 'parasites with degrees in economics or sociology.' Carlson, Peter, 'Nobel Chemist Kary Mullis, Making Waves as a Mind Surfer', *Washington Post*, 3 November 1998.

. . . eleven of their seventy-six patients on dopamine drugs (all at very high doses) were creative. Lhommée, Eugénie, et al. (2014), 'Dopamine and the biology of creativity: Lessons from Parkinson's disease', *Frontiers in Neurology*, 5.

Obviously I'll take health. But I miss being so creative. Armsden, Catherine, 'An Alert, Well-Hydrated Artist in No Acute Distress–Episode Nine', *Medium*, 9 December 2015.

And Openness to Experience predicts creativity . . . John, Oliver P., Naumann, Laura P., and Soto, Christopher J. (2008), 'Paradigm shift to the integrative big five trait taxonomy', *Handbook of Personality: Theory and research*, 3, pp.114–58.

But actually a creative response is easily defined. Kaufman, James C., and Sternberg, Robert J. (eds.) (2010), *The Cambridge Handbook of Creativity*, Cambridge: Cambridge University Press.

The Wiley Handbook of Genius. Simonton, Dean Keith (2014), *The Wiley Handbook of Genius*, New Jersey: John Wiley & Sons.

. . . unmedicated patients who had developed Parkinson's in their forties had markedly reduced novelty-seeking. Bódi, Nikoletta, et al. (2009), 'Reward-learning and the novelty-seeking personality: A between- and within-subjects study of the effects of dopamine agonists on young Parkinson's patients', *Brain*, 132.9, pp.2385–95.

These ancient migratory patterns have recently been associated with variants of a gene called DRD4. Matthews, Luke J., and Butler, Paul M. (2011), 'Novelty-seeking DRD4 polymorphisms are associated with human migration distance out-of-Africa after controlling for neutral population gene structure', *American Journal of Physical Anthropology*, 145.3, pp.382–9.

In a study of Harvard students, the most eminently creative were seven times more likely to have reduced latent inhibition . . . Carson, Shelley H., Peterson, Jordan B., and Higgins, Daniel M. (2003), 'Decreased latent inhibition is associated with increased creative achievement in high-functioning individuals.', p.499.

Whether magic mushrooms also inspired the work of these mural artists is unknown. Akers, Brian P., et al. (2011), 'A prehistoric mural in Spain depicting neurotropic psilocybe mushrooms?', *Economic Botany*, 65.2, pp.121–8.

A hallucinogenic mushroom cult of sorts, psychedelics perhaps an intrinsic element of their creative process. Samorini, Giorgio (1992), 'The oldest representations of hallucinogenic mushrooms in the world', *Integration*, 2 3.

A dawning realisation that they are 'part of a bigger, universal cosmic oneness'. Sessa, Ben (2008), 'Is it time to revisit the role of psychedelic drugs in enhancing human creativity?', *Journal of Psychopharmacology*, 22.8, pp.821–7.

Notes

Patients described spiritual and mystical experiences and moved towards a dreamlike dimension. Ross, Stephen, et al. (2016), 'Rapid and sustained symptom reduction following psilocybin treatment for anxiety and depression in patients with life-threatening cancer: A randomized controlled trial', *Journal of Psychopharmacology*, 30.12, pp.1165–80.

. . . developed frontotemporal dementia and began to paint for the first time at the age of fifty-six. Miller, Bruce L., et al. (1996), 'Enhanced artistic creativity with temporal lobe degeneration', *The Lancet*, 348.9043, pp.1744–5.

A man in his fifties began to paint churches and haciendas remembered from childhood . . . Miller, Bruce L., et al. (1998), 'Emergence of artistic talent in frontotemporal dementia', *Neurology*, 51.4, pp.978–82.

A seventy-four-year-old woman who had been a brilliant inventor with exceptional visuospatial abilities . . . Miller, Bruce L., et al. (2000), 'Functional correlates of musical and visual ability in frontotemporal dementia', *The British Journal of Psychiatry*, 176.5, pp.458–63.

. . . cognitive resources in semantic dementia are redirected towards areas that oversee visuoconstructive and visuospatial skills. Kapur, Narinder (1996), 'Paradoxical functional facilitation in brain-behaviour research: A critical review', *Brain*, 119.5, pp.1775–90.

There was no semantic link between this artistry and the object – for him, there didn't need to be. Liu, Anli, et al. (2009), 'A case study of an emerging visual artist with frontotemporal lobar degeneration and amyotrophic lateral sclerosis', *Neurocase*, 15.3, pp.235–47.

It turned out that he was having seizures during each of these artistic outbursts – this was epilepsy. Finkelstein, Yoram, Vardi, Jacob, and Hod, Israel (1991), 'Impulsive artistic creativity as a presentation of transient cognitive alterations', *Behavioral Medicine*, 17.2, pp.91–4.

Professor Simone Shamay-Tsoory and colleagues in Haifa, Israel . . . Shamay-Tsoory, S. G., et al. (2011), 'The origins of originality: The neural bases of creative thinking and originality', *Neuropsychologia*, 49.2, pp.178–85.

'Lonely Cowboy's Thoughts' was a case study I read that made me think about how easily that expression might be overlooked. Antérion, Catherine Thomas, et al. (2002), 'Lonely cowboy's thoughts', *Neurology*, 59.11, pp.1812–13.

In 2004, Australian researchers used a technique called repetitive transcranial magnetic stimulation to switch off the frontotemporal lobe. Young, Robyn L., Ridding, Michael C., and Morrell, Tracy L. (2004), 'Switching skills on by turning off part of the brain', *Neurocase*, 10.3, pp.215–22.

'I don't want Columbia's filthy lucre.' Nini, Paul, 'Across the Graphic Universe: An Interview with John Berg', *AIGA*, 30 October 2007.

The influence of LSD on Crumb's work was explored in a 2011 piece . . . Jones, Matthew T. (2007), 'The creativity of Crumb: Research on the effects of psychedelic drugs on the comic art of Robert Crumb', *Journal of Psychoactive Drugs*, 39.3, pp.283–91.

'For the next couple of months, I felt like the guy in Eraserhead . . . everything was dreamlike and unreal.' Crumb, R., Introduction, in, Groth, G., and Fiore, R. (eds.) (1989), *The Complete Crumb Comics, Vol. 4: Mr Sixties!* Seattle, Washington: Fantagraphics Books.

'. . . I began to really enjoy being able to concentrate in this way that I'd forgotten how to do from being stoned all the time.' 'Artists on Film: The Confessions of Robert Crumb', TV episode, directed by Mary Dickinson, UK, BBC Arena, 1987.

'If everybody's walking forward, I want to walk backwards.' Armitstead, Claire, 'Robert Crumb: "I was born weird"', *Guardian*, 24 April 2016.

Before that, they had been used throughout the Second World War. Rasmussen, Nicolas (2011), 'Medical science and the military: The Allies' use of amphetamine during World War II', *Journal of Interdisciplinary History*, 42.2, pp.205–33.

In a 2016 study in Israel, thirty-six healthy adults were given either methylphenidate (also known as Adderall) or placebo. Gvirts, Hila Z., et al. (2017), 'Novelty-seeking trait predicts the effect of methylphenidate on creativity', *Journal of Psychopharmacology*, 31.5, pp.599–605.

To make things worse, creative novelty-seeker types . . . Leyton, Marco, et al. (2002), 'Amphetamine-induced increases in extracellular dopamine, drug wanting, and novelty seeking: a PET/[11C] raclopride study in healthy men', *Neuropsychopharmacology*, 27.6, p.1027.

It was his 'unconscious work', he said, that led him to his best discoveries. Poincaré, Henri (1908), 'Science and Method, in 1913', *The Foundations of Science*.

In one study, 'Inspired by Distraction. Mind Wandering Facilitates Creative Incubation' . . . Baird, Benjamin, et al. (2012), 'Inspired by distraction: Mind wandering facilitates creative incubation', *Psychological Science*, 23.10, pp.1117–22.

Studies that placed jazz musicians and rappers . . . De Pisapia, N., et al. (2016), 'Brain networks for visual creativity: a functional connectivity study of planning a visual artwork. *Sci. Rep.*, 6, p.39185.

PART III
Chapter 7: *Disintegration*

Take the 1937 report of a French man with four of them . . . Sivadon, P. (1937), 'Phénomènes autoscopiques au cours de la grippe', *Annales Médico-Psychologiques*, 95.

Life-threatening danger (falls or avalanches) . . . Brugger, Peter, et al. (1999), 'Hallucinatory experiences in extreme-altitude climbers', *Cognitive and Behavioral Neurology*, 12.1, pp.67–71.

A 1957 survey of aviators . . . Clark, Brant, and Graybiel, Ashton (1957), 'The break-off phenomenon: A feeling of separation from the earth experienced by pilots at high altitude', *The Journal of Aviation Medicine*, 28.2, pp.121–6.

'. . . *turning a somersault and then flying with my legs up!'* Titov, Gherman Stepanovich, and Caidin, Martin (1962), *I Am Eagle!* Indiana: Bobbs-Merrill.

. . . *an inbuilt neural vulnerability.* Braithwaite, Jason J., et al. (2013), 'Evidence for elevated cortical hyperexcitability and its association with out-of-body experiences in the non-clinical population: New findings from a pattern-glare task', *Cortex*, 49.3, pp.793–805.

'Everywhere in the world, self starts with body.' Baumeister, Roy F. (1999), 'The nature and structure of the self: An overview', *The Self in Social Psychology*, pp.1–20.

Neuroscientist Henrik Ehrsson conducted the experiments . . . Ehrsson, H. Henrik (2007), 'The experimental induction of out-of-body experiences', *Science*, 317.5841, p.1048.

By 2008, they had performed a body swapping experiment. Petkova, Valeria I., and Ehrsson, H. Henrik (2008), 'If I were you: Perceptual illusion of body swapping', *PloS one*, 3.12, p.3832.

And by 2011, a group of Swiss researchers led by neuroscientist Olaf Blanke . . . Lenggenhager, Bigna, et al (2007), 'Video ergo sum: manipulating bodily self-consciousness', *Science*, 317.5841, pp.1096–9.

'It is made of pure information, flowing in the brain.' Metzinger, Thomas (2009), 'Why are out-of-body experiences interesting for philosophers?: The theoretical relevance of OBE research', *Cortex*, 45.2, pp.256–8.

It sufficed to drive me back into my body. Waelti, E. (1983), 'Der dritte kreis des wissens', *Ansata, Interlaken* (Translation by Thomas Metzinger).

. . . *represented a multisensory impairment of body perception.* Serino, Silvia, et al. (2016), 'A novel technique for improving bodily experience in a non-operable super-super obesity case', *Frontiers in Psychology*, 7.

Similar findings have been reported in women with anorexia. Keizer, Anouk, et al. (2016), 'A virtual reality full body illusion improves body image disturbance in anorexia nervosa', *PloS one*, 11.10, p.0163921.

A 2015 experiment provided participants with the option of an entirely invisible one. Guterstam, Arvid, and Ehrsson, H. Henrik (2012), 'Disowning one's seen real body during an out-of-body illusion', *Consciousness and Cognition*, 21.2, pp.1037–42.

. . . *the Nintendo Wii gaming system in this case.* Saposnik, Gustavo, et al. (2016), 'Efficacy and safety of non-immersive virtual reality exercising in stroke rehabilitation (EVREST): A randomised, multicentre, single-blind, controlled trial', *The Lancet Neurology*, 15.10, pp.1019–27.

. . . *the effect was most marked for people with higher levels of prejudice to begin with.* Gutsell, Jennifer N., and Inzlicht, Michael (2010), 'Empathy constrained: Prejudice predicts reduced mental simulation of actions during observation of outgroups', *Journal of Experimental Social Psychology*, 46.5, pp.841–5.

The idea behind the mirror neuron system. Di Pellegrino, Giuseppe, et al. (1992), 'Understanding motor events: A neurophysiological study', *Experimental Brain Research*, 91.1, pp.176–80.

Take the results of a Chinese study. Xu, Xiaojing, et al. (2009), 'Do you feel my pain? Racial group membership modulates empathic neural responses', *Journal of Neuroscience*, 29.26, pp.8525–9.

. . . *the more positive their implicit racial attitudes became.* Maister, Lara, et al. (2013), 'Experiencing ownership over a dark-skinned body reduces implicit racial bias', *Cognition*, 128.2, pp.170–78.

A 2017 study delved deeper. Hasler, Béatrice S., Spanlang, Bernhard, and Slater, Mel (2017), 'Virtual race transformation reverses racial in-group bias', *PloS one*, 12.4, p.0174965.

Chapter 8: *Slumber*

'. . . *along with a letter initialled A.J. T. to M. A. B.*' Cohen, Daniel A. (1990), 'The Murder of Maria Bickford: Fashion, passion, and the birth of a consumer culture', *American Studies*, 31.2, pp.5–30.

A *characteristic 'hot zone' towards the back of the brain.* . . . Siclari, Francesca, et al. (2017), 'The neural correlates of dreaming', *Nature Neuroscience*, 20.6, pp.872–8.

A *2013 Japanese study published in Science found just that.* Horikawa, Tomoyasu, et al. (2013), 'Neural decoding of visual imagery during sleep', *Science*, 340.6132, pp.639–42.

. . . *a twenty-five-year-old blond-haired female Finnish student.* Revonsuo, Antti, (2005), 'The self in dreams' in Feinberg, Todd E., and Keenan, Julian Paul (eds.), *The Lost Self: Pathologies of the Brain and Identity*, Oxford: Oxford University Press, pp.206–19.

In *one early study the dream self* . . . Revonsuo, Antti, and Salmivalli, Christina (1995), 'A content analysis of bizarre elements in dreams', *Dreaming*, 5.3, p.169.

'*Despite thousands of years of dream interpretation . . .*' Wamsley, Erin J. (2013), 'Dreaming, waking conscious experience, and the resting brain: Report of subjective experience as a tool in the cognitive neurosciences', *Frontiers in Psychology*, 4

'. . . *the entire room was filled with wine*' (1605), de Cervantes, Miguel, *Don Quixote de La Mancha*, 1995 edition, Barcelona: Editorial Juventud, S.A., p.364 (author's translation).

. . . *is crucial for paralysing skeletal muscle during REM sleep.* Schenck, Carlos H., and Mahowald, Mark W. (2002), 'REM sleep behavior disorder: Clinical, developmental, and neuroscience perspectives 16 years after its formal identification in SLEEP', *Sleep*, 25.2, pp.120–38.

'. . . *culminating in a defensive posture.*' Jouvet, M. (1981), 'Toward an etho-ethology of dreaming', *Psychophysiological Aspects of Sleep*, pp.204–14.

'. . . *and he spiked the football in the end zone.*' Boeve, Bradley F., et al. (1998), 'REM sleep behavior disorder and degenerative dementia: An association likely reflecting Lewy body disease', *Neurology*, 51.2, pp.363–70.

'. . . *and swarms of bees who were attacking me*' Schenck, Carlos H., et al. (2009), 'Potentially lethal behaviors associated with rapid eye movement sleep behavior disorder: Review of the literature and forensic implications', *Journal of Forensic Sciences*, 54.6, pp.1475–84.

What *happened next was described in a case report some years later.* Broughton, R., et al. (2009), 'Homicidal somnambulism: A case report', *Sleep*, 17.3, pp.253–64.

But *what's also crucial is the pathways that seem to become hypoactive during sleepwalking* . . . Bassetti, Claudio, et al. (2000), 'SPECT during sleepwalking', *The Lancet*, 356.9228, pp.484–5.

But when it is no longer moderated by the frontal lobes, unwarranted aggressive behaviour surges forth. Siclari, Francesca, et al. (2010), 'Violence in sleep', *Brain*, 133.12, pp.3494–509.

Chapter 9: *Calling Time*

'*I couldn't see me in there. It was disturbing.*' Hamzelou, Jessica (2015), 'Looking out from behind someone else's face', *New Scientist*, 228.3045, pp.28–30.

Meanwhile her donor's daughter, Miranda, saw her late mother . . . Goodnough, Abby, 'For Victim of Ghastly Crime, a New Face, a New Beginning', *The New York Times*, 25 October 2013.

Nicholas Schiff and research colleagues at Weill Medical College of Cornell University . . . Voss, Henning U., et al. (2006), 'Possible axonal regrowth in late recovery from the minimally conscious state', *Journal of Clinical Investigation*, 116.7, p.2005.

'. . . *if the brain is dead, the person is dead.*' Pallis, C. & Harley, D. H. ABC of Brainstem Death (BMJ, London, 1996). There are variations world-wide on these definitions.

A 2010 French study tracked patients . . . Luauté, J., et al. (2010), 'Long-term outcomes of chronic minimally conscious and vegetative states', *Neurology*, 75.3, pp.246–52.

. . . *and three months after non-traumatic brain damage.* Laureys, Steven, and Boly, Melanie (2007), 'What is it like to be vegetative or minimally conscious?', *Current Opinion in Neurology*, 20.6, pp.609–13.

But even then around a third of patients said to be in a vegetative state are misdiagnosed. Childs, Nancy L., Mercer, Walt N., and Childs, Helen W. (1993), 'Accuracy of diagnosis of persistent vegetative state', *Neurology*, 43.8, pp.1465–7.

'*It was like magic, it found me.*' Cyranoski, David (2012), 'The mind reader', *Nature*, 486.7402, p.178.

Adrian Owen and his team persisted . . . Owen, Adrian M., et al. (2006), 'Detecting awareness in the vegetative state', *Science*, 313.5792, p.1402.

All of this eventually led to a New England Journal of Medicine study in 2010. Monti, Martin M., et al. (2010), 'Willful modulation of brain activity in disorders of consciousness', *New England Journal of Medicine*, 362.7, pp.579–89.

'*I couldn't believe it. I just cried and cried.*' Boggan, Steve, 'Reborn' *Guardian*, 12 September 2006.

'*Extraordinary arousal from semi-comatose state on zolpidem.*' Clauss, R. P., et al. (2000), 'Extraordinary arousal from semi-comatose state on zolpidem', *South African Medical Journal*, 90.1, pp.68–72.

Zolpidem seems to shift the balance of inhibition and stimulation of brain networks. Schiff, Nicholas D. (2010), 'Recovery of consciousness after brain injury: A mesocircuit hypothesis', *Trends in neurosciences*, 33.1, pp.1–9.

Five years later, he was still responding to zolpidem. Clauss, Ralf, and Nel, Wally (2006), 'Drug induced arousal from the permanent vegetative state', *NeuroRehabilitation*, 21.1, pp.23–8.

In Israel, a fifty-year-old woman had suffered a cardiac arrest . . . Shames, Jeffrey L., and Ring, Haim (2008), 'Transient reversal of anoxic brain injury-related minimally conscious state after zolpidem administration: A case report', *Archives of Physical Medicine and Rehabilitation*, 89.2, pp.386–8.

. . . only one of fifteen patients responded to it in a 2009 placebo-controlled trial in Pennsylvania. Whyte, John, and Myers, Robin (2009), 'Incidence of clinically significant responses to zolpidem among patients with disorders of consciousness: A preliminary placebo controlled trial', *American Journal of Physical Medicine & Rehabilitation*, 88.5, pp.410–18.

Another study that examined sixty patients . . . Thonnard, Marie, et al. (2013), 'Effect of zolpidem in chronic disorders of consciousness: a prospective open-label study', *Functional Neurology*, 28.4, p.259.

'*He was noted to pull head upright, reach for objects, play "thumb war", and hug mother and girlfriend.*' Whyte, John, et al. (2014), 'Zolpidem and restoration of consciousness', *American Journal of Physical Medicine & Rehabilitation*, 93.2, pp.101–13.

Acknowledgements

My deep appreciation goes to the patients I have met along the way – in Ireland, the UK, Mozambique and India. I have learnt so much from you – not just about your brain or mine, of course, but about our lives, about life. I hope I have done right by you.

A special thank you to Will Francis, my supremely talented, erudite, and enthusiastic agent. In fact, the literary agent of all literary agents. *Lost and Found* only came to be because of him. I'm also indebted to the rest of the superb people at Janklow & Nesbit including Rebecca Folland, Kate l'Anson, Kirsty Gordon, and Rachel Balcombe.

What an outstanding team at Sceptre – I have truly landed on my feet. Drummond Moir has been a wise and perpetually encouraging editor. All authors should have a Drummond. I'm sincerely grateful to the rest of the Sceptre family who have welcomed me with open arms – including Jenny Campbell, Fleur Clarke, Ruby Mitchell, Francine Toon, Lucy Hale, Ellie Wood, Richard Peters, Catherine Worsley, and Carole Welch.

I'd like to recognise a few mentors I've been lucky enough to encounter as a neurologist. The compassion they show towards their patients has profoundly impacted upon me – here's to Raymond Murphy and Michael Hutchinson in Dublin. And to Jeremy Gibbs, Lionel Ginsberg, Andrew

Gale, and Tom Warner in London. They are, quite simply, good people.

I'm eternally thankful for my wonderful friends whose support and enthusiasm for this book has only recently been outweighed by their keenness to come to the launch party. My heartfelt gratitude for your friendship. I've done this in alphabetic order, just to be on the safe side: Aoife L, Aoife M, Athena and the Cypriots, Bianca, Brian, Bríd, Carrie, Catríona, Clodagh, Daryl, Davina, Declan, Emma M, Emma R, Graham, Jen, Jo, Kate, Kerry, Rina, Rowena, Sharon, Siobhán, Trish and Úna.

My thanks also go to two special family friends I'd like to mention: Matt Moylan and Sam Andrews.

Finally, to my family – for their unwavering support and love. I dedicate this book to you.

Picture Acknowledgements

Index

Index

and psychological connectedness 17–18, 27, 32, 111, 148, 265–6

during sleep and dreaming 211–16, 221–30

and storytelling 24–6, 61–3, 87, 89–90

a succession of selves 16–17

illusory body experiments 203–5, 206–7

James, William 44

Janet, Pierre 79, 134–5

Janiger, Oscar 172

Jones, Matthew 172, 174, 175

justice

and false witness 55–61, 63

and personality change/disorders 128–33, 139–48, 264

sleepwalking defence 209–10, 221–30

Keats, John 183

Kerouac, Jack 177

King, Larry 133

Kitwood, Tom 31

Kopelman, Michael 82

Korsakoff, Sergei 35

Korsakoff's syndrome 33–6, 37, 63–4

Kray twins 18n

Kulik, James 43–4

Kyle, Benjamin (William Powell) 74, 77, 80, 81, 85–8, 91–5, 265

Lancet 163, 205, 248

Lanchester, John 177

latent inhibition 159–60

Le Doux, Joseph 48–51

Leithauser, Brad 29–30

Letterman, David 42

levodopa 151, 155

Lewis, Donald 50n

Locke, John 16n

Lockerbie disaster trial 55–9, 60–61

Loftus, Elizabeth 56, 58

Logan, Judge 143n

LSD 149, 160, 171–6, 182

Lynn, Steven Jay 136–7

magic mushrooms 149, 160–62

Malcolm and Barbara: Love's Farewell 19

malingering 85

marijuana 175, 176

Mason, Shirley 132, 138–9

Maxwell, Juanita 131–2

McAdams, Dan 62

McCrae, Robert 156–7

Megrahi, Abdelbaset al- 55–9, 60–61

memory–identity relationship 7, 15

and dementia 15, 19–32

and embodiment 19–24, 62, 189, 190–91, 264

and the mountain of memories 15–16

and social interaction and reflection 26–32

and the stories we tell 24–6, 61–3

and a succession of selves 16–18

memory formation 49

memory loss/amnesia/forgetting

with dementia *see* Alzheimer's; dementia

dissociative amnesia and fugue 74–82, 85–90, 91–5

everyday forgetting 65–74; absent-mindedness 72–3; childhood amnesia 65, 66–9;